10 0608110 0

D0707972

The Bitter-Sweet Awakening

The Legacy of the

Sydney 2000 Olympic Games

The Bitter-Sweet Awakening

The Bitter-Sweet Awakening

The Legacy of the
Sydney 2000 Olympic Games

Richard Cashman

Walla Walla Press, Sydney
in conjunction with
the Australian Centre for Olympic Studies
University of Technology, Sydney

Published by **Walla Walla Press**
P.O. Box 717
Petersham NSW 2049
Phone: 612 9560 6902
Website: www.wallawalllapress.com
Email: info@wallawallapress.com

ISBN 1 876718 90 0

Designed and formatted by Ed 'n' Art, Newport, Sydney
Printed by Ligare Pty Ltd, Sydney

1006081100

TABLE OF CONTENTS

ACKNOWLEDGMENTS

I have had a long-standing interest in legacy having published my first paper on the subject in 1999. I was encouraged to further pursue this subject and made more aware its potential by the Barcelona team — Miquel de Moragas, Ana Belen Moreno, Chris Kennett and Berta Cerezeula at the Centre for Olympic Studies at the Autonomous University of Barcelona as well as Nuria Puig of the Olympic Studies Centre at the IOC. I enjoyed many long and helpful legacy discussions at Barcelona, when I held the Olympic Chair there in 2002. The paper that I presented at the legacy conference at Lausanne in November 2002 was much improved as a result.

Many people have assisted me with their comments on chapters or sections of chapters including Philip Bell, John Black, Simon Darcy, Kevin Dunn, Stephen Frawley, Beatriz García, Greg Hartung, Harry Hiller, Sandy Hollway, Chris Kennett, Bruce Kidd, Roger March, Andy Miah, Miquel de Moragas, John O'Hara, Kristy Ann Owen, Deo Prasad, Ray Spurr, Kristine Toohey, A.J. Veal and Eric Winton. Thanks are also due to many others have answered specific queries and provided me with research information and papers. My thanks to John MacAloon, Daniel Bell, Christina Bianchi, Janet Cahill, Debra Good, Chito Guala, Rob Harris, John Huxley, Anne and Ian Jobling, Charles Leski, Judy Macarthur, Martha McIntosh, Tara Magdalinski, Norbert Müller, Roy Panagiotopoulou, Jim Parry, Holger Preuss, Hai Ren, Matthew Ricketson, Otto Schantz, Mark Snow, Dominique Tremblay and Wayne Wilson.

Many individuals and institutions have freely responded to requests for information including James Bell (Mirvac Projects Pty Ltd), Michael Bland and Damien Lynch (Greenpeace), Greg Blood (National Sport Information Service), Helen Brownlee, Craig Phillips and Michelle Smith (AOC), Christine Deaner, Andy Greenway, John Johnstone and Michelle O'Shea (SOPA), Kevin Fewster (Powerhouse Museum), Matt Hamilton (Newington Village Real Estate), Paul Hartmann (RALC), Peter Holden and Helen Kebby (TAFE GLOBAL), Melissa Kimmerly, Martha McIntosh, Craig McLatchey and Nuria Puig (IOC), Doreen Payne (Corrs Chambers Westgarth), Simonetta Lo Po' (Penrith Whitewater Ltd), David Studham and Mary Monaghan (Melbourne Cricket Club Library), Councillor Ian Sneddon and Craig Moffitt (Jerilderie Shire Council).

It is impossible to acknowledge all the international colleagues and students who have contributed to this book over a decade when I met them at Olympic events and conferences or taught and supervised them in a university context. I have listened and learned from what they have said and written. I have also presented papers on the Olympic Games and legacy and thank those people who have facilitated international visits to a range of countries including Brazil, China, Denmark, Greece, Italy, Singapore, South Korea, Spain and Switzerland. Those who have facilitated visits include John Bale, Chito Guala, Nikos Filaretos, Kostas Georgiadis, Miquel de Moragas, Hai Ren, Katia Rubio and Kang Shin-pyo.

For the best part of a decade I enjoyed a good research and teaching partnership with Anthony Hughes. We collaborated on a wide range of Olympic activities from Olympic conferences to publications.

The illustrations in the book have been supplied courtesy of Scott Barbour (Getty Images Sport), Torsten Blackwood (AFP), Jeff Brown (Riverlands Visual Media), Simon Darcy, Paul Hartmann (RALC), Frank Hubbard (James Hardie Industries), Angie Knott (SOPA), Chris McGrath (Getty Images Sport), Pauline McGuirk and Kevin Dunn (Cartolab), Matthew Newton Photography and Penrith Whitewater Ltd, David Studham (Melbourne Cricket Club), Janelle Mikkelson (National Film and Sound Archive), Eric Winton (DRSD). Thanks are also due to Bruce Hayllar, head of the School of Leisure, Sport and Tourism, at the University of Technology, Sydney, who provided funds to cover the costs of the cover illustrations and some other photographs.

I am pleased that my colleagues at the Australian Centre for Olympic Studies, which was launched on 6 October 2005, have agreed that this book be in published in conjunction with ACOS. My thanks to Bruce Hayllar, Tony Veal, Stephen Frawley and Jackie Edwards for their endorsement of this publication and for their wholehearted support of ACOS.

I would also like to thank John O'Hara of Walla Walla Press for his continuing friendship, encouragement and constructive suggestions. Carol and Gordon Floyd from Ed 'n' Art have been invariably helpful and professional in a wide range of matters ranging from editing and design to project management. David Edwards of Ligare has been his usual efficient and reliable self.

Margaret has been by my side for the entirety of my Olympic journey and I deeply appreciate her unfailing support, helpful suggestions and tolerance of this project.

ABBREVIATIONS

ABC	Australian Broadcasting Corporation
ABS	Australian Bureau of Statistics
AGOSOM	Australian Gallery of Sport and Olympic Museum
AOC	Australian Olympic Committee
APC	Australian Paralympic Committee
ASC	Australian Sports Commission
ATC	Australian Tourist Commission
ATHOC	Athens Organising Committee for the Olympic Games
BOCOG	Beijing Organising Committee for the Olympic Games
DET	Department of Education and Training
DSRD	(NSW) Department of State and Regional Development
EKS	Event Knowledge Services
GGW 2000	Green Games Watch 2000
HREOC	Human Rights and Equal Opportunity Commmission
IOC	International Olympic Committee
IPC	International Paralympic Committee
OBR	Olympics Business Roundtable
OCA	Olympic Co-ordination Authority
OGGI	Olympic Games Global Impact
OGKS	Olympic Games Knowledge Services
OPDAS	Olympic and Paralympic Disability Service
ORTA	Olympic Roads and Transport Authority
NCCRS	National Centre for Culture and Recreation Statistics
PGR	Post-Games Report (*Official Report of the XXVII Olympiad*)
PPGR	*Paralympics Post-Games Report*
RALC	Ryde Aquatic Leisure Centre
PWC	PricewaterhouseCoopers
RWC	Rugby World Cup (2003)
SCVB	Sydney Convention and Visitors Bureau
SMH	*Sydney Morning Herald*
SOCOG	Sydney Organising Committee for the Olympic Games
SPOC	Sydney Paralympic Organising Committee
SOPA	Sydney Olympic Park Authority
SSC	SOCOG Sports Commission
SVCB	Sydney Visitors and Convention Bureau
STA	State Transit Authority
TOK	Transfer of Know How

Chapter 1

WHEN THE CARNIVAL IS OVER

For the final act of the Paralympic Games the celebrated Australian pop group from the 1960s, The Seekers, was flown from London to perform one and only one song, which lasted barely three minutes. It was an inspired move, partly because the lead singer, Judith Durham, was confined to a wheelchair — not permanently, like many of the Paralympic athletes, but because she was recovering from an operation. The group sang the haunting lyrics of the 'The Carnival is Over' which topped the charts for 17 weeks in 1965. The song was strangely at odds with the general celebrations which featured athletes cavorting around a stadium festooned with bunting and balloons. The song consisted of a simple melody repeated over and over:

> Say goodbye my own true lover
> As we sing a lover's song
> How it breaks my hear to leave you
> Now the carnival is gone.
> High above the dawn is waiting
> And my tears are falling rain
> For the carnival is over
> We may never meet again.
> Like a drum my heart is beating
> And your kiss was sweet as wine
> But the joys of love are fleeting
> For Pierrot and Columbine.
> Now the harbour light is calling
> This will be our last goodbye
> Though the carnival is over
> I will love you till I die.

The parallels between the end of an individual relationship and a sporting festival were clear to everyone — the moment of joy, the pain of the last goodbye and the final separation. For the athletes, the organisers, the spectators and the citizens of the Olympic city, the once-in-a-lifetime carnival was over. It was a poignant end to the Olympic and Paralympic festivals, which had taken place over 44 days — from 15 September to 29 October 2000 — with a break of only 16 days between these two mega sporting events. It was the culmination of a decade of accelerating excitement beginning in the period before the bid was submitted in 1991.

A few hours before The Seekers performed, the flag had been lowered, the flame extinguished and the Games proclaimed closed by the president of the International Paralympic Committee (IPC). The Sydney Paralympic Games, like the Sydney Olympic Games, had secured the 'best ever' accolade. After the Seekers' song, as if to fill the awkward silence, an official intoned banally: 'Ladies and gentlemen, this concludes the closing ceremony of the 2000 Games. On behalf of everyone here tonight we congratulate the athletes.' While the Games had officially ended, athletes, officials and spectators partied on into this final Games night.

I have long wondered what happens to that heightened emotion and the festival-like atmosphere that affected all involved in the event. Does it disappear overnight? Is it savoured for some time before it fades gradually over time? Is it pragmatically shelved to reappear when another sports caravan returns to an Olympic city? Is it suppressed because it is too painful?

This book starts where I think it should: with the personal and emotional legacy of the Games, something that has attracted far too little attention in public and scholarly debate. There has always been more interest in the tangible and monetary benefits resulting from the staging of a mega event — ones that are obvious and can be measured (even if somewhat imprecisely) — such as increased tourism, greater global promotion and recognition, enhanced business and the aspiring city's success in winning the competition to host the Olympics. These are 'bigger picture' issues which are the agendas of the business and power elites. The comment by landscape architect James Weirick before the Sydney Olympic Games describes this perspective. He wrote that 'the main impulse behind the Games is to promote Sydney as a "global city"' and added that the 'Sydney Olympic experience is only partially to do with sport and the Olympic Movement'.[1] Urban sociologist Harry Hiller has contended that the decision to host a mega event 'is legitimated in economic terms and the event itself has economic impacts'. He added that the 'economic justification' for staging a mega event 'is so compelling to key elites that other impacts are considered minor'.[2] The economic validation cannot be disputed if one takes the perspective of the organisers of the event — which is a top-down view.

But there is another story to be told. The Olympic Games also inspire the emotional investment of individuals, including athletes, volunteers, spectators, the paid Games work force, and the families who host visitors. Maurice Roche, author of *Mega-events and Modernity*, reminds us that mega events are embraced both by the 'power elites' and by 'ordinary people'. While such events 'provide power elites with "flagships" and catalysts to promote their visions of society and of the future', they also invest 'ordinary people with opportunities to connect with and affirm or contest collective identities'.[3] This book turns the usual discussion of the Games' legacy on its head by looking first at the impacts the Games has on the people of the host community. While it would be foolish to question the significance of economic legacy, it is worth focusing on a neglected aspect of the legacy first. Perhaps an upside-down view may lead to new questions and perspectives.

The literature on festivals and mega events attests to the fact that ordinary people have a heightened sense of awareness at such times, enabling them to recall the events more clearly and vividly than at more mundane times. On such occasions they feel more alive. A mega event, and particular happenings within that festival, is used by ordinary people to mark the passing of time.

This book is written partly as a personal journey, since I was heavily involved in the Sydney 2000 Olympic and Paralympic Games, particularly from the time that the Centre for Olympic Studies at the University of New South Wales was launched on 21 May 1996. (The closure of the Centre on 31 March 2004 is another Olympic outcome and an aspect of Sydney's post-Olympic environment that will be touched on in Chapter 2.) Being a participant in the Games was memorable, as was the experience of being at the centre of the biggest and most prestigious sporting event staged in Sydney. For five years I was on an academic and sporting roller coaster that brought many challenges, much excitement and a few frustrations. I was greatly enriched by the experiences, whether they related to ongoing contact with local and international media or with international Olympic scholars and students. I

The author (runner number 53, on day 99) holds a lit torch at the beginning of his run of 500 metres at Enmore Park on 14 September 2000.

also had the opportunity to witness a pivotal event for Sydney and Australia first-hand: I was runner number 53 on day 99 — the day before the opening ceremony — of the torch relay and had the privilege of carrying the torch for 500 metres around Enmore Park, not far from my home. I thus experienced first-hand the pre-Games euphoria which brought a heightened sense of place and community. I was also stretched, intellectually and physically, by the demands associated with this event. Because I was present from the beginning — the opening ceremony of Olympic Games on 15 September — to the end — the closing ceremony of the Paralympic Games on 29 October 2004 — I too experienced a sense of loss after The Seekers finally brought down the Paralympic (and Olympic) curtain. Since then, I have keenly followed the ongoing debate on legacy issues in the Olympic city and was present on two significant Olympic occasions when the cauldron was relit, on 15 September 2001 (the first anniversary) and on 4 June 2004 (the arrival of the Athens torch in Sydney).

John Ferguson of SOPA noted that the lighting of the cauldron, which is at the discretion of the AOC, is mainly confined to significant Olympic dates. Since 2000, it has been lit on each 15 September, to commemorate the opening of the Sydney Olympic Games. The cauldron was also lit on each day of the Athens 2004 Olympic Games though not for the Salk Lake City 2002 Winter Olympic Games. It has also been lit for occasional community events, such as carols by candlelight.

The lighting of the cauldron towards the end of the carols provided a spectacular climax to this event (see chapter 2).

The initial chapters focus on memory, identity and culture, issues that relate to the popular imagination of the Games. Other chapters examine business and economic outcomes, including international investment and the transfer of Olympic knowledge. There are also chapters that look at the pre- and post-Games history of venues, the fate of Sydney Olympic Park, sporting legacies, environmental outcomes and community impacts. A later chapter explores the legacy of the Paralympic Games: looking at how they advanced the cause of the Paralympic athlete and enhanced disability awareness. A concluding chapter sums up the positive and negative impacts of the Games and considers their worth.

This book is published soon after the fifth anniversary of the Sydney 2000 Olympic Games. It's a long time to wait to write such a book. Another Olympic Games have come and gone and the interest in what happened at Sydney seems to have long ago subsided in the public memory. It's possible that the market for another book on the Sydney Games, written five years down the track, will be small in Australia,

Sydney's cauldron, designed along classical lines, was an attractive and familiar presence during both Sydney Games (Simon Darcy).

though more significant internationally. So, why bother? The reasons are relatively straightforward. Firstly, a clearer evaluation of the impacts of the Games, whether in terms of the environment, sport or tourism, can be made after some time has passed. An assessment made a year or two afterwards is provisional at best because it is based on a limited range of data. Secondly, no Olympic researcher has previously undertaken a study of the legacy of an Olympic Games in the longer term.

Samaranch, Rogge and others: public assessments of the Games

It is an assumption of this work that the celebrated 'best-ever' judgment of the Sydney 2000 Olympic Games made at the closing ceremony by the former president of the International Olympic Committee (IOC), Juan Antonio Samaranch, was at best an immediate and a provisional assessment of the Games. It continued his tradition of rating the Games at the closing ceremony. In 1988 Samaranch had declared that the Seoul 1988 Olympic Games were the 'best ever'. Barcelona was rewarded with the best-ever mantle in 1992, which meant that he thought it had bettered the achievement of Seoul. Atlanta, by contrast, gained a lesser accolade in 1996, being described as the 'exceptional Games'. Samaranch then raised the benchmark again in 2000 when Sydney was awarded the ultimate accolade. Samaranch thus perpetuated the phenomenon, much loved by the media and host city public, of what Moragas and Kennett referred to as semantic synthesis, involving reduction and reproduction, by which complex issues of assessment are reduced to a simple phrase. They argue that the media focus on a narrow range of images and issues, so that Olympic interpretation conforms to the expectations of readers and the 'cultural production routines of each media'.[4]

At no point did Samaranch spell out precisely what were the criteria behind his judgments, though he commented in general terms on some of the positive achievements of various host cities. Olympic scholar Holger Preuss has questioned the grounds on which Samaranch based his judgment. He asked whether Samaranch referred to financial, social, organisational or sports success.[5]

In all probability the Samaranch judgment in 2000 was based on four factors. Firstly, there was the operational success of the Games from an athletic perspective, the smooth running of the events and the operation of facilities to the satisfaction of athletes. The absence of any major infrastructure problems, in terms of transport, media arrangements and potential disruptive local protests was a second factor. Thirdly, there was the positive support of the local community as volunteers, spectators and Games hosts. A final factor included the absence of an unwanted disruption from outside, such as a terrorist attack or a natural disaster, which could detract from the event.

In making his assessment Samaranch was undoubtedly influenced by the judgment of the international media, because the media do more than report on the athletic events: they assess how well the Games were organised and make numerous judgments about the host country and its society. The international media help to define the reputation of an Olympic Games. Samaranch recognised their role when he made the following comment before the staging of the 1996 Atlanta Olympic Games: 'the foreign media more than anyone else measure the success of the Games'.[6] However, the international media focus primarily on immediate issues, such as the operational efficiency of the Games, and largely ignore longer-term outcomes of the Games.

Since he became president of the IOC, Jacques Rogge has been more circumspect in his assessment of Olympic Games when he addresses the closing ceremony. He proclaimed the 2002 Salt Lake City Winter Games to be 'superb Games' and chose to refer to the 2004 Athens Summer Games — in somewhat ambiguous and imprecise terms — as 'unforgettable dream Games'. (He also referred to them as the 'surprising Games'). Why were they unforgettable? Was it because they were unforgettably good or was it that the tortured path to success could not be forgotten? Why the dream Games? Did it refer to an ancient dreaming time, the era of gods, when many features of western civilisation were born? Did the word dream refer more specifically to the long-nurtured Olympic dream of ancient Greece?

Whatever Rogge intended, his remarks represented a diplomatic, politically correct and cautious assessment which satisfied the Athenian hosts. Rogge undoubtedly felt a huge sense of personal relief that the first Summer Games of his presidency had not ended in disaster. The IOC had invested much in the operational success of Athens.

At a press conference on the final day of the Athens Games Rogge elaborated on why he had abandoned the Samaranch practice of declaring a Games the 'best ever':

> The Games are a competition between athletes and not between Organising Committees. And [to] say that the previous one or that the next one is going to be better than the actual one, this is not how things work. You cannot compare Games that are held at different times, in different countries with different political and cultural environments.[7]

Rogge undoubtedly believed that the rivalries between organising committees and cities also fuelled gigantism. He has consistently argued in favour of more modest and sustainable Games. Rogge also claimed that each Games reflect the idiosyncratic culture of the host country. This may be a reason why he used the phrase the 'dream Games', in that the Games were idiosyncratically Greek — which is yet another interpretation of his much reported words.

However, Rogge was effusive in his praise for the Athens Games: he stated that 'the organisation of ATHOC [the Athens Olympic Organising Committee for the Olympic Games] was outstanding' and he added that 'our Greek friends have delivered in a splendid way'. He commented that he was 'very happy about the transportation', 'technology has worked extremely well', 'security has been flawless' and 'broadcasters were ecstatic'. He added that the competition in the 'state-of-the-art' venues proceeded smoothly. Rogge did use the 'best ever' epithet when he stated that the athletes believed the village to be 'the best ever built'[8] but he referred to a particular facility rather than the Games as a whole. Australian IOC member and chef de mission John Coates acknowledged that the Athens village was better than Sydney's.[9]

Nonetheless Rogge did note that there was a problem of poor spectator response in the early days of the Greek Games, which he attributed to the Greek holidays. He could have added that the week-long controversy surrounding the Greek sprinters, Kostas Kenteris and Ekaterina Thanou, had cast a pall over the start of the Games, particularly as Kenteris was reported to be the athlete chosen to light the cauldron. The staging of the marathon on the final day was disrupted when an Irish ex-priest tackled the leading runner.

Rogge's decision to avoid giving comparative assessments after each the Olympic Games has had one interesting side effect. It is unlikely that any future IOC supremo will use those words so beloved of Samaranch. So Sydney will never lose its 'best ever' status for the Olympic and the Paralympic Games.

Unlike Sydney in 2000, when the international media seemed to speak with one voice of unqualified praise in the immediate aftermath of the Games, there were mixed messages after the 2004 Games. On the one hand, there was obvious relief that from an operational success the Games had proceeded smoothly despite a slow beginning when the media dwelt on the 'no-show' spectators. *Sydney Morning Herald* journalist John Huxley was very positive in his assessment of the Games during the Games and his final report on 30 August 2004 followed under the banner headline, 'Thanks Athens, you pulled it off. An Olympics to be proud of':

> Ultimately they [the Athenians] produced a Games that was different from, but easily the equal of Sydney's. Spectacular, safe, friendly, efficient and without the edginess many expected would inevitably flow from the omnipresence of security.

This assessment by a Sydney-based journalist is particularly interesting because even though Rogge purposely avoided the Olympic reductionism of Samaranch, journalists continued the practice of scoring the success of the Games. By equating Athens as the 'equal of Sydney', Huxley was, perhaps unintentionally, suggesting that Athens was not better than Sydney, thereby perpetuating the reputation of Sydney.

Others, such as Sydney opening ceremony organiser, Ric Birch, believed that Athens had raised the bar when it came to the staging of ceremonies. In his Channel 7 commentary during the opening ceremony Birch praised the ceremony as 'adventurous' and 'spectacular'.[10] He added that the technology employed in the Athens opening ceremony, which he regarded as superior to Sydney's, was 'difficult' and 'dangerous', thereby making the end result even more praiseworthy.

The Athens opening ceremony set a new benchmark for Olympic ceremonies. The cultural presentation was half the length of previous ceremonies, enabling the opening ceremony to be completed in under four hours. The IOC had expressed concern about the length of the opening ceremonies at Sydney and Atlanta which both lasted well over four hours. An interesting feature of the Greek cultural presentation in the opening

Dick Pound, who appeared at an Olympic conference at the University of New South Wales on 8 September 2000, was later critical of the costs of Athens 2004 Olympic Games.

ceremony was that it represented an abstract and intellectual synthesis of Greek history and culture. It did not feature the entertainment package of song, dance and humour that was part of the Sydney opening ceremony. Popular culture was shifted to the closing ceremony at Athens.

The Athens opening ceremony advanced the idea of the stadium becoming a film location. Whereas the Sydney Olympic stadium became an imaginary ocean in the initial segment 'Deep Sea Dreaming' — featuring creatures in the depths of the ocean with swimmers suspended in the air above them — the Athens stadium became an actual sea. The impressive parade through Greek history was another interesting innovation. It was produced more for the television audience, that could more readily observe its fine details, than the spectators at the stadium.

In contrast to Sydney — where criticism emerged after years rather than days — discordant voices surfaced before the Olympic dust had settled at Athens and before the Paralympic Games had commenced. An American newspaper commented that 'Greece woke up on Monday [the day after the closing ceremony] to the reality of an Olympic-size bill that might take decades to pay off':

With the projected cost of the Athens Games at $12 billion and rising [having more than doubled from the initial projection of 5.5.billion], Olympic historians and economists predict that the major legacy of the most expensive Games in history will be a string of little-used white-elephant venues that will cost tens of millions annually to maintain and a multibillion-dollar debt that will drain money from government programs well into the next decade.[11]

Prominent IOC member Dick Pound endorsed this view in a scathing attack of the Games only a month later. Pound compared the Athens Games to the 1976 Montreal Olympic Games in that both were 'plagued by cost overruns, delays and white elephant structures'. Pound added that 'late construction is expensive construction'.[12] Even a member of the Greek Government, the public order minister George Voulgarakis, admitted that 'we really spent more than we could afford'.[13]

A possible side effect of the escalating costs of the staging of the Athens Olympic Games was that the organisers of the Beijing 2008 Olympic Games promoted the concept of a 'frugal' Games. This new emphasis on the frugal Games may be a Chinese response to the Rogge campaign for more modest and sustainable Games but equally it may have been a Beijing response to the spiraling costs of venues, particularly the main stadium. It was proposed in 2004 that the retractable roof of the 'bird's nest' — the name for its roof design of interweaving steel bands — might be scrapped thereby saving an estimated $36,000 million.[14] However, the grandeur of Beijing's Olympic developments rather undermines the case for the frugal Games.

Commenting on the parlous financial state that Athens had found itself after the Games, Wright State University economist Evan Osborne argued that Olympic cities generally overestimate the worth of the Games and underestimate the cost. Because each successful bidding city 'talks up' the worth of the event, it can become the victim of what Osborne defines as the 'winner's curse'. Osborne elaborated his view:

> It's called the winner's curse because the cities that win the Olympic bids [or other mega events] are the cities that most overestimate what they [the Games] are worth [and also underestimate what they will cost] ... [In Olympic bidding] everybody is bidding on

> assumptions. What's tourism going to be like? What's the exchange
> rate going to be like? The people that are the most optimistic are
> the people that bid the most. And the people that bid the most are
> the people that usually win, so there's a built-in bias.[15]

Writing in 2005 on a future mega event, the 2006 Melbourne
Commonwealth Games, Australian scholar Bob Stewart endorsed
Osborne's view that the local organisers 'talked up' the benefits of the
event and indulged in 'an enormous amount of hyperbole' relating to the
potential economic and social impacts. He claimed that 'nobody really
knows' if this event will generate a 'net community benefit'.[16]

A document produced by the Sydney Olympic Games Review
Committee in 1999 for the NSW Premier portrayed the coming Games
as a great economic and sporting panacea that would produce improved
infrastructure, increased investment and tourism, and even greater
sporting participation:

> An Olympic Games that is successfully staged and financially
> managed leaves a positive legacy for the host city in terms
> of new and upgraded sporting facilities and venues; new and
> improved infrastructure; enhanced international recognition;
> enhanced international reputation; increased tourism; new
> trade, investment and marketing opportunities; and increased
> participation in sport.[17]

The report's glowing assessment and forecast of a 'positive legacy'
was inevitable, because such reviews never countenance the idea of
negative legacy.

Rogge's assessments of the worth of any specific Games, like
Samaranch's previous judgments, will never be accepted as the final
word. Olympic scholars will always sift through longer-term variables in
the decade after a Games — looking at costs and benefits, community
impacts, tourism and the post-Games use of facilities and many other
issues — to develop a more rounded picture. Scholars, as well as the
media, are the final arbiters of an Olympic Games.

This book is partly a product both of a desire to make some longer-
term assessment of the Sydney 2000 Olympic and Paralympic Games
and to reflect on how and in what ways a mega event should be assessed.
What should be the criteria? What is an appropriate methodology of

assessment? In the burgeoning literature on mega or hallmark events — a category which includes cultural events and world expos as well as sporting festivals — there is an increasing interest in just this sort of evaluation of mega events and their outcomes. Roberts and McLeod suggested in 1989 that 'while the staging of a hallmark event can provide a significant boost to the economy of a city or region' it is also the case that 'a common legacy of many past events has been a huge debt and a great deal of underutilised infrastructure'. Their chapter was part of a work edited by Geoffrey Syme *et al* entitled *The Planning and Evaluation of Hallmark Events.* However, since 1989 there has been limited systematic study of outcomes.[18] A similar point made by Maurice Roche in 1992 that 'pre-event projections are seldom tested against post-event accounting' remains true in 2005.[19]

Assessing legacy: some processes and practices

Although the existing practice of Olympic assessment is inadequate, some does occur nonetheless. While organising committees and other Games-related organisations close down soon after the Games are over, all city, state and even national governments undertake some post-Games assessment, even though it is more focused on economic rather than other impacts. The New South Wales Government, for instance, commissioned a report which was completed in 2002, by the firm PricewaterhouseCoopers to appraise the business and economic benefits of the Games (see Chapter 4). An earlier study, *The Keys to Success*, is a pioneering scholarly work written after the 1992 Barcelona Olympic Games, though the focus is almost entirely on the successful delivery of the Games rather than its outcomes.[20]

Another area of interest in terms of evaluation is the creation of post-Games institutions and the role they play in the post-Games period. Sydney's Olympic Co-ordination Authority (OCA), the organisation responsible primarily for building the venues, ceased operations in 2001 but some its functions were taken over by a successor body, the Sydney Olympic Park Authority, whose activities are examined in Chapter 6. Institutions, such as libraries, museums and archives, continued to play an Olympic role arranging and cataloguing the documents and memorabilia of the Games. For example, the Powerhouse Museum in Sydney became the repository for the artefacts from the opening ceremony. National Olympic Committees and Centres for Olympic Studies continue the evaluation process.

Evaluation is crucial because outcomes should be related back to the stated aims. Assessment introduces the twin notions of accountability and sustainability. If Olympic promises cannot be delivered, they represent empty rhetoric and may also contribute to the problem of gigantism. The issue of legacy is thus of important practical interest.

The Legacy of the Olympic Games 1984–2000

Olympic legacy was the theme of an international symposium at Lausanne in 2002 that was jointly sponsored by the Centre for Olympic Studies at the Autonomous University of Barcelona and the IOC. The papers at this conference, which were subsequently published, documented the importance of legacy and presented a cogent case that there had been

International Olympic scholars relax after a UNSW Centre for Olympic Studies forum on 12 September 2000. (From the left) Miquel de Moragas (Barcelona, Spain), Alan Tomlinson (Brighton, UK) and Peter Horton in a volunteer uniform (James Cook University, Queensland).

insufficient attention to outcomes in the past. It was also suggested that there was a need for greater research into outcomes.[21]

Harry Hiller suggested at this conference that the term 'legacy' usually came with a 'golden halo', in that it was believed to produce a 'positive end result' that enhanced a city. Hiller preferred the word 'outcomes' to 'legacy' since he sees it as a more neutral term that can indicate the possibility of both positive and negative, planned and unplanned outcomes.[22]

I prefer to use the term legacy — even though I use it in the same way as Hiller uses outcomes — because the word has such a standing in official Olympic discourse. The word legacy, however, is elusive, problematic and even dangerous word for a number of reasons. When the term is used by organising committees, it is assumed to be entirely positive, there being no such thing as negative legacy when used in this context. Secondly, it is usually believed that legacy benefits flow to a community at the end of the Games as a matter of course. The post-Games history of Sydney Olympic Park suggests that this was not the case (see Chapter 6). Thirdly, legacy is often assumed to be self-evident, so that there is no need to define precisely what it is. The Sydney Olympic Park Authority, for instance, stated in 2001 that it was its aim to preserve Sydney's 'Olympic legacy' without stating what it was or how it might be preserved. Finally, while the word legacy has a specific meaning in English — as either an individual bequest or anything that is left over from an event — there is no precise equivalent in other languages such as French. The French word *legs* has a narrow and specific meaning relating to individual legacy. This resulted in an odd occurrence: the 2002 symposium was advertised as a conference on legacy in English and a conference on *heritage* in French. If there is such a difference in the meaning of legacy from one European language to another there may be even greater ambiguity when the word is translated into non-European languages.[23]

Rogge declared at the 2002 conference that the legacy of a Games could be 'dangerous' if it resulted in luxury developments that became white elephants. He argued that an Olympic Games should produce a sustainable legacy that was of long-term benefit to the community of the host city and country. The conference documented the need both for legacy studies and for legatee institutions to develop an appropriate process of post-Games policies.

However, in June 2004, Rogge reiterated his belief in the value of the legacy of the Games:

> [The] Olympic Games ... represent an extraordinary sporting, social, cultural and environmental legacy for the host city, the region and the country. The International Olympic Committee is dedicated and committed to ensuring that its legacy is the best possible one.[24]

Scholars at this conference also documented the varieties of legacy. While bid cities mostly regarded legacy in economic terms — the increased prosperity and global standing of a city — delegates suggested many other kinds of legacy — outcomes in terms of the built and physical environment; public life, politics and culture; sporting facilities and culture; education and information; and symbols, memory and history.

The Olympic Games Global Impact Project

The IOC had already recognised the importance of legacy when it commissioned the Académie International des Sciences et Techniques du Sport (the International Sports Science and Technology Academy [ISSTA]) to develop an 'analysis tool' to identify and measure the global impact of the Olympic Games. The researchers, headed by Christophe Dubi, developed a methodology which became known as the Olympic Games Global Impact Project (OGGI). It came into partial operation — since it was not possible to include a full 11-year cycle (see below) — for the first time at the Salt Lake City 2002 Olympic Games. The objective of OGGI was to collect and capture the wider impacts of the Games — the social, environmental and economic dimensions — 'in a consistent and comparable manner' so that they could be passed on from one Olympic city to another. The period of measurement for the OGGI program stretches over 11 years; it starts two years before the selection of the host city and ends two years after the Games. (So an almost complete 11-year study will be possible for the first time with the 2008 Beijing Olympic Games.) Data for OGGI is collected and analysed by ISSTA in partnership with a research institution in the host city. The primary purpose of OGGI is to 'provide information' to future bids and Olympic cities 'to help them build stronger foundations'. OGGI then is now the core part of the transfer of Olympic knowledge that has become an important part of the IOC culture since 2000 (see Chapter 5).[25]

OGGI is an important part of the Rogge agenda. It is an instrument to advance the potential for positive impacts and also to further the goals of the Olympic Games Study Commission (OGSC), set up in early 2002, to deal with the increased size and popularity of the Games and the related problem of gigantism. An aim of OGSC is to assemble material to assist in efforts to 'contain the growth and manage the growth and costs [of the Games] in a more efficient way'. OGGI will provide OGSC with data to improve 'Games management efficiency'.[26] The IOC now requires the publication of a fourth volume of the *Official Report* on the Olympic Games based on the data collected and analysed through OGGI. This is a welcome development.

While OGGI is a valuable initiative to assess the impacts of the Games and the transfer of knowledge, there are some areas that are not addressed by this program. First of all, impacts are studied in terms of 150 indicators grouped in three broad dimensions — environmental, social and economic. While the dimensions are extensive — the social dimension includes culture, education, sport and media — less attention is paid to the more intangible indicators such as memory and symbols, and the Paralympic Games are not included. Secondly, the focus on OGGI seems to be more on what can be measured and quantified which means that the less tangible and more qualitative aspects of legacy are given less importance. Thirdly, all OGGI studies are concluded two years after the Games so that they only capture the dimensions that are evident in the immediate post-Games period. It will be argued in this book that some economic indicators, such as tourism, need to be measured over a longer time. This book considers the OGGI indicators in various chapters and suggests some additional indicators and approaches that may enhance the operation of the OGGI program.

OGGI was of course not in place in 2000 so there is no OGGI analysis, nor was a fourth volume published on the impacts of the Sydney 2000 Olympic Games. Hence there is a need for a study such as this. However, even the publication of a fourth volume on outcomes by future Olympic cities will not replace the value of an individual history of legacy for each Olympic city. An advantage of this history is that it locates legacy in the context of a particular city and engages with debates that continue to resonate in an Olympic city in the post-Games period. Such a work will have value for the citizens of an Olympic city who wish to understand the meaning of the Olympic Games. It will also help to define the place of the Games in the history and public life of a city. OGGI studies, by contrast, are more directed to the needs of future Olympic cities. There is, however, clearly a case for two approaches to legacy, one which deals with the transfer of knowledge from one city to another and the other which is focused more on a city's experience of legacy.

Approaching legacy: focus and range

The approach in *A Bitter-Sweet Awakening* is eclectic in that it draws on the various methodologies employed at the Lausanne conference to study legacy. The first principle is that legacy is considered in its widest possible perspective: public and private; tangible and intangible; short and long-term. Secondly, the study of legacy provides the opportunity to draw on a wide number of disciplines, such as history, anthropology, sociology and media as well as disability, environmental and urban studies.

While the Lausanne legacy conference looked at legacy as a whole, and specifically at legacy in the Olympic Games since 1984, this book is the first of its kind to look at outcomes in the context of one particular Olympic Games. It also includes a chapter on the legacy of the 2000 Paralympic Games, since cities are now required to stage both Games. I trust that this book will encourage other scholars to undertake similar studies, which will add to the comparative data available on this subject.

There are a number of reasons why this book is necessary. One is that most of the post-Games literature has focused only on one or two aspects of legacy — outcomes in terms of tourism and investment, community impacts, Games venues, costs, or volunteers, to name a few — rather than the Games as a whole. This evaluation, by contrast, aims to broaden this focus.

Another problem with most Sydney post-Games studies is that they do not sufficiently compare outcomes with the stated objectives made to the host community at the time of the bid. A central issue of this book is to address such issues: whether the promises made in 1993 were realised in full, or in part, or not at all. The stated promises are a useful starting point for a book on legacy, though this history also attempt to evaluate unstated promises or hidden agendas.

In terms of the stated promises, it is interesting to note that Sydney's three-volume 1993 bid books, which advanced Sydney's case to stage the 2000 Games, were a product of their time. They elaborated Sydney's case for the Games, providing detailed plans for the staging of each sport, but they included little material on post-Games impacts and issues such as sustainability and long-term community benefits. They made a number of claims that will be examined in this book. For instance, the Sydney bid books forecasted a modest Games surplus of US$15 million, on the basis of receipts of US$975 million, and the operation of price-control measures for hotels before and during the Games.[27] A book on the outcomes of the Sydney Olympic and Paralympic Games is also necessary because since the almost universal chorus of praise in 2000 there have been a number of critical and even discordant voices chipping away at Sydney's best-ever reputation. So while some authors continue to praise the Games as 'the time of our lives' and an event which produced great political, cultural and economic benefit for the city and country, others have been more critical, pointing to post-Games problems and even, in one instance, questioning the Samaranch assessment of the best-ever Games.[28] (The post-Games literature and the assessment of the Games will be discussed in Chapter 2). So there is a need to evaluate such alternative assessments of the Sydney Games and to explore why, to some, the Games look so different in 2005 to the way they appeared in 2000.

A central question posed by this book is whether the Games changed Sydney in any significant way and whether any such changes were temporary or long-lasting. David Richmond, director general of the OCA when it was established in 1995, believed that Sydney would never be 'quite the same after the Games'. He likened the challenge facing Sydney in 2000 to 'grabbing hold of the city and shaking it':

> You had to take it, shake it hard, put it on its side for three weeks ... that's your city ... then afterwards you shake it again and put it back. It will never be quite the same again ... It has had this rare, amazing experience.[29]

So has this 'rare, amazing experience' left any enduring mark? Is Richmond right when he claims that the city will never be the same again?

My assumption is that a study of the legacy of the Games will reveal much about how Sydneysiders and Australians dealt with this major event in their lives. Some have suggested that the Australians, like the Greeks, have been reckless in their pursuit of the 'winner's curse' and of fool's gold.

Obviously, I contest the view (as I did in 1999) of Emory sociologist Alvin Boskoff that nothing could be gained by revisiting a mega event in a city's history. He wrote one year after the Atlanta 1996 Olympic Games that a city should move on after the event and not concern itself with Olympic legacy:

> The Olympics is a temporary thing. It's like a rocket that shoots into the sky, a big expensive rocket, and then it's gone … Maybe the best thing is to forget about the Olympics and go about the business of becoming a first-class city.[30]

Finally, this book attempts to look at the legacy of the Sydney Olympic and Paralympic Games in the greater context of the importance of festivals in the life of a community. In writing it, I return to a long-held interest in festivals. My first publications explored how an Indian nationalist politician, Bal Gangadhar Tilak attempted to appropriate a popular Indian festival honouring the elephant-headed god Ganapati.[31] I have always enjoyed reading anthropological studies of festivals, which are high points in the life of the community, and memories of festivals past are savoured, while future festivals are eagerly anticipated. Observing a society at 'deep play' — a term coined by anthropologist Clifford Geertz in his classic study of cockfighting in Bali — provides some clues as to what it values and the meaning it places on public rituals.[32] A similar point was made by Handelman, who argued that public events consist of 'dense concentrations of symbols' and are 'locations of communication that convey participants into versions of social order'.[33] Despite their limitations and their critics, the Olympic and Paralympic festivals seemed to have left a deep mark on the people of Sydney and Australia. It would be astonishing if some of this did not last in some form or another.

Former senior *Sydney Morning Herald* journalist Milton Cockburn told an interesting anecdote about a favourite Alan Moir cartoon of the Sydney Olympics (Moir is a celebrated cartoonist who regularly appears in the same newspaper). The cartoon featured a young child staring up at his father who was sitting in a lounge chair reading a newspaper that had headlines such as 'rail-link in time for the Olympics', 'airport in time for the Olympics' and 'republic in time' and so forth. The young child is asking: 'Daddy, is there life after the Olympics?' There is, of course, life after the Olympics. But what kind of life there is constitutes the subject of this book.[34]

Chapter 2

THE MEMORY OF THE GAMES

The Sydney Olympic Games, according to some observers, left a powerful stamp on the public mind. Harry Gordon, author of a book on the Sydney Olympics, noted in 2003 that the Games had provided Australians not only 'with memories that we'll treasure always, but with a period of sheer, enduring happiness, possibly unmatched in Australian history'.[1] In his foreword to that book, Australian Olympic Committee (AOC) president John Coates commented on how Australians savoured 'the warm memories evoked' by the Games.[2] Novelist Thomas Keneally made a similar point in 2001 when he suggested that the Olympic Games were still a 'dominant memory'.[3] Australians, noted journalist Matthew Ricketson in 2004, still have 'fond memories' and a 'protective pride' about the Sydney Games.[4] Former SOCOG CEO Sandy Hollway, who gave many talks around Australia in 2001 as part of the International Year of Volunteers, discovered that many in his audiences harboured positive Olympic memories which were 'just below the surface'. His talks provided an occasion for many in his audience to enthusiastically express such Olympic experiences.[5]

While many believe that individuals retain positive memories of the Olympic Games, it is more difficult to locate any individual or collective Olympic memory and to point to a place or time where it was manifested. Olympic scholar Kristine Toohey even came to a different conclusion to the above writers. She commented in 2004 that it was 'perplexing' that there was an apparent public disinterest in 'the glory, the benefits, the costs, or the legacy of the Games' once they were over.[6] There is evidence, which is cited below, that supports her view that the Games quickly receded in the public mind after 2000.

This chapter will explore many issues relating to the memory of the Games in Sydney and Australia after 2000. The strength or weakness of Olympic memory also provides evidence of the perceived worth of the Games in the longer term. Three categories of memory will be considered. First, there is individual or private memory. It will be of interest to consider whether Olympic participants — such as volunteers and torch-bearers — continue to value their Games experience more so than the general public. Secondly, there are spontaneous effusions of a collective public memory that may occur at the time of a Games anniversary. Finally, there are attempts by civic authorities and media to cultivate public memory, such as planned commemorations and public monuments.

There are many questions to ponder in 2005. Is memory sustained by the grass-roots or is it the media that develops and sustains memory? Why do politicians seek to promote memory and what are the political uses of memory? Did the 2003 Rugby World Cup, which culminated at the Olympic stadium, rekindle an Olympic memory?

Memory and sport

Memory, which often takes the form of nostalgia, is an important element of sport and sporting ideology. The modern Olympic Games evolved because of a European fascination in the nineteenth century with Hellenism — an admiration of the achievements of classical Greek society — which led to an idealisation of the ancient Olympic Games. This romantic view underplayed their commercial, violent and cultic features. 'Dressing the Games in the image of antiquity proved to be a masterstroke of public relations', noted Olympic scholar Bruce Kidd, because although the modern Games were based only loosely on the ancient Games, they were built on the 'myth of the ancient Games'.[7]

The importance of nostalgia has been evident in many modern team sports such as baseball, cricket and the various codes of football.[8] Cricket, for instance, was elevated to become the most 'English of English' games from the eighteenth century. More than any other sport, cricket was believed to epitomise 'Englishness' because it was represented as a bucolic pursuit of a pastoral England which was fast disappearing as England became more urban and industrial.[9] Colonials in far-flung imperial outposts played cricket for nostalgic reasons, to remind themselves of 'home' and to prove that English society could be successfully transplanted elsewhere. Cricket paintings, which adorned some great English houses from the eighteenth century, depicted an idyllic game played in villages.[10]

In Australia, nostalgia for the Melbourne 1956 Olympic Games has progressed so that it came to be regarded as the cornerstone of a golden decade of Australian sport. The achievements of Australian athletes and the general success of the Games — which 'ended in 'a huge tide of

The Melbourne cauldron on display at the Australian Gallery of Sport and Olympic Museum in 1999. Although it was much smaller and less substantial than the Sydney cauldron, it attracted the interest of onlookers. This cauldron will again tour Victoria prior to the Melbourne 2006 Commonwealth Games (Melbourne Cricket Club image).

goodwill' — were celebrated both at the time and since, with the Games becoming known as the 'friendly Games'. In fact, nostalgia for the Games has increased in recent decades. The Australian Gallery of Sport and Olympic Museum (AGOSOM) at the Melbourne Cricket Ground was opened by Prime Minister Bob Hawke on 22 November 1986, the anniversary of the opening ceremony of the Games. This 30th-anniversary event included an Olympians dinner for 900 persons and the re-lighting of a replica of the cauldron by Marcus Clarke, son of Ron Clarke, who lit the cauldron in 1956. Invited guests for the anniversary included some prominent Olympians as well as John Ian Wing, a Chinese-Australian whose 1956 proposal, when he was just a boy, for athletes to mix informally at the closing ceremony was embraced by the organising committee.[11] A full-scale reenactment of the opening ceremony will be staged on 22 November 2006, on the 50th anniversary of the Games.

The post-Games history of the 1956 cauldron provides an interesting insight into Melbourne's post-Games legacy. Unlike the more substantial Sydney 2000 cauldron, the Melbourne cauldron was 'constructed quickly' by local sheet metal engineers Rayson Industries and 'was not intended to last for longer than the period of the Games'.[12] (Legacy was less of an issue in 1956 than 2006). After the Games the cauldron was exhibited briefly around the state of Victoria to raise money for charity. 'Subsequently it was lost and its whereabouts unknown for 30 years. In 1987 the cauldron was found in a city council warehouse in West Melbourne and donated to the AGOSOM by the Melbourne City Council', where it was given a new life as a display.[13]

Nostalgia for the 1950s and the lure of another home Olympics proved irresistible in later decades because many Australians believed that winning another bid would usher in another golden era of Australian sport and provide the catalyst for an exceptional Australian sporting performance. It undoubtedly spurred various Australian cities to bid again to host the Olympic Games: Brisbane bid first for the 1992 Games, then Melbourne for the 1996 Games and finally Sydney bid for the 2000 Games.

Of course, Brisbane did not win the 1992 Olympics: Barcelona

When Ron Clarke lit another Olympic cauldron in 2000 — a replica of the 1956 cauldron — the Melbourne Cricket Ground was filled to capacity. Clarke opted not to wear the 2000 torch-bearer uniform (Melbourne Cricket Club image).

did. The post-Games experience of Barcelona provides an interesting comparative model to Sydney of what happens to Olympic memory after the Games and the character of the post-Olympic environment. Miguel Moragas, Ana Belen Moreno and Christopher Kennett, have published an informative article on 'The Legacy of Symbols' which considers various aspects of communication including memory, anniversaries, images and symbols in the context of the 1992 Barcelona Olympic Games.[14] There are some remarkable parallels between the Olympic experiences of Barcelona and Sydney which are noted later in the chapter.

Moragas and Kennett have argued in another article that the conservation of memory — its appropriate documentation in archives and its expression in public monuments — is important to restore a proper and considered understanding of an event which suffers from Olympic reductionism (see Chapter 1) so that the memories of it are reduced to a few events which are repeatedly mentioned in public discourse.[15] Olympic films, videos and books tend to focus on a narrow range of highlights, excluding many other important events and achievements. Olympic reductionism by the media has compacted the Sydney 2000 Olympic Games to a handful of major events: Samaranch's 1993 declaration that Sydney had won the bid, the lighting of the cauldron, Cathy Freeman's success in the 400 metres and Samaranch's 'best-ever Games' verdict.

After the Games: an overview of public response

How did Sydney deal with the end of the Games? Initially there was great public relief and pride in the virtual universal acclaim and the unqualified plaudits of the local and international media. Bud Greenspan, the official Olympic Games documentary maker, rated Sydney a 'perfect 10': 'the torch relay merited a perfect 10, the opening ceremony a perfect 10 and the standard had been maintained throughout'.[16]

Australian politicians and civic boosters invoked sportive nationalism spelling out all the wider social, political and cultural lessons of the Games. They talked up the legacy of the Games. Prime Minister John Howard wrote in the *Australian* on 25 October 2000:

I do not think there is another country that can look to the future with such optimism, or that faces such an array of opportunities ... We should recommit ourselves to ensuring that the Australian spirit on display during the Olympics is not only maintained during our second centenary of Federation [the first century having ended in 2001], but is extended so that we can also achieve our full potential as a nation.

Bob Carr, premier of New South Wales, exulted in the 'gold medal Olympics performance' of Australia and believed that it would inspire emulation in other areas of public life. He added that 'what we're attempting to do is to move seamlessly from the gold medal Olympics performance of Australia into delivering excellence into all other areas (of government)'.[17]

If there was any post-Games depression after the closing ceremony, it was not apparent because another Games started at the same venues just 16 days later. There was a second torch relay, the cauldron was relit and another large Australian team, which marched in the same uniform as the Australian Olympians, was celebrated. While there was much less media coverage of the Paralympic Games — after Channel 7 had declined to broadcast the event, enabling the national broadcaster, the Australian Broadcasting Corporation (ABC) to cover it — the Sydney and Australian public embraced these Games. The opening ceremony of the Paralympic Games was watched by 4.2 million Australians on 18 October 2000 and it achieved a peak rating of 49.2 per cent in Sydney — the ABC's highest-ever audience.[18]

Clearly Australians had enjoyed the first Sydney Olympic experience so much that they flocked back in large numbers to Sydney Olympic Park. Attendances at the Sydney Paralympic Games created new records for these Games. The Australian Paralympic team achieved a better result than the Australian Olympic team (which was placed fourth), finishing in first place in the medal table by a wide margin. (See Chapter 10 for a fuller discussion of the Paralympic Games).

While there has been frequent reference to the idea of a post-Games depression, there has been little analysis of what it is, how long it lasts and who is affected by it and to what extent. Most discussion assumes that there is a temporary flat period — a case of the 'blues' after a great party — making the resumption of mundane work difficult. It is a problem that organising committees are aware of but not something that they plan for, considering it a matter related to the psychological health of the community. Occasionally a post-Games depression has a wider economic application. The *Salt Lake Tribune* of 23 September 2004 stated that the hotel industry had an 'unusually strong rebound for the second year following the Olympics' there. It added that 'while many individual Utahns fell victim to the blues after the 2002 Olympics ended, the post-Games performances of Salt Lake City's hotel industry has avoided the depression that afflicts most host cities of Winter Games'.

Thomas Keneally was one of the few to reflect on how the community faced the end of the Sydney Games. He suggested that at the end of the Games there was a sort of 'relaxed gratification' because of the success of the event — Sydney's reputation as a superb host and outstanding event manager had been securely established. However, Keneally's contention that Sydneysiders dealt with the end of the Games 'fairly pragmatically' invites further reflection. Was this really the case? Where is the evidence? Was a deep sense of loss to the ending of the Games hidden from view?

If the public response to the ending of the Games was pragmatic, it will be argued later that Sydney had an extended post-Games depression and suffered from an Olympic recession. For three to four years after the Games there appeared to be a profound public disinterest in matters Olympic. The buoyant pre-Olympic atmosphere in the nine years before 2000 was replaced by a sluggish post-Games one.

Games anniversaries

Why are anniversaries important? Do they provide a justification for large-scale spending? Are they an opportunity for collective expression of memory? Do they provide opportunities for politicians to capitalise on the legacy of the Games?

Moragas, Moreno and Kennett have noted that 'the celebration of [Olympic] anniversaries serves as a good indicator of the evolution of public opinion and memory of the Games'. They added that the celebration of the first anniversary of the Barcelona 1992 Olympic Games was 'characterised by strong institutional involvement, with speeches and commemorative acts, and considerable press coverage, but with limited public participation'. There was also public debate about the merits of 'nostalgia for the past' and the need 'to find new objectives'.[19]

Moragas, Moreno and Kennett noted that celebrations in the succeeding years were subdued:

Over the years that followed, nostalgia was transformed into forgetting, as if Barcelona society wanted 'to change the subject' and speaking publicly of the Games almost became 'politically incorrect'. The second and third anniversaries, 1994 and 1995, almost passed unnoticed. Only a group of ex-volunteers met under the cauldron at two minutes to ten on the eve of 25 July, in order to open a few bottles of champagne and to toast happy memories. Although the memories were still alive among the population, newspaper references were imperceptible and official acts were non-existent.[20]

The staging of the 1996 Atlanta Olympic Games provided the catalyst for a revival of this memory as did the tenth anniversary of the Barcelona Games in 2002 (see discussion below).

It is uncanny how similar has been Sydney's post-Games experience. In Sydney, like Barcelona, it was regarded as politically incorrect to make a public association with the past Games. Toohey noted that it was common to hear 'snide comments' about volunteers who continued to wear their uniforms after 2000.[21] This occurred because the public regarded them as 'Games tragics' who could not come to terms with the fact that the Games had long gone.

Sydney, like Barcelona, had an official event to mark the first anniversary of the Games. Sydney's celebration — known as the *Ignite* festival — was held over three weekends in September 2001 with its climax at dusk on 15 September 2001, when the relocated and revamped (deconsecrated) cauldron was relit after a spectacular laser light show. Unlike in 2000, no one lit the cauldron; it was switched on during the laser show. This 'secular' ceremony had echoes of the opening ceremony: singers and drummers performed music composed specially for the occasion. The cauldron remained alight for the duration of the 16-day festival.

The cauldron was removed to Overflow Park, between the main stadium and the railway station, because the Olympic stadium was soon to be downsized from 110,000 to approximately 83,500 seats. This involved the removal of the uncovered seating at the two ends of the stadium which included the stand that had housed the cauldron. The cauldron was moved from its lofty pedestal high in the Olympic stadium, was transformed and became an accessible and attractive sculpture in a public park. The cauldron was reconfigured so that water

Following a specially-composed work, performed by a choir backed by drummers, the cauldron was relit in a spectacular ceremony on 15 September 2001 during the Ignite festival (SOPA).

cascaded from its perimeters while the flame burned at its centre. It thus replicated the fire and water that were central to the cauldron-lighting ceremony of the Olympic Games. Journalist Anthony Dennis, writing before the re-lighting, described the character of the reconfigured cauldron in the *Sydney Morning Herald* of 9 September 2001:

> A curtain of water will cascade beneath the cauldron, shrouding
> the 24 stainless-steel support columns and emulating the moment

last September 15 when it rose from the water after it was lit during the Opening Ceremony. Below, [the] names of all Olympic and Paralympic medal winners will be recorded in paving made from Greek white marble and Australian black granite.

During the heat of summer children played near the cauldron and adults inspected the names of the Olympic and Paralympic medallists that were recorded in paving beneath it.

The choice of the name *Ignite* by festival spokesman Leo Schofield is an interesting one. The event was organised by three event-marketing companies with a budget of $2 million. While the name related specifically to the relighting of the cauldron, it was also chosen because it represented an attempt to rekindle the spirit that was so evident 12 months before. It was, then, an effort to use the memory of the Games to recreate public interest in Sydney Olympic Park. Journalist Anthony Dennis stated, before the event, that the festival was an attempt 'to exorcise the Games ghosts'. He added that:

It's tempting to say that *Ignite!*, like its venue, a post-Games

The cauldron in Overflow Park aroused much public interest during the Ignite festival. Note that the uncovered northern stand (to the left of the cauldron) has yet to be removed.

Olympic Park, is yet to set Sydney on fire.

In the year since the glory of the Games, an inglorious perception of Olympic Park seems to have developed: the pariah of Sydney precincts; a wasteland of white elephants; a massive multibillion-dollar monument to a triumph that cannot — and will not be repeated.[22]

Dennis described how people were 'working around the clock at a park beside Olympic Boulevard with an intensity not witnessed since the Games' to create this 'signature event' for the Park. Bold red, yellow and orange banners fluttered on numerous ceremonial poles and a nearby man-made hill was emblazoned with thousands of tiny flags of the same colours. Dennis added that if 'all goes well' the festival will become an annual event though he doubted it because 'Sydney's hunger for Olympics nostalgia is fast fading'.[23]

Unfortunately for the organisers, the event occurred just four days after the world was transfixed by the terrorist attacks in the United States on 11 September 2001, so any celebrations were subdued and a smaller crowd than anticipated — an estimated 25,000 — attended the event.[24] However, it was clear that many wanted to reconnect with the Sydney 2000 Olympic Games. Some individuals wore their volunteer uniforms. One person even wore her torch-bearer uniform and carried her Olympic torch.

There was no festival at the time of the second anniversary, which attracted far less public interest. However, Premier Bob Carr unveiled 'Games memories' on 15 September 2002, near the entrance to the main stadium, primarily to honour the contribution of some 74,000 Olympic and Paralympic volunteers. 'Games Memories', which cost $4.5 million, consists of a V-shaped forest of 480 poles that include the names of all the volunteers. There are an additional 50 special poles that evoked Games memories using graphics, video and audio. A multi-media pod was located at the heart of the poles and it plays continuous archival footage of Games highlights. The choice of the phrase 'Games Memories' is significant because it represents another attempt to cultivate the memory of the Games, this time by the state government. The path of 530 poles adds to the symbolic significance of the Park.

The third anniversary of the Games passed without an event or media notice as was the case in Barcelona. The Sydney cauldron was relit on 15 September and an annual dinner was held at Sydney Olympic

Park for NSW Olympians. The visit of the Athens torch to Sydney and Melbourne in 2004, on 4 and 5 June 2004, revived Olympic memory (see below). The cauldron was relit on 4 June 2004 by Steve Waugh, a popular former captain of the Australian cricket team. The cauldron was lit on each day of the Athens 2004 Olympic Games when a live site was established at Sydney Olympic Park.

Sydney has thus closely followed the post-Games experience of Barcelona. Professor Miquel de Moragas, director of Barcelona's Centre for Olympic Studies, pointed out that there was limited interest in things Olympic immediately after the end of the Games in 1992 but that little by little, year by year, local interest returned, so that by the tenth anniversary of the Games, there was a major celebration at the Olympic stadium (see below). Barcelona's experience provides evidence of a continuing public memory of the Games. Whether memory is submerged for a few years or whether it continues to exist close to the surface in the public mind, as Hollway suggested, it re-emerges over time.

Canadian scholar Harry Hiller reported that Calgary's experience of anniversaries was similar to Barcelona's and Sydney's. In February 1989, the year after the Calgary Winter Olympic Games, there was a worthwhile anniversary event but when the city attempted to stage an annual commemorative festival it 'just died'. Hiller was uncertain as to whether this failure occurred for organisational reasons or due to a lack of public interest.[25]

An Olympic recession: 2001 to 2003

In the two to three years after the Games, as we have seen, Sydney replicated the Barcelona experience. Nostalgia gave way to 'forgetting' and Sydneysiders no longer wanted to remember the Games. This Olympic trough can better be described as a recession rather than a temporary depression because it occurred over a longer time-frame and had economic, social and political dimensions.

Sydney Olympic Park became a focal point for this Olympic recession, as it was a stark reminder that the Games had come and gone and all that seemed to remain was a 'white elephant', as the media often referred to it. The problem was that, as one resident stated in 2001, 'before and during the Olympics the place pumped ... but now it's like a ghost town'. Keneally, who grew up in Homebush, believed that

Sydneysiders were now staying away from Homebush Bay because they did not want to experience this emptiness. At the time of the 2001 anniversary event he mused:

> Homebush Bay can be a lonely and desolate place … It's a wonderful site to visit when it's full … It's atmospheric … But I think that the Olympics are still a dominant memory. It's so dominant that, outside of events, I don't want to go there and perhaps experience the nostalgia of lost glory that Homebush represents. We're staying away from Homebush Bay perhaps due to a fear of encountering our own wistfulness.[26]

Keneally implied that the memory of the Games had an aspect of pain and a sense of loss that he preferred to avoid, and in so doing was partly suppressing his memory of the Games.

Any positive feeling towards Sydney Olympic Park was not encouraged by continuing national and international media criticism of it, nor by the suggestion that Sydney's post-Games planning had been deficient, which it was (see Chapter 6). Former Victorian Premier Jeff Kennett argued Sydney had failed to plan for life after the Games and was suffering from 'post-Olympic inertia'. The newly installed IOC President Jacques Rogge referred to Stadium Australia as a 'white elephant' because the largest stadium in Olympic history was surplus to the post-Games needs of the Sydney population and was downsized afterwards (see Chapter 6).

Publications: pre- and post-Games

Another significant indicator of a profound public disenchantment with the Olympic Games was the rapid decline of the Olympic market for books and memorabilia, which had been buoyant before the Games. After the Games there were 'remains of the Games' sales and auctions in which Olympic memorabilia, artefacts, sports equipment and miscellaneous material was rapidly disposed of at bargain prices. After that there was little ongoing interest in Olympic literature, memorabilia or merchandising. One of the first pre-Games books to capitalise on the public appetite for Olympic books after Sydney won the bid in 1993 was Harry Gordon's authoritative official history entitled *Australia and the Olympic Games*, published in 1994. This book celebrated Australia's continuing involvement with the

Summer Olympic Games and recounted the stories of many athletes who had overcome obstacles to achieve Olympic success. A three-hour video of the book was released in the Olympic year, before the Games. Rod McGeoch, who headed the Sydney Bid Limited, also published a book in 1994 that was co-authored by Glenda Korporaal, *The Bid: How Australia Won the Games*. Olympic sponsors also contributed to the boom in Olympic books. Australian Mutual Provident (AMP), the Australian Millennium Partner for the Sydney Olympic torch relay, underwrote the printing of over 20,000 copies of Janet Cahill's 1999 book, *Running Towards Sydney 2000: The Olympic Flame & Torch*. Well-subscribed tertiary courses on the Olympic Games encouraged the production of works that served as texts. The University of New South Wales Press published *Staging the Olympics: The Event and its Impact* (edited by Richard Cashman and Anthony Hughes) in 1999. Within two years all 2000 copies of the book had been sold. Kristine Toohey and Tony Veal, Olympic scholars from the University of Technology, Sydney, published *The Olympic Games: A Social Science Perspective,* in early 2000. A number of other books and monographs were published with titles such as *The Green Games* and *The Festival of the Dreaming*. Dennis Phillips also published a second edition of *Australian Women at the Olympic Games* in 1996. Many other Olympic monographs and articles were published in the pre-2000 period.[27]

The popularity of *The Games*, a long-running television program which satirised the organising committee as bumbling and inefficient, demonstrated that Australians had a large appetite for Olympic news before 2000. By poking fun at those who took the Games too seriously, the program helped make the Olympics part of everyday life and indicated that any Olympic news was of public interest in the Olympic city. Comedians Roy Slavin and H.G. Nelson (their real names are Greg Pickover and John Doyle) produced a popular comedy program, *The Dream*, on each night of the Games. With its light-hearted and irreverent approach to the Olympic Games, the program catered both for dedicated sports fans and a large number of non-sports watchers which were drawn into the festival. Journalist Tony Stephens noted that 'both programs were clever correctives to the hype surrounding the biggest show on earth'.[28]

In contrast to this pre-Games appetite for Games publications, the post-Games market was sluggish. There was no better illustration of this sluggish market and the puzzling lack of interest than the public response to the publication in 2003 of Harry Gordon's book, *The Time of*

Our Lives, which was sub-titled *Inside the Sydney Olympics. Age* journalist Matthew Ricketson noted in his review of January 2004 that Gordon's book was 'an outstanding work of sports history, thoroughly researched, finely judged and beautifully written. A must-read in the lead up to the Athens Olympics, this book is also remarkably well priced considering its size and illustrations'. Ricketson added that it was a 'literary scandal' that the book had 'been virtually ignored since its release late last year'. His check of three different search engines revealed just one short review, in the *Sunday Mail,* and a news story in *iSport7.*[29] A third edition of Dennis Phillips's book on Australian women and the Olympic Games published in 2001, which included a chapter on the prominent role played by Australian female athletes in 2000, sold about one quarter of its print run of 2000 copies. *The Collaborative Games* by Tony Webb, also published in 2001, documented how government, Games organisations, private companies and trade unions combined in a 'culture of collaboration' which was critical to the building of infrastructure on time and the smooth organisation of the Games. However, like other post-Olympic books it received only limited public notice. Two books published in 2001 on the contribution of volunteers likewise failed to achieve a worthwhile readership (see below).

While some post-Olympics books celebrated the achievement of the Games, there was a growing number of authors who were now critical of some aspects of the Olympic Games. Writing from a radical perspective and focusing on social aspects, Australian-born but Canadian-based scholar Helen Lenskyj questioned the reputation of the Sydney Games in the *The Best Ever Olympics?,* which was published in 2002. Lenskyj contended that Olympic 'legacy benefits accrue to the already privileged sectors of the population' while the disadvantaged bear a disproportionate share of the burden.[30] Given that she was a long term Olympic critic and a member of the Toronto anti-Olympic coalition, Bread Not Circuses, her stance was to be expected. Kristine Toohey, by contrast, was more supportive of the Sydney Games in that she had worked for SOCOG, becoming a manager in the communications department. She also became the editor of the *Official Report of the XXVIII Olympiad.* However, in an article on the legacy of the Olympic Games published in 2005, she was highly critical of the economic, social and sporting outcomes of the Games. Toohey wrote that 'now that the ongoing economic report cards on the Games are beginning to be known, the Olympic rapture appears to have worn off in Sydney, NSW and Australia. With the current troubles in NSW health, transport and other state government sectors, some are questioning the costs and benefits of the Games.' [31] Toohey and Veal also published a paper in 2005 in which they questioned whether the Olympic Games had had any positive effect on sports participation. [32] Urban planning scholar Glen H. Searle published a number of papers that documented Sydney's mixed legacy in terms of urban outcomes. There was the problem of an 'oversupply of large stadiums' some of which were a continuing economic drain on the state revenues. Although Sydney became a popular location for conventions, tourism numbers fell below expectations. Searle also pointed out that largely Olympic-related spending on sport and recreation from 1996 to 1999 had resulted in a significant decrease in State spending on health and education in this period (see Chapter 9).

Closure of the UNSW Centre for Olympic Studies

The closure of the Centre for Olympic Studies at the University of New South Wales (UNSW) on 31 March 2004 — surprisingly in an Olympic year — provided further evidence of an Olympic recession. After the Centre was launched on 31 May 1996, it achieved international prominence between 1996 and 2000 through its research, publications, teaching and documentation. Three major international Olympic conferences were organised in 1999 and 2000, in which the Centre collaborated with the three other major international Centres for Olympic Studies at Barcelona, Lausanne and Western Ontario.

After the Centre operations were reviewed by a UNSW committee in September 2003, a decision was taken to close the Centre on 31 March 2004. This occurred largely for internal reasons. UNSW believed that it had too many centres and that they were not sufficiently integrated into existing schools and faculties. Another reason was that since 2000 the Centre had struggled to gain sufficient resources and income to adequately fund its operations, so it was deemed expendable. Looked at in another way the Centre's demise was a product of the flat Olympic environment after 2000: UNSW concluded that the scale of operations were not sufficient to justify its continuance. Nonetheless UNSW left itself open to criticism that it had established a Centre for short-term gain and had no serious long-term educational interest in Olympic studies. The closure did not assist the university's efforts to market itself in China. It ignored the invitation of Chinese President Hu Jintao, who visited Sydney in October 2003, to 'come over and help us with [our] Olympics projects'.[33]

It is a matter of great irony that as local public interest in the Centre's activities diminished, international interest in the Australian Olympic experience increased. This is illustrated dramatically by the growing international interest in the Centre's website in 2001 and 2002, even though resources to manage the website were so scaled down in this period that the contents of the website were changed only infrequently. From 2001 to 2002 there was a remarkable surge of 'hits' on the Centre website; hits more than doubled, increasing from 271,299 to 657,765. Although there were many unidentified 'hits', international 'hits' were two to three times greater than Australian. The comparative use of the Centre website was also far greater than another six websites in the Faculty of Arts, where the Centre was located. The figures provide quantitative evidence that as Olympic interest in the host country declined in 2001 and 2002, international interest in Australia's Olympic experience increased.[34]

Fortunately for Olympic studies in Sydney and Australia, the University of Technology, Sydney (UTS), saw some longer-term value taking over this role because it had set up an Olympic Committee, to coordinate Olympic activities across the campus, soon after September 1993. An Australian Centre for Olympic Studies (ACOS), based in the School of Leisure, Sport and Tourism, was launched on 6 October 2005. ACOS was the recipient of the library and archives built up by the UNSW Centre. UTS will use the Centre to add value to its sports teaching programs in China, which are related indirectly to the staging of the Beijing 2008 Olympic Games. A continuing international interest in Australian Olympic expertise is a more positive post-Games story. The transfer of Australian Olympic knowledge and expertise to future Olympic and bidding cities and even to future Commonwealth and other mega event cities are significant developments (see chapter 5).

So Sydney's Olympic recession was long-lasting and amounted to a disinterest, bordering on a revulsion, in anything to do with the Olympics. This lasted at least three years. Why did it occur? Perhaps it was a necessary corrective to the decade before 2000 when the Olympics dominated everything in Sydney. Australians had devoured so much Olympic news — good news, bad news, including scandals

The name of every Olympic and Paralympic volunteer appears on poles in front of the Olympic stadium.

and controversies, and news of what the rest of the world thought of the preparations — that after 2000 there was a sense of relief that it was over. However, the experiences of Melbourne and Barcelona suggest that an Olympic memory will resurface in time and that the Sydney 2000 Olympic and Paralympic Games will be romanticised and mythicised.

Memory and the volunteers

Volunteers were the one Games group committed to 'keeping the [Games] spirit alive' said an unofficial website of the Sydney 2000 volunteers set up shortly before the 2000 Games. The website, the brainchild of ceremonies volunteer Rick Matesic, was begun as a social club for ceremonies volunteers, those who wished to maintain the camaraderie developed during the Olympic training period. By 2002 the website had over 1000 subscribers and it continues to operate in 2006. Matesic noted in 2005 that the website continued to produce quarterly newsletters and that new subscribers continued to be attracted to the website.[35]

One journalist suggested that the website was based on nostalgia, noting that it was as if 'on the Internet the Olympics never ended'. However, the website evolved into something more and was sustained by a broader commitment to volunteering in general. Newsletters and postings advertised volunteer opportunities in other sporting festivals, including the 2003 Rugby World Cup, the 2004 Athens Olympic Games and the 2006 Melbourne Commonwealth Games. The website was sufficiently prominent to attract the interest of non-sports groups, such as the Kidney Foundation, which used the website to recruit volunteers. More than four years after the Sydney 2000 Games, there is a clear and continuing volunteer legacy.

All told there were over 70,000 volunteers in the Sydney Games: 40,917 were accredited for the Olympic Games and 12,635 for the Paralympic Games; the universities provided another 6,000 volunteers, and there were approximately 12,000 ceremonies volunteers.[36] Most volunteers were trained by TAFE (Technical and Further Education). Brendan Lynch, SOCOG's Program Manager Volunteer Recruitment, noted that the attrition rate was relatively low — 31 per cent from 1997 to 2000. Some of this was caused by poaching by sponsors and the practice of raiding when a volunteer was lured to a more attractive position.[37]

It is not surprising that some of the Sydney volunteers wished to maintain the memory of the Games, because they had been highly praised for their Olympic role, which gave them a strong sense of their own worth. In the closing ceremony of the Olympic Games President Samaranch praised them as the 'best ever'. The volunteers were recognised by the state government which organised a special tickertape parade through the streets of Sydney to thank them, and later created 'Games Memories' in 2002 (see above). They were equally popular with the community as the human face of the Games. When the Sydney Swans Australian football team played their first home match for the 2001 season, the club paid a tribute to the effort of the volunteers 'by inviting them to go to the match free if they were wearing their uniform'.[38]

If any group was likely to nurture a post-Olympic memory it was the volunteers. Three weeks before the first Olympic anniversary in 2001, prominent volunteer Laurie Smith — who had been a volunteer at seven successive Olympic Games — published a book, *Living is Giving: The Volunteer Experience*. Lavishly-illustrated with over 700 colour photographs in its 300 pages, it was 'an expensive coffee table book' that was promoted as a 'tangible souvenir'. Thirty thousand copies of the book were printed. Smith noted that he and his wife, who put up the money for the book, 'spent a lot of money' on its advertising'.[39]

Unfortunately for Smith, former international cricketer Max Walker and prominent New South Wales public servant Gerry Gleeson published a paperback, *The Volunteers*, a week later at half the price. It included a foreword by former IOC President Samaranch and included a list of the volunteers at the Olympic and Paralympic Games. The authors included a 'Volunteers Honour Roll' listing the volunteers for both Games. Walker and Gleeson added a note to any volunteers who were inadvertently missing from the roll: 'Please let us know if you were a volunteer at the Sydney Olympic or Paralympic Games and your name is not on the list, or if you would prefer to be removed from the list, and we will adjust future editions'.

Both books failed to tap into the post-Games volunteer market. There were no future editions of *The Volunteers* and the book was remaindered after a relatively short period. The situation was worse for Laurie Smith, who incurred a substantial financial loss when less than a third of the printed copies were sold. Smith was also dismayed when 20,000 copies of his book were pulped (without his knowledge) after the publisher went into receivership. He attributes the disappointing sales of his book to the competition of the Walker book and 'the apathy of some volunteers who have said that they should be given a copy because they were volunteers!'[40]

Lynch asserted in 2004 that there was a volunteer legacy. The International Year of Volunteers in 2001 'capitalised on the lift that Sydney 2000 had given the image of volunteering for a short while'. Several hundred Sydney volunteers participated in the Athens volunteer program, though many of these were former SOCOG staffers of Greek descent (see Chapter 5). Lynch himself has advised the organising committees of Olympic and Commonwealth Games cities including Salt Lake City, Manchester, Athens, Melbourne and Vancouver and has written for the Olympic Games Knowledge Service. Lynch noted that while only 1 per cent of Sydney's volunteer applications were from overseas, the figure for Athens was 25 per cent. He noted that this represented a 'huge risk' given the challenge of finding accommodation, attending training and test events.[41]

A volunteer legacy was also evident in 2005 when the Fairfax company, publisher of major dailies in Sydney and Melbourne, announced that it was supporting the recruitment of volunteers for the 2006 Melbourne Commonwealth Games. The *Sydney Morning Herald* stated that it would publish a *Volunteer Update* every two months, to assist in the 'recruitment of volunteers' and to keep them 'informed in the countdown to the Games'. The editor of this paper, Robert Whitehead, stated that he was delighted that his newspaper was supporting the Games: 'Following the success of the volunteers programs at the Olympics in Sydney I am sure Sydneysiders will be delighted if we can help ensure these will be the best Commonwealth Games yet'.[42] Despite the limited success of two volunteer books, there was clearly a continuing positive memory of the volunteer contribution in 2000.

The post-Games history of artefacts

The fate of the many artefacts used in the opening ceremony is an interesting issue. Do they have any post-Games use and value? After the Games four Games organisations (OCA, ORTA, SOCOG and SPOC) transferred 700 items, including many of the props used in the opening ceremony, to the Powerhouse Museum, near the central Sydney business district. The Powerhouse Museum retained 614 of these objects distributing the remainder to other cultural institutions. The 614 objects, which were individually listed and can be accessed electronically, form the basis of its Sydney 2000 Games Collection. The collection categories include:

- Broadcasting
- Games force (volunteers)
- Green Games 2000
- Look and image
- Opening and closing ceremonies
- Pins, coins, medals and stamps
- Sport
- Torch relay
- Transport

Since the donation of the 700 objects the collection has been broadened to include a range of material, including interviews of those involved in Olympic ceremonies, such as David Atkins. Kevin Fewster, director of the Museum, noted that 'we use objects from the collection very regularly in a host of exhibitions and programs'. He added that the website gained significant usage from researchers and the general public.[43]

Fewster added that the Sydney Olympic Collection represents 'the nearest thing that Sydney has to an offical Sydney Olympic Games museum'. The usage figures for 2004 and 2005 indicate an increasing interest in this microsite and demonstrate the value of this collection. This occurred in part because the site became part of the NSW Department Education and Training's portal in March 2005, directly linking the Museum's online education products to students and teachers throughout the state. (The Powerhouse Museum Olympic Collection includes educational modules).

Table 2.1 Unique visitors to Sydney Olympic Collection by month from April 2004 to September 2005. (Unique visitors remain at the site for eight to nine minutes so the figures do not include 'hits' which are often for a much shorter time).

2004		2005	
Apr.	206	Jan.	208
May	203	Feb.	677
June	145	Mar.	1223
July	218	Apr.	1521
Aug.	224	May	1424
Sept.	120	June	1696
Oct.	127	July	1427
Nov.	126	Aug.	1525
Dec.	204	Sept.	1790

Ned Kelly's horse, which featured in the 'Tin Symphony' segment — when it changed from a horse to a windmill before reverting back to a horse — was too big for the Powerhouse Museum. It found a permanent home at Jerilderie, a small town in southwest New South Wales with a population of approximately 2000.

Jerilderie was an appropriate place for this horse-cum-windmill because its main claim to fame was that the Kelly gang took over the town for two days in 1879, locking up the police and robbing the bank of more than £2000. Jerilderie's Telegraph Office Museum has a display of relics from the Kelly gang, so this was an opportunity to add to the town's Kelly heritage.

The then mayor of Jerilderie Shire Council, Councillor Ian Sneddon, accepted the gift of the 'horse' in 2001 and placed it in an attractive location overlooking Lake Jerilderie. Councillor Sneddon witnessed many tourists stopping to admire the horse and to read its plaque which states:

The Ned Kelly Horse

Part of the Sydney 2000 Games Collection. Gift of the New South Wales Government 2001.

The Ned Kelly Horse was one of the major objects from the Opening Ceremony of the Sydney 2000 Games.

The Horse is made up of a welded iron structure on a large vehicle chassis. During the Opening Ceremony, the Horse 'changed' into a windmill and then back to a Horse, then left the arena after eating an apple given to it by Nikki Webster.

The Olympic torch relay passed through Jerilderie on 15 August 2000 with members of the Jerilderie community participating.

The Jerilderie Shire Council acknowledges the cooperation of the Powerhouse Museum, the Melbourne Museum and the New South Wales Government.

The Council has yet to determine the long-term future of this Olympic artefact, and the surrounding fence and plaque are temporary. Sneddon hoped that funds can be found to re-animate the machinery of the horse and the windmill so that tourists to Jerilderie can observe how it worked in the opening ceremony.

Auctions conducted by Charles Leski, one of the leading auctioneers in Australia since 1973, provide further insights into memory and the worth of Games artefacts. Although more than 11,000 torches were produced, and each torchbearer had the opportunity to purchase his or her own torch at a cost of around $330, relatively few have been sold at auction since 2000 indicating the value placed on Sydney Olympic Games torches. Leski estimated that he had probably sold less than a dozen in five years at a consistent average price of around $3000 — almost ten times their original cost. He believed that the high price of the torch had been maintained because there were insufficient torches to satisfy the market. He added that the greatest demand for Sydney torches came from overseas collectors.[44] Fatso, the counter-mascot who became popular on Roy and H.G.'s program *The Dream*, was sold for a reported $80,450 on the internet to Kerry Stokes, the owner of Channel 7 (see Chapter 3).

The Rugby World Cup 2003: a new life for Sydney Olympic Park

The staging of the 2003 Rugby World Cup (RWC 2003) in Australia was a great boon for the New South Wales Government and the promoters of Sydney Olympic Park. The Rugby World Cup is ranked third, after the Olympic Games and the FIFA's Football (soccer) World Cup, as a global sporting festival. The 2003 tournament was broadcast to 194 countries and had a cumulative international television audience of 3.4 billion viewers. This event ensured that the Olympic precinct once again became a vibrant sporting focus for a major international sporting festival. The

Ned Kelly's horse from the opening ceremony found an appropriate and peaceful home overlooking Lake Jerilderie.

successful RWC 2003 countered the doomsayers who had contended in 2001 and 2002 that Sydney Olympic Park was a white elephant.

The Rugby World Cup coincided with a softening media attitude towards the park. Journalist Steve Meacham wrote in the *Sydney Morning Herald* of 8-9 March 2003 that:

> We've tagged our Olympic Stadium 'a white elephant', dismissed the entire Olympic precinct as a monumental vanity, and complained that there's nothing to do 'out there'. And yet, with virtually no fanfare, Sydney Olympic Park — as we're meant to call it now — has been reshaping itself as a stately pleasure dome.

Meacham outlined a growing number of cultural and sporting events that were transforming the park and making it 'as cool as a fat-arsed wombat'.

RWC 2003 was originally to be shared by Australia and New Zealand, but when the New Zealand planning was deemed deficient it was decided that the entire tournament would be played in Australia. Seven of the most important games were played at Telstra Stadium — Stadium Australia having been renamed in 2002 — including the opening match, the two semi-finals and the final.

The Rugby World Cup was far easier to organise than the Olympic Games because the 48 matches in one sport were played in various cities around Australia. The event lasted for six weeks rather than 16 days. Games took place at existing venues, so there were limited capital expenditures for rugby authorities or state governments. However, in New South Wales, the RWC 2003 benefited from the established Olympic infrastructure, such as the Olympic stadium and the rail link to Sydney Olympic Park.

Sydney, and Australia, slipped easily into celebration mode in October and November 2003. It was as if the Olympic or festival switch was again turned on. Rugby was the talk of the town and it dominated the media and rugby clothing and merchandise featured prominently in shops. People who knew nothing about the sport were swept along by the tide of public enthusiasm. The tournament went according to script with the old adversaries, Australia and England, meeting in the final. Although England defeated Australia in extra time, with a last minute field goal, it was an exciting and dramatic final; and did not disappoint about half the crowd, who were English tourists.

The Rugby World Cup received great support from the Australian public. There were bumper crowds at almost every match and a total attendance of 1,837,547 at the 48 matches. Even the smallest crowd of 15,457 at York Park, Launceston, was remarkable because this was an inconsequential match (in terms of advancement prospects) between two rugby minnows, Namibia and Romania, staged in an Australian football stronghold. The revenue from tournament ticket sales was $202 million.[45]

RWC 2003 achieved a glowing economic report card. Whereas 40,000 international tourists were expected, many more came. A survey conducted on behalf of the Bureau of Tourism Research estimated that 64,296 international visitors came to Australia specifically for the Rugby World Cup. The total number of international tourists who visited individual states and territories numbered 110,250, indicating that many travelled to two or more states and territories. Because of the length of the tournament, many rugby tourists stayed for much longer periods than the 2000 Olympic tourists.[46] A 2005 report on the business and economic benefits arising from the RWC 2003, commissioned by the

There were echoes of the Olympic Games opening ceremony in the opening ceremony of the 2003 Rugby World Cup, which included Aboriginal images. The removal of two uncovered stands enabled a roof to circle the stadium (Chris McGrath and Getty Images Sport).

NSW Department of State and Regional Development, stated that:

> Average spending on tourism activities by those attending RWC
> 2003 may have been larger than that of visitors attending the
> [Olympic] Games; with substantial time between each RWC
> 2003 match, RWC 2003 visitors had greater opportunity to
> enjoy the tourist activities available in and around the RWC
> 2003 venues.[47]

The report added that Australian Hotels Association (AHA) had reported far fewer last-minute cancellations in accommodation than had occurred at the time of the Olympic Games. AHA members also reported that regional tourism, to places such as the Blue Mountains, was better supported during the RWC 2003 than at the time of the Olympic Games (see Chapter 4).[48]

The Rugby World Cup provided a boost the nation's shops, hotels and restaurants, and was estimated to be worth up to $1 billion to the Australian economy.[49] NSW benefited most, with the Rugby World Cup attracting over 110,000 visitors — 38,048 international and around 72,854 from interstate, It was estimated that international tourists contributed $196,488,168 and interstate visitors $42,072,070 to the state economy, and had created an estimated 5100 job equivalents.[50] The demand for rugby clothing, both for men and women, was exceptional.

Because income from the Cup greatly exceeded expenditure, the immediate legacy of the event was one of profit both for the Australian Rugby Union (approximately $44.5 million) and the International Rugby Board ($37 million), with the latter body receiving another $120 to 150 million from its commercial operations. The Australian Rugby Union stated that one-third of its windfall profit would be directed towards the sport's development. Some believed that the success of the Cup could enhance the status of rugby in Australia. Journalist Peter Jenkins predicted that rugby was 'now poised to move into the No. 2 sport' behind the Australian football and move ahead of its rival, rugby league.[51]

Although it was a one-off event, the 2003 Rugby World Cup provided a boost for the image of Telstra Stadium and Sydney Olympic Park. If nothing else it demonstrated that there was life for the precinct after the Olympic Games. There were some 700,000 visitors to the Olympic precinct during the tournament, including 550,000 who attended matches at Telstra Stadium. The Merivale Group operated a popular 'live site' in Overflow Park, next to the stadium.[52] The RWC 2003 also provided further employment for sporting event organisers. Andrew Walsh, who was a producer of the opening and closing ceremonies for RWC 2003, was involved in the staging of the opening and closing ceremonies for the Athens 2004 Olympic Games.

The contrast between the business and economic outcomes of the 2003 Rugby World Cup and the 2000 Olympic and Paralympic Games was stark. The legacy of the Rugby World Cup was entirely positive and there were no concerns for struggling sporting venues and precincts. However, the success of this tournament was built on the back of Olympic organisation and infrastructure. Without the contribution of the Olympic Games Sydney would have lacked a stadium with a capacity of 83,500 and a transport infrastructure to service it.

The successful staging of the 2003 Rugby World Cup demonstrated the importance of capitalising on Olympic infrastructure and expertise with follow-up events, or as former Victorian State Premier Jeff Kennett stated, the 'feeding' of a mega event with more events. Barcelona has proven the benefits of such a policy: following the tenth anniversary Olympic celebration in 2002, it staged the Barcelona Universal Forum of Culture in 2004, which built on Barcelona's previous international event success.

The staging of another Olympic Games

The staging of the 2004 Athens Games reignited Australia's interest in the Olympic Games. Olympic merchandise once again flooded the shops and Sydney retailers reported 'healthy sales of Olympic books', ranging from Phil Cousineau's The Olympic Odyssey which was subtitled Rekindling the Spirit of the Ancient Games to a largely pictorial work, The Athens Dream, which featured the athletic bodies of Australian Olympians.[53] Olympic billboards, wishing Australian athletes well, reminded the Australian public of the coming festival. Of course, the build-up to Athens in Australia was relatively brief compared to the extended and intense public involvement in 2000. In a sense this was all part of the normal Olympic cycle, when the staging of another Olympics and the saga of Australian athletic success (and failure) absorbed the Australian public once again.

But in 2004 there was an added dimension. An inter-city rivalry between Sydney and Athens provided the catalyst for a re-surfacing of Olympic memory. In the lead-up to the Athens Games the Australian media made much of the apparent tardiness of the Greek preparations, the roofless aquatic venue and the saga of the late erection of the Olympic stadium roof. There were, as Kristine Toohey noted, 'gleeful media reports' about the problems faced by the Athens' organisers 'juxtaposed with flashbacks to Sydney's success'.[54] The Australian media and Australian Olympic authorities raised the security bugbear after the detonation of three small bombs just 100 days before the opening ceremony. The Australian Government, to the consternation of the Athens Olympic Organising Committee (ATHOC), even issued warnings about travelling to Greece. It was all too much for Gianna Angelopoulos-Daskalaki, president of ATHOC, who complained: 'Australia chose, in the middle of an overwhelmingly successful IOC Coordination Commission meeting, to release a warning about travelling to Greece. This is damaging to the Olympic Games.'[55]

It's not hard to detect what was behind this inter-city rivalry. Some believed that if Athens succeeded, Sydney's might lose its status as the 'best-ever Games' — as the Olympic benchmark city. If Sydneysiders and Australians had been blasé about the country's achievements, it now became clear that they were protective about its sporting reputation. The Australian production and screening of *Atlanta Blues* in 1997, which documented Atlanta's shortcomings, was an earlier manifestation of an intercity rivalry.

Moragas, Moreno and Kennett report a similar Olympic 'remembering' in Barcelona in 1996 when the failures of Atlanta led to a 'surprising public revitalisation'; the closing ceremony of the Atlanta Games made 'the Barcelona Games even better' as the *Avui* newspaper put it on of 25 July 1996.[56] The criticisms of Atlanta provided the incentive for the Barcelona City Council to organise a huge public party, and a fireworks and musical display lasting 40 minutes and attended by 180,000 people. Barcelona reinstituted the ritual of lighting the cauldron in the stadium and the 1992 Games again became the focus of journalistic attention. The Barcelona Games once more returned to the front pages of the press.

It didn't quite happen that way in Sydney because the Athens Games, while not perfect, confounded the doomsayers. The Athens opening and closing ceremonies were stylish and technologically sophisticated. The venues, if not always full in the first few days, looked good and worked smoothly. The Greeks recovered from the scandal of its two leading track stars in the first week to record some stirring performances and to achieve their best medal haul since 1896. The fears of a security crisis did not eventuate.

The 'remembering' of the Sydney Games was, as a result, not as spectacular as Barcelona in 1996. Athens did provide an opportunity to re-connect with the memory of the Games and to relive another round of Australian athletic success. Bob Carr and Sydney Lord Mayor Clover Moore nominated the symbolic date of 15 September for a tickertape parade in honour of the homecoming Olympians, so there was a major event on the fourth anniversary. Roy and H.G. repeated their popular show, renamed *The Dream in Athens*, during the Games. However, the live sites at Sydney Olympic Park — which were immensely popular in 2000 — were thinly peopled in 2004 because the event was held far away, the still-wintry nights were colder than those in the early spring of 2000, and key events took place in the early hours of the morning.

Barcelona may provide a model of how Olympic memory might be played out in Sydney in the future. The celebrations there from the fifth to the ninth anniversaries were low-key and discreet. However, the tenth anniversary in 2002 was an impressive event. Its importance was enhanced by two factors. Barcelona and Catalonia paid homage to Juan Antonio Samaranch, who had stepped down as president of the IOC in 2001. The commemorative acts were used to publicly launch a large-scale campaign to promote the Universal Forum of Culture in 2004, demonstrating the value of linking new projects with the past.

Catholic World Youth Jubilee 2008

Sydney and Sydney Olympic Park received another boost when Pope Benedict XVI announced to a cheering crowd of 800,000 at Cologne Germany on 21 August 2005 that Sydney had won the bid for this major Catholic festival, which will be held from 15–20 July 2008. The euphoria of Australian delegates reminded many in the Australian media of that 1993 day when Samaranch had declared Sydney the winner of the Olympic bid. A 2500-strong Australian contingent at Cologne cheered, waved Australian flags and sang 'Waltzing Matilda'. Like the Olympic bid, the bid for the jubilee had been well-developed. Cardinal George Pell, Archbishop of Sydney, stated that 'we put in a coherent and well-prepared bid with tremendous help from the state and federal governments'.[57]

The opening mass, expected to attract 100,000 to 150,000 pilgrims, will be held at Telstra Stadium on 15 July. (The previous Pope, John Paul II, had celebrated a mass at Randwick racecourse). As many as 250,000 pilgrims will sleep overnight at Sydney Olympic Park before the final mass there on 20 July attended by an estimated 500,000. The *Australian* of 22 August 2005 reported a tentative plan that 'the mass will be staged on the 1.7km Olympic Boulevard, with huge video screens to accommodate what would be largest crowd in Australian history'. With the prospect of 80,000 to 100,000 international visitors, the NSW Tourism Minister Sandra Nori talked up the benefits of the event, stating that the jubilee could lead to 'massive' tourist profits. While the event would cost taxpayers $20 million, Nori stated that 'we are expecting a minimum of a three-to-one return, possibly as high as $110 million'.[58]

Conclusions

Moragas, Moreno and Kennett wrote that 'in one of the final scenes of the closing ceremony of Barcelona '92, [the mascot] Cobi could be seen in a paper boat going up in the air and waving goodbye, appealing to post-Olympic positive nostalgia'.[59] It seems that this appeal fell on deaf ears initially, in Barcelona, and later in Sydney. While there were a handful of dedicated Olympic supporters — notably volunteers — who wanted to maintain the spirit, most Catalans and Australians wanted simply to forget. There are probably two main reasons for this forgetting. The awakening from the Olympic dream was a bitter-sweet experience and in the initial post-Games years it seems that pain was more evident than pleasure.

Sydney, like most other previous Olympic cities, went through a long Olympic recession after 2000 when most citizens did not want to be reminded of the Games, in spite of their success. Kevin Fewster, director of the Powerhouse Museum, commented in 2005 that 'apart from the marathon blue line and one statue at Darling Harbour there was nothing in the city to indicate that Sydney had staged an Olympic Games. It was as if they hadn't occurred.'[60] This situation will change gradually, as Moragas has suggested. By 2010 and in 2030 any lingering pain will be replaced by nostalgia when the Sydney Olympic Games, like the Melbourne Olympic Games previously, will be elevated in public memory.

While some efforts to cultivate a positive public memory of the Olympic Games have achieved limited success, the symbolic marking of Sydney Olympic Park is likely to be of long-term benefit. The organisation of another mega event at Sydney Olympic Park in 2003 helped to restore the public confidence in this precinct.

Have the people of Sydney and Australia been legacy winners or losers in the aftermath of the Games? Given the continuing media criticism of Sydney Olympic Park, it seems that the memory of the Games in 2001 and 2002 has been for a time problematic and even painful. Despite this, many Sydneysiders have positive memories for the Games in general and even Sydney Olympic Park. David Morrow, a popular ABC sports broadcaster, refuses to refer to Telstra Stadium by this name: he invariably continues to refer to it as the Olympic stadium.

There are many agendas involved in the cultivation of Olympic memory. The NSW Government has an interest in making the Olympic precinct popular, thereby endorsing its past plans to develop the area and reduce costs in maintaining Sydney Olympic Park. By contrast, it suits the media to indulge in Olympic reductionism dwelling initially on an empty Sydney Olympic Park and other seeming Olympic white elephants, thus reducing the Sydney Olympic Games and its memory to simple formulas. It is the task of the scholars, as Moragas and Kennett, have noted, to encourage a broader understanding of such memorable events and to locate them in the longer-term history of a city.

Chapter 3

MEDIA, IDENTITY AND CULTURE

Olympic cities attempt to use the Games to promote new and more interesting images of themselves; images designed to appeal domestically and internationally. Images of the city and country are re-branded and exported through international media, primarily to stimulate greater tourism. These re-branded images may also have domestic outcomes, in that many event organisers believe that an Olympic Games can act as a catalyst to promote an enhanced sense of identity and community. It is also an opportunity, as Canadian scholar Harry Hiller has noted, for politicians and civic leaders to indulge in urban boosterism.[1] In Sydney, the then NSW Premier Bob Carr believed that the Games helped 'unite and energise' the community.[2]

The distinction between international and domestic outcomes is frequently blurred. An editorial in the Sydney *Daily Telegraph* of 7 August 1996 linked the two processes:

> The 2000 Olympics pose many challenges for Australia. Not the least of which is the question of the symbols we should use to identify and promote the nation ... The 2000 Games provide us with an extraordinary opportunity, not merely to re-examine ourselves, but to redefine our nation for the rest of the world.

The two outcomes share similar media space. The cultural presentation of the nation in the opening ceremony, for instance, was constructed both for local and international consumption. A ceremony has many layers and nuances which are read differently by diverse audiences internationally. Television stations around the world cater to local audiences in that they choose which part and how much of the official television 'feed' is broadcast to a particular country. The commentary is also geared to an audience's understanding of the country in question.

The re-branding exercise — the development of *Brand Australia* (see below) — is directed more to the international market. *Brand Australia* was carefully planned and generously funded by national tourist organisations and backed by the various levels of government in the belief that it would generate tangible financial returns as a result of increased tourism. By contrast, an increased sense of national identity and community is regarded as a more indirect benefit of staging the Games.

Culture is another important aspect of the Olympic Games in that it is one of the three dimensions of Olympism, the other two being sport and the environment. The cultural emphasis of the founder of the modern Olympic Games, Pierre de Coubertin, was based on the notion that sport should play an educational role and be part of the balanced development of both the individual and the community. De Coubertin also believed that sport and culture should be closely aligned. He promoted an Olympic Arts competition which became an official part of the Olympic Games after 1912 and entered himself in the first competition, winning a bronze medal for a poem.

Although the Olympic cultural program exists on the periphery of the sporting festival, each Olympic city is required to stage it in conjunction with the Olympic Games. In recent times the cultural program has been overshadowed by the cultural presentation in the opening ceremony, which has grown in significance in the last two decades to become the most prized and popular event of an Olympic Games. Its growing importance has coincided with the growing prominence of television coverage.[3]

The contemporary opening ceremony plays an important role in the re-packaging of a regional or a national identity both for local and international consumption. There is a strong belief among Olympic cities that such advertisement promotes its local and global interests and brings increased tourism. As a result there is intense competition between cities to stage the 'best ever' opening ceremony.[4]

Moragas, Moreno and Kennett have noted that planners carefully redefine the image of the city to be promoted in the opening ceremony and through tourist promotion:

> The image of an Olympic city is, therefore, the result of a long process … Once the nomination has been obtained, one of the first challenges consists, precisely, in defining (and selecting) the image of the collective identity of the host city (the briefing) to be publicised not only on an international scale, but also locally.[5]

In his work on world fairs anthropologist Burton Benedict made a comment that was equally applicable to the opening ceremony of an Olympic Games:

> [Each one] is a collective representation that symbolizes an entire community in a massive display of prestige vis-à-vis other communities ... They are about power and economics, but they are also about culture.[6]

Anthropologist John MacAloon has approached the Olympic Games as a complex cultural form of 'performance' or 'communication' which involves four distinct genres that operate at the same time — festival, ritual, spectacle and game.[7] Maurice Roche noted that this has 'always been a complex and at times contradictory mixture' with the 'spectacle dimension' achieving priority over the 'other dimensions' in more recent times. This has sometimes resulted in a clash between the Olympic values promoted in opening ceremonies and in the cultural program, such as internationalism and equality, and those promoted in the sports spectacle which celebrates 'the inequalities and hierarchies of sports "stars"'.[8]

There are many questions that can be asked about the international and domestic consumption of the Olympic Games. Did the coverage of the Games and the efforts of the Australian tourism industry to develop a new *Brand Australia* have an impact on international perceptions of Australia? Did it provide a boost for the Australian tourism industry? The economic aspects of this are dealt with in Chapter 4, but this chapter focuses on the aspects of image and identity.

Did the Olympic Games act as a catalyst for local and national identity in the short and even long term? Did the Olympic Games act as a change agent contributing to greater reconciliation of the majority of the Australian population and its indigenous communities? Did the cultural program produce any significant outcomes?

The Olympic Games Global Impact (OGGI) Program (see Chapter 1) includes relatively few social indicators relating to media, culture and identity. The listed indicators are:

Media
- Television and radio audiences and broadcasting time
- Media image
- Media accreditation

Culture
- Cultural venues
- Arts and architecture
- Ceremony participants
- Cultural program
- Television and radio audiences for the ceremonies

There is only one item that may relate to identity — opinion polls — but this refers to the host-city community's acceptance of the Games, particularly in the lead-up period, rather than identity.

Identity and community cohesion are important subjects because politicians invariably talk up the benefits before and after of the Games. These are also elusive subjects because of their non-tangible character and because there have been few previous studies of such subjects.

Australian identity

Much was read into the significance of the Olympic Games for Australia's self-image by the politicians, city leaders and the public. From the time that Sydney won the bid, Australian politicians and the media made sweeping claims about how much the country would benefit from the Games. Shortly after Sydney was announced as the winner, Australian Prime Minister Paul Keating announced that the successful bid was a major step in Australia's search for a new international identity. 'It's a defining decision', Keating added, 'that marks out the Australian nation as one that can carry the greatest international pageant of our time, the Olympics'. Keating believed that the bid decision was 'a great confidence builder and a great nation builder'.[9]

By strengthening the sense of Australian nationalism, Keating also believed that the Games would quicken the pace of the movement towards an Australian republic, which he was keen to champion. Keating added that the winning of the bid put Australia 'in the swim with the big boys'.[10] Keating's metaphor was apt because swimming was one sport where Australia could mix it with the best. The winning of the bid, like victories in international sport, enable countries to seize the opportunity 'to display national accomplishments in ideology, economics, politics, science, diplomacy, religion and race'.[11]

Whether or not the Olympic Games changed Australia in any significant way, there can be no doubt that the Australian public was intensely interested — even to the point of hyper-sensitivity — in the representation and re-branding of the country at the time of the Olympics.

The seven-minute-19-second presentation of Australia — known as the Olympic Flag Handover Ceremony — at the Atlanta closing ceremony generated huge media coverage and sustained public outrage. The public scorn was directed to one small segment, the kangaroos on bikes involving 12 boys riding bicycles covered with inflated plastic kangaroos, featuring multi-coloured Aboriginal motifs. By contrast, there were few comments on the rest of the ceremony, which featured the Aboriginal Bangarra Dance Theatre, Australian flora and fauna (cockatoos and waratahs), the Sydney Opera House and lifesavers bearing Olympic flags.

While the Atlanta stadium audience 'loved the whole thing' including the 'roos on bikes',[12] Australian newspapers were inundated with letters to the editor, with the vast majority expressing embarrassment at this representation of the country. The letters column of the *Sydney Morning Herald* of 7 August 1996 was headed by the comment that 'We must do better in 2000'. Extracts from two of the letters convey typical responses:

Ric Birch discovered in 1996 that most Australians were hyper-sensitive about the representation of Australia overseas (Scott Barbour and Getty Image Sport).

Ramin Jahromi of Neutral Bay wrote that:

> Fauna (such as kangaroos) might seem the quintessential Australian icon, but plastic kangaroos with Aboriginal motifs on bikes are a tacky, unintelligent interpretation of our national emblem.

Frank Watters of East Sydney was equally critical:

> If the closing ceremony at Atlanta is any indication of Australia's plans for the future, we should win at least four medals:
> Gold for bad taste;
> Gold for vulgarity;
> Gold for mediocrity;
> Gold for schlock.

The director of this presentation and the opening ceremony, Ric Birch, was astounded by the controversy, because he had included the kangaroos on bikes as an element of fun. He recounted later that 'when I saw the biker boys in full kangaroo formation I laughed so hard I nearly fell off the scaffolding'. The presentation, Birch added, tapped into Australian 'deep-seated insecurity complexes about their image overseas' with many believing that Australia had become the 'laughing-stock' of the world. Controversy raged for weeks and 'never really went away until after the Sydney opening ceremony'.[13]

Media commentator Enno Hermann agreed with the Birch view of the kangaroos on bicycles, regarding them as an example of 'irony, parody and self-reflexivity' which had become part of the advertising of Australia. This was part of the advertisement of Australia as a postmodern and postcolonial society, which provided a model for a more globalised world.[14] However, such irony was lost on the majority of the Australian public. As if to make fun of the hysterical public reaction in 1996, Birch brought back the kangaroos on bikes in the Sydney closing ceremony of the 2000 Paralympic Games, when the cycling 'roos were greeted with 'great affection'.[15] By that time the public reckoned that Birch had 'redeemed' himself with an acclaimed opening ceremony (see below).

Historian Graeme Davison noted that Australians have long suffered from a sense of insecurity, which he believes is a 'mental relic of colonialism'. It was noted at the time of the 1956 Melbourne Olympic

Games that 'we seem to be terrified of offending anyone, frightened what people might think of us'. From the late nineteenth century and for much of the twentieth Australians entertained an 'uneasy feeling', as novelist David Malouf noted, that they were 'second-rate' in all those aspects of life that had anything 'to do with education and culture'.[16] Davison suggested that Australians believe that they perform in front of an 'imaginary grandstand of international spectators' because they have developed a habit of seeing themselves 'through the real or imagined eyes of others'.[17] ABC broadcaster Amanda Smith even suggested that a fear of failure — and avoiding disgrace — was a key factor in public concern about the Games and was why so much effort and money were invested in staging a successful Games.[18]

The opening ceremony

If there was any public nervousness about how Australia would be presented in the Ric Birch-organised opening ceremony, it was alleviated by the production. It attracted no criticism and drew unstinting acclamation within Australia and internationally. Bob Carr had no doubts about the worth and merit of the performance, describing it in grandiose terms as 'the greatest single work of the imagination by Australians, about Australia'.

There was the occasional critic, even within Australia, who did not share Carr's view that the opening ceremony was an artistic masterpiece. John MacDonald, head of Australian art at the National Gallery of Australia dismissed the opening ceremony as 'kitsch from start to finish'. 'Kitsch', he added:

> is crap with pretensions to sincerity. Kitsch takes all the emotions associated with great art, and packages them in the most compact, user-friendly fashion: editing out anything that may be disturbing or complex.[19]

Although MacDonald may not have intended it, this may be a back-handed compliment to Birch. A ceremonies director is required to produce something that is spectacular, entertaining and accessible for a mass international audience. Opening ceremonies are not occasions for the display of 'great art' though there are opportunities the expression of artistic imagination.

Why did the opening ceremony appeal to such diverse international audiences? First of all, it was a skilful, technologically sophisticated and innovative event with a large cast of 12,600 and a sizeable budget — it used most of the ceremonies budget of $67 million. It brought together a wide range of talented directors from theatre, dance and performance. Ric Birch had had a distinguished career as a 'master of ceremonies': his involvement in opening and closing ceremonies included the 1982 Brisbane Commonwealth Games and the 1984 (Los Angeles) and 1992 (Barcelona) Olympic Games. 'The list of Australian creative minds who contributed to the opening ceremony' read 'like a Who's Who of the Australian arts elite'.[20] David Atkins, the artistic director, had starred in, produced, directed, or choreographed over 20 musicals in Australia and overseas. Choreographer Meryl Tankard, who produced the 'Deep Sea Dreaming' segment, had directed two dance companies in Australia since 1989. Dancer and choreographer Stephen Page, who co-produced 'Awakening' has been the artistic director of the Bangarra Dance Theatre from 1991. Peter Wilson, who produced 'Nature', is acknowledged as Australia's leading puppeteer. Nigel Jamieson, the producer of 'Tin Symphony', founded the London Festival of New Circus and the London International Workshop Festival before he migrated to Australia in 1992. Lex Marinos, who produced 'Arrivals', had been the director of Carnivale, Sydney's multicultural arts festival, since 1997. Nigel Triffit, who directed 'Eternity' designed the 'wildly successful' tap musical, *Tap Dogs*, which included elements of theatre, dance and rock concert. Richard Wherrett, a seminal figure in Australian theatre, directed the cauldron segment.[21]

Much of the music of the cultural presentation was composed and even conducted by Australian musicians. 'Nature' was composed by Chong Lim who conducted the Sydney Symphony Orchestra. 'Tin Symphony' was composed by Ian Cooper, John Frolich and Paul Grabowsky. 'Fire' was composed by Michael Askill and performed by the Michael Askill Fire Percussion.[22] Musicians were joined by the country's leading costume designers and choreographers. In short, many of the leading members of the Australian arts community brought the full weight of their creative talents to the event.

Although previous opening ceremonies — notably at Seoul in 1988, Barcelona 1992 and Atlanta in 1996 — had celebrated the culture of their countries, the Sydney ceremony introduced a seven-part narrative of Australia which operated at a number of levels.

In the prelude the stadium was transformed into Australia's dry centre, which exploded into life when a lone horseman galloped in followed by 120 stockhorses and their riders. The seven parts were as follows:

1. Deep Sea Dreaming
In this segment the stadium became a dreamscape — a metaphorical beach, and an ocean — in which an innocent 13-year-old girl, Nikki Webster, lay down on a beach and began to dream. She dreams about the sea, where she swims in a tropical sea surrounded by exotic fish. 'Deep Sea Dreaming' introduced the idea of the Aboriginal dreamtime, the importance of the ocean and the Australian love of swimming.

2. Awakening
The meeting of Nikki Webster with the songman, Djakapurra Munyarryun, depicted young white Australia learning from the ancient wisdom of Aborigines, which enables Nikki Webster to awaken from her deep-sea dreaming 'cleansed of history to reconcile the indigenous and non-indigenous'.[23]

3.Fire
This sequence showed the ancestral spirit Wandjina bringing forth lightning that engulfs the arena and starts a bush fire that regenerates the land.

4.Nature
In this segment, the charred earth was regenerated by rain, which fills the billabongs so that the arena becomes a living garden in which the waratah, Sturt Desert Peas, water lilies and banksias bloom. Kangaroo, echidna, swan, wombat, turtle, platypus and goanna relish this flowering of nature.

5.Tin Symphony
This segment focused on the coming of the Europeans — an often 'wildly funny tribute' to the European migrants with 'its sheer energy, its humour, its sense of "larrikinism", a distinctly Australian sense of irreverence, wit and mistrust of authority'.[24] It involved depictions the taming of the outback and familiar clichés such as Ned Kelly, settlers' huts and windmills. 'After the sacrament', recounted media scholar

Philip Bell, 'came a circus and variety show parodying the post-colonial colony, a comical celebration of a successful European society no longer seen as just plain folk, but still folksy'.[25]

6. Arrivals

This part of the ceremony showed the welcome of immigrants from the five continents — Africa, Asia, the Americas, Europe and Oceania — that are symbolised by the Olympic rings. The immigrants depart, leaving only children, who represent the hope for a tolerant and understanding multicultural society.

7. Eternity

Triffit produced this tap segment, which featured workers in flannel shirts and Blundstone boots. Dancer Adam Garcia, 'led a crew of workers through the construction of a 30 m high bridge ... The completed bridge was the Bridge of Life, a walkway towards connection and Reconciliation ... '[26] The completed structure represented the creation of a modern industrial society. Djakapurra Munyarryun and Nikki Webster rose high into the sky at the end, symbolising the realisation of reconciliation.

Bell noted how this pageant worked to engage its international viewers and commented on how 'these televisual mediations of self-proclaimed Aussie narratives were open to other interpretations'. The opening ceremony achieved this objective 'by narrating its imaginary history as dream, as sacrament, and as carnival, consummating its humanistic ritual with a transcendental act of reconciliation, albeit on behalf of only very abstracted historical actors — colonial powers and indigenous Australians'.[27]

Bell referred to the 'innocence' of the opening pageant in which Australia was depicted as 'fun and funny'.[28] Social commentator Hugh Mackay suggested that both the opening and closing ceremonies were 'sensational examples of pop culture on parade'.[29] The prominence of humour in the opening ceremony also helped the presentation appeal to the local audience; they appreciated the gentle mocking of the exuberant and ranting Australian Olympic swimming coach, Laurie Lawrence, who epitomised the Australian larrikin tradition. International audiences may not have appreciated the cameo appearance of Lawrence and the appearance of dozens of powered lawn mowers manicuring suburban backyards though they could not miss the general idea of 'Australian character'.

Australia's tourism marketing, in the opinion of Bell, has become increasingly directed at selling images of an 'exotic trans-historical place, a place of tradition, but also a place of post-colonial innovation and fun'. Bell added that:

> From the perspective of Europe, these re-enchanted antipodes
> ... are unsullied by such vices as recent, televisually inescapable
> racism, including the genocidal wars in the former Yugoslavia
> ... 'Australia' is easily created as a label for a kind of European-
> originated *innocence*. Innocence connotes youth, fun, irony (of an
> unserious kind) and domestic hospitality. In short, the fresh face
> of the child as the newest, smiling version of European modernity,
> or perhaps 'new-age', transcendent version of post-modernity.[30]

Moragas and Kennett noted that during this process when the cultural model for the ceremonies is selected and the symbols are designed 'there is a tendency to reinforce dominant and widely accepted values that are of a non-conflictive nature, which are often "politically correct" so as to avoid controversial or divisive themes'. They added that as

The closing ceremony of the Olympic Games was an occasion for cultural clichés: the hat of Crocodile Dundee, 'shrimps on the barbie' and 'roos on bikes (Simon Darcy).

with any promotional activity, negative aspects — such as pollution, marginalisation, poverty, prostitution, noise, urban inequalities, congestion and so forth — tend to be left out of image making and semantic processes.[31]

Although it took a slightly left-of centre view — in terms of its advocacy of reconciliation which was a cause passionately supported by some Australians but not others — few quibbled about the foregrounding of this issue and prominence of Aborigines in the opening ceremony partly because it was abstract and could be read in multitude of ways — like the entire opening ceremony itself.

The opening ceremony aimed to defuse one of Sydney's and Australia's largest potential negatives: the physical, social and economic plight of Aborigines in the country, and to sidestep the issue of relationships between indigenous and non-indigenous Australians and ongoing issues relating to human rights and land rights. (These issues are discussed further below and in Chapter 9). The prominence of indigenous people and themes in the opening ceremony implied that Australia was dealing constructively with what the international community saw as a 'problem'.

Brand Australia

The Olympic Games provide the opportunity to re-brand the country as a desirable tourism destination when the existing images and stereotypes are considered outdated. There is a need to continuously revise — or 'refresh' in the jargon of the industry — the appeal of a tourist destination. Barcelona attempted to avoid outdated tourist stereotypes such as bullfighting, flamenco, sangria, sun and folklore. Olympic organisers and tourism officials in Australia tried to avoid similar hackneyed and time-worn images of Australia such as the wide-open and largely empty land, the unique flora and fauna of the country, and semi-naked tribal Aborigines standing on one leg with a spear in their hand.

When *Brand Australia* was launched in 1995, it brought a new dimension to tourism promotion. Before that date, travel advertising tended to portray a broad view of the land, particularly focusing on the physical dimensions of the country. *Brand Australia*, by contrast, was a more specific and targeted approach to tourism in that it focused on particular destinations as well as the benefits and experiences that would derive from an Australian holiday. An Australian Tourism Commission (ATC) paper in 2004 on *Brand Australia* elaborated on this new approach to tourism:

> The good news for Australian tourism is that within this turbulent world, people are trying to re-discover themselves, with many looking for transforming experiences as part of that journey. The opportunity for Australia and the ATC to market and provide incredible emotional experiences and leave indelible memories with visitors has never been stronger.[32]

A short promotional video entitled *Australian Games*, produced by ATC in 1997, demonstrated this changed approach to tourism marketing. Although there were the almost obligatory glimpses of the land and familiar landmarks, the video emphasised the range of Australia experiences, which included fine wining and dining as well as night life and all manner of leisure and recreation. Its focus was more on the vibrant life in the cities than on the emptiness of the country, though this was in part because the primary focus was on the Olympic city. *Brand Australia* presented Australia as a lively and technologically advanced society. *Australian Games* included positive images of Asian Australians, suggesting that Australia was a successful multicultural society — an important message given the increasing importance of tourists from Asia. The video also emphasised the diversity of rural and regional Australia — grazing land, vineyards, forests, wetlands, and desert — rather than the simple reductionism of the outback. It thus reflected many of the themes advanced in the opening ceremony.

It is ironic that the *Brand Australia* trade mark includes a yellow kangaroo, framed by a red sun, with blue lines representing the sea, and the word 'Australia' below. Olympic marketers, by contrast, avoided the kangaroo preferring to choose lesser-known animals and birds as mascots — the platypus (Syd), the echidna (Millie) and the kookaburra (Olly) — whose names suggested the phrase Sydney Millennium Olympics. They were, as Tara Magdalinski noted, designed as 'animated creatures that are easily transformed into cuddly toys' and 'unashamedly constructed to appeal to children and to contribute to the familial marketing of the Games'. Magdalinski contended that Syd, Millie and Olly were too 'cute' and 'similar' and failed to appeal to the public.[33]

The popular mascot Fatso achieved Olympic recognition when he was placed atop one of the poles of Games Memories. None of the Olympic mascots were similarly honoured.

SOCOG's three mascots and the AOC's boxing kangaroo were upstaged by Fatso the fat-arsed wombat, who appeared nightly on Roy and H.G.'s *The Dream* on Channel 7 and was presented as a 'battler who puts in' and the 'people's prince'. Fatso captured the imagination of the public because of his unathletic body and because he had no link with any official merchandising. He also appealed to athletes, and swimmer Michael Klim carried Fatso to the victory ceremony even though officialdom preferred athletes to carry the boxing kangaroo in order to enhance sales.

Why was Fatso so popular? Was he a subversive icon who undermined the official mascots? Tara Magdalinski thinks not. She believes that allowing Fatso, a counter-mascot, to star on the official Olympic broadcast humanised this global festival, disguising its hegemonic character.[34] She noted that Fatso:

> operated successfully in and for a commercial enterprise. His
> presence on *The Dream* contributed in no small part to its

> success ... Whilst he may have appeared to be an anti-Olympic
> hero, he was a critical part of Channel 7's marketing program.[35]

It certainly suited Channel 7 to allow Klim to temporarily own the one and only Fatso and to feature the mascot in his victory ceremony, because it provided free publicity for *The Dream*.

However, there are other possible readings of the Fatso phenomenon. It could be argued that Fatso was a product of the Olympics of everyday life. Because the Olympic Games, like the Melbourne Cup, attract many people who have limited understanding of the intricacies of sport, there is need to include elements of popular culture, including humour, to make them more accessible. Fatso was lovable, eminently ordinary and a figure of fun, in contrast to the formal and serious Olympic pageant. Roy and H.G. helped transform this global event into one that was attuned to Australian popular culture.

Harry Hiller argued that the residents of Calgary had negated the elitism associated with the 1988 Winter Games and transformed it into a carnival event. Eddy the Eagle (a ski jumper from England who finished last) and the Jamaican bobsled team became 'urban heroes'[36] is the same way that Eric the Eel Moussambani appealed to the Australian public for his lone, courageous and exceptionally slow 100 metres in the pool.

Although Fatso was an unofficial mascot and did not exist outside *The Dream*, Fatso became part of Olympic culture. He appeared on official stamps, one of which featured Klim holding Fatso on the victory podium. Fatso was also included in Games Memories (see Chapter 2) and sits atop of a pole in front of the entrance to the Olympic stadium.

Fatso, as mentioned in the previous chapter, was sold on the internet, shortly after the Games, to raise money for charity. He was purchased for the astonishingly large sum of $80,450 by Kerry Stokes, the owner of Channel 7. Perhaps Stokes was appreciative of the contribution of Fatso to the success of the high-rating program, *The Dream*.[37]

Although the original Fatso was retired in 2000, Roy and H.G. reinstated Fatso in *The Dream in Athens*, their nightly program during the 2004 Athens Olympic Games. Early in the program Roy and H.G. revealed to their audience that a wombat — another Fatso — had been excavated from ancient Greek ruins.[38]

Did the opening ceremony and tourism promotion change perceptions of Australia and the perceived attributes of Australians?

Anecdotal reports in 2001 confirm that there was a greater depth in the perception of Australia and Australians in Asia after 2000. There was greater understanding of attributes such as the Australian character, multiculturalism and indigenous culture.

Preuss quotes a study by Young and Rubicam of how 48 German tourists evaluated *Brand Australia* in 2000 and 2002. They found that the following attributes were highly rated: 'friendly', 'fun', 'different' and 'trustworthy'. Less highly rated were attributes such as 'high quality', 'reliable' and 'good value'. Preuss believed that such attributes demonstrated the increased attraction of Australia as a tourism destination. Increased tourism, he added, 'is a very important Olympic legacy'.[39]

Reflections on identity after the Games

In the post-Games euphoria and the universal acclaim of the international media, there was much full-blown rhetoric about how the staging of the Olympic Games had changed Australia and enhanced its world standing. Several months after the Games, the then Premier Bob Carr argued that the Games had united the community:

> One of the many lessons of the Olympics was that a great public festival — and that is essentially what the Olympics were — can unite and energise an entire community. What we are really doing during the Games is celebrating our achievements, character and history in a world where success is more than ever measured in terms of creativity and ideas. This is why the festival is needed, and why my government supported it so generously.[40]

Left-inclined academic Robert Manne believed that the Games had demonstrated some of the positive features of the Australian way of life:

> The Games were in their efficiency, friendliness and exuberance an expression of much that is attractive about the Australian way of life. Australia is now, in every sense, a fully independent, quirkily idiosyncratic nation state.

Reiterating the Keating view that the Games might stimulate the republican movement, Manne added: 'what a pity that the Games could not have doubled as a festival of the republic'.[41]

There were even more specific claims that the Games had progressed the relationship between indigenous and non-indigenous Australians and had advanced the reconciliation process. Writing in the *Weekend Australian* of 21-22 October 2000, journalist Stuart Rintoul argued that 'for many Australians, the Olympics marked a pivotal point in the quest for reconciliation' and he argued that 'we should seize the day':

> From the moment the Sydney Olympics began, with Nikki Webster and Djakapurra Munyarryun, walking hand in hand, they had a sub-theme that was as clear to the watching world as it was to Australians: the idea of a nation awakening and hoping to be at peace with itself and with its history. It penetrated the opening ceremony that culminated in Cathy Freeman's lighting of the Olympic cauldron, her nation-stopping run for gold, and the closing ceremony that did everything John Howard has not done to say sorry for the wrongs of the past ... Freeman arrived on her mark to the sound of didgeridoos. Kim Beazley called her run '400 metres of national reconciliation'.

Bob Carr advanced this theme:

> Rising nobly above all their disadvantage, Australian Aborigines showed in the past three weeks they are fully committed to this Australian experiment in nation-building. They did not withdraw to the margins in protest. They performed in the opening ceremony, competed in sport, sang their song of survival and protest at the closing. In this new Australia, the indigenous — yes, with their real grievances — see themselves as part of the whole, as do the unionists and board members. It seems we all now realise that one part of Australia can't prosper at the expense of the rest.

The *Australian* was more cautious in an editorial published the morning after the opening ceremony, but it too believed in the power of the Olympics to advance inclusiveness:

> The big issues for our nation, such as reconciliation with the Aborigines, may not have gone away this morning. They are,

however, etched forever in the minds of more people here and overseas, thanks to the immense power of the Olympics to be inclusive.[42]

Reflections on reconciliation after the Games

Aboriginal Cathy Freeman was the Australian star of the Games. She lit the cauldron and won (as she was expected to) the 400 metres on the track. On her victory lap she draped the Australian and Aboriginal flags on her back, an action which drew no public reprimand from officialdom, unlike the occasion when she did the same thing at the 1994 Vancouver Commonwealth Games. Her action in 2000 was read as an inclusive gesture. The 400 metres was for Australians the race of the Games. Freeman's celebrated victory, had perhaps, indeed advanced the cause of reconciliation, as Kim Beazley suggested.

Michelle Hanna, author of a book on *The Festival of the Dreaming* — the first stage of the Cultural Olympiad in 1997, which focused on Aboriginal culture — was more circumspect but still positive in her

Above and opposite page: indigenous dancers perform during the ceremony before the lighting of the cauldron during the 2001 Ignite festival (SOPA).

assessment of what the festival and the Olympics could achieve. She wrote in 1999 that:

> *The Festival of the Dreaming* cannot of itself generate greater reconciliation in Australia, nor can the Olympics. However, the Olympics have provided an opportunity to extend and enhance the reconciliation process, by educating both Indigenous and non-Indigenous Australians about the reality of Australia's Indigenous people in the past and present of the nation. Perhaps, most significantly, this was achieved not in the context of protest and *marginality*, but of authority and in the *mainstream* … in the Cultural Olympiad itself … A new constructive dialogue has been opened up between Indigenous and non-Indigenous Australia in the 'in-between' spaces of the nation and it is not one where the non-Indigenous Australia invariably determines what is said.[43]

While the *Festival of the Dreaming* empowered Aboriginal artists, Bell noted that the elevation of Cathy Freeman in the public mind did not translate into wider respect for the Aboriginal community:

So, an athlete who, within Australia, is obligated to wear her 'Aboriginality' like a Nike logo to help consumers to identify her, and to identify with her, gave closure to the ritual. In so doing, she might be said to have re-stated the paradox so concisely noted by Marcia Langton. She recently claimed that: 'The paradox of the high consumption of ideas about Aborigines as against the failure to engage with aboriginal life, lies at the heart of the quintessential post-colonial identity'.[44]

Enno Hermann made a similar point when she noted that 'as a result of tourism market research, Australia increasingly advertises itself with images of Aboriginality'. Hermann added that following the announcement of funding cuts to the Aboriginal and Torres Strait Islander Commission (ATSIC) in 1996, Peter Yu, the chairman of the Kimberley Land Council had complained that 'they want us to pull our culture out of a suitcase for the … Olympic Games, but are not willing to give recognition to what culture means on a day-to-day basis'.[45]

Lifesavers bearing the great Australian thong featured in the closing ceremony of the Olympic Games (Simon Darcy).

In the years after the Games the public admiration for Cathy Freeman continued — she became the Australian of the Year in 2001 — and the consumption of Aboriginal ideas, artefacts and, in particular, paintings, remained high. Despite the high hopes of many, there was a continuing failure to engage with Aboriginal life and no apparent evidence of any advance in the reconciliation process. Freeman's close friend, Lou Glover, made the apt comment that 'Freeman's power' partly derives from her being 'the only person to have united this nation, if only for a moment'.[46] There was undoubtedly an enhanced sense of belonging to an imagined nation for this one moment but, like any similar sporting triumph, the moment was short-lived. However, it would be surprising if the prominence placed on Aborigines did not have some lasting symbolic effect, in that in this most-watched narrative of Australia, Aborigines were presented as an interesting and integral part of Australian culture and one in which Australians could take some pride (see also Chapter 9). Given the hostile attitude of many Australians to the boat people in 2001 — who were lumped together as 'queue jumpers' and 'illegals' rather than desperate refugees — the international image of Australia as the tolerant and welcoming multicultural society that had been promoted in the opening ceremony appeared to some as a glossy advertisement without real basis.

Reflecting six months after the Games, social commentator Hugh Mackay expressed scepticism about the idea that the Olympic Games were a 'mystical visitation' that 'transformed our society in unique and lasting (and positive) ways'. Mackay concluded that the Olympic Games were not a change agent:

> It's certainly true that, at the time, many believed the Games *would* change us forever. Six months on, though, I'm even struggling to recall what the changes were supposed to be. (I do remember one: we were all going to be nicer to each other).[47]

Culture and the Cultural Olympiad

The organisers of the Barcelona 1992 Olympic Games enhanced the status of the cultural program (outside the opening ceremony) by instituting the practice of a Cultural Olympiad, staged over the four years

A celebrated pest, the blowfly, appears in the closing ceremony of the Paralympic Games (Simon Darcy).

before the Games. Atlanta, Sydney and Athens followed the Barcelona model, although Moragas and Kennett contended that the value of new Cultural Olympiad was limited in that they 'constituted nothing more than another sub-brand' that was 'incorporated into the annual program of cultural activities organised by the host city'.[48]

The organisers of the Barcelona Cultural Olympiad believed that neither Los Angeles in 1984 nor Seoul in 1988 were 'culturally rich enough' to put on a 'substantial cultural festival'. Beatriz García has argued that the Barcelona Cultural Olympiad achieved a measure of success and managed to engage the local arts community because its budget of $74 million was considerably more than that devoted to the cultural program in most contemporary Olympic cities, before and after 1992. Atlanta, which located its arts festival within the Olympic ring, allocated a budget of only $30 million.[49] Like its predecessors, it was 'swamped by the sporting Games'.

The Sydney Cultural Olympiad consisted of four discrete segments, beginning with *The Festival of the Dreaming* in 1997. Andrea Stretton was appointed artistic director of *A Sea Change*, which took place across Australia from April to November 1998. This Olympiad focused on exploration and immigration as well as Australia's place in Oceania. Stretton was also the artistic director of the third festival, *Reaching the World*, which took the form of an international touring exhibition taking Australian artistic works to the five continents. Leo Schofield was the artistic director of the fourth festival, *The Harbour of Life*, which took place in Sydney from August to October 2000. It was based on 'physical and imagined notions' of Sydney Harbour and featured new works, exhibitions and performances.[50]

Craig Hassall, director of Sydney's Olympic Arts Festival, believed that Sydney's ambitious four-year arts festival would enable Sydney's Cultural Olympiad to avoid being overwhelmed by the sporting festival. Stretton regarded it as a 'wonderful opportunity for Australia to showcase its arts to the world under the Olympic "umbrella"'. She added that it was an opportunity for 'Australians themselves to learn about what we are doing artistically around the world'.[51]

The Cultural Olympiad made a promising start with the six-week *The Festival of the Dreaming*, which was the first contemporary indigenous festival of its size and the first international arts festival directed by a woman, Rhoda Roberts. It was popular and achieved critical acclaim even though it was confined to Sydney, where it played to full houses. This festival confronted some of the most controversial issues in Australian life and was an event that, Roberts suggested, should have been staged in 1988, when the majority of the population had celebrated the bicentennial of 'white settlement'. It also confronted the 'central motif of the Olympic opening ceremony and did so more on Aboriginal terms … and it engaged and empowered the Aboriginal artistic communities and communities more generally'. *The Festival for the Dreaming* introduced many new works to the Sydney public giving 'them a taste of what indigenous works are about in the 90s' as Rhoda Roberts noted. The largely non-indigenous audiences were introduced to a less stereotypical view of Aboriginal culture. Whereas Aborigines were often portrayed in the media as angry protesters, audiences became more aware of other parts of Aboriginal life, such as their humour. After the festival Roberts added that 'we achieved what I always intended to achieve, which was to change stereotypes ... It was unique and it was very unknown'.[52]

Linda Meekison examined some of the ambivalences and contradictions in *The Festival of the Dreaming*. She quoted one member of the indigenous arts community who believed that the festival was a 'cynical move on SOCOG's part to appropriate and sell indigenous arts because they have value'. Despite this, she believed that there was no sense that 'non-indigenous interests controlled either the event itself or subsequent interpretations'. The ceremony's participants 'held their heads high' and 'performed what they wanted, and resisted being interpreted only according to SOCOG's agenda'.[53]

The *Official Report of the XXVII Olympiad* contended that there were important outcomes from the four-year cultural program. It stated that

> An important aspect of the four-year Festival program was a commitment to facilitate longer-term benefits and legacies for Australian artists and arts companies. These legacies included the commissioning of a number of new works, including plays, musical works, dance works, fine art print portfolios, publications and anthologies.[54]

The Festival for the Dreaming was the only festival to achieve some of these goals. The next three festivals failed to gain any significant notice and were largely ignored. With sizeable cuts in the Cultural Olympiad budget after 1997 later directors operated with pitifully small budgets. Good wrote that the $51.5 million listed in the bid documents had been cut by almost 40 per cent to $32.6 million, less than half the budget of the Barcelona Cultural Olympiad. Stretton had a paltry budget of only $1.3 million for *A Sea Change* and there was even less funding for *Reaching the World* — $1 million. (By contrast the ceremonies budget of $67 million, most of which was spent on the opening ceremony, was not cut.) The Cultural Olympiad also failed to engage the Australian arts community and gain their support and attract arts sponsorship money. Good noted that many in the arts community had complained 'that Olympic [sporting] sponsorship has diverted sponsor funds and locked out the cultural industry'.[55] Finally, *The Harbour of Life* — with a budget of $4 million — had no coherent theme, and was an assortment of theatre, music, exhibitions and displays which happened to coincide with and form a backdrop to the Olympic Games.

There were relatively few positive outcomes of the Sydney Cultural Olympiad other than a successful Aboriginal arts festival. However, 'Sculpture by the Sea', which was part of *A Sea Change,* has continued as an annual festival. The sculptures are arranged along a popular ocean walk of several miles between Bondi and Bronte beaches in Sydney.

Good concluded that 'despite the number, quality, range, and national and international cultural significance of the programs at recent festivals, the modern Cultural Olympiad has remained one of the least known of international arts festivals among art world professionals and the general public'.[56] The Sydney Cultural Olympiad failed to achieve a higher profile than any of the recent Cultural Olympiads. The problems inherent in staging arts festivals alongside a major sporting event remain. It is ironic that while prominent members of the arts community were involved in the opening ceremony, the Cultural Olympiad failed to enlist their interest.

García documented the disappointment of the Australian arts community in the Olympic arts festival. She added that 'many Sydney critics focused on what they saw as cosmetic about the event, created to benefit the privileged' and promoting 'a safe and flat view of Australia that excluded the often difficult and controversial voices from marginal communities'.[57] García identified three key weaknesses of the Sydney Olympic Arts Festivals. Firstly, there was a 'lack of integration mechanisms', meaning that the cultural program had a marginal status compared to the main sporting events. She noted that even the successful *The Festival of the Dreaming* 'failed to establish a clear Olympic affiliation'. Good reiterated this point, noting that *The Festival of the Dreaming* had 'little acknowledged connection to the Olympics or Olympism'.[58] Secondly, the cultural program had an ambiguous status in the Olympic Games and lacked a clear function or role. Thirdly, there were 'ineffective programming elements'. It was difficult to market the cultural festival given its operation over such a long period and in so many different locations.[59]

However, García noted that the 'promotional difficulties' associated with the Sydney Cultural Olympiad 'were remarkably similar to the limitations' evident at Barcelona in 1992 and Atlanta in 1996. She argued that there was a need to develop new directions for the cultural program, to break down barriers between sport, education and culture. The fusion of these three elements in the opening ceremony provides an example of what might be achieved. García added that Sydney's successful live sites programs, which generated a festival atmosphere, may provide 'the opportunity to promote cultural activities (and messages) in a popular way'.[60] The live sites programs were organised at strategic city sites and included non-stop displays of sports competitions on large screens along with the simultaneous staging of popular music concerts and acrobatics. This free entertainment, which was organised by the Sydney City Council supported by OCA, enhanced the party atmosphere of the city.

The role of the media

One of the paradoxes of the Sydney Games was the extent of local media criticism in the years before and after the Games, especially when compared with the universal chorus of approval from both the local and international media during the Games and in their immediate aftermath. The reasons for the media praise of the Games themselves are easier to establish, but the continuing negative attitude of the local media — apart from during September 2000 and the following few months —is more difficult to comprehend.

The unstinting media praise during and after the Games occurred for three main reasons. Firstly, the Games were an operational success and gained the ultimate accolade from President Samaranch.

Secondly, the management of the media was far superior to Atlanta in terms of facilities and communications at the Main Press Centre and media transport. Reg Gratton, manager of the Main Press Centre, learnt from the mistakes of Atlanta and realised that an 'angry' and 'disgruntled' media were more likely to write negative stories about the city and the Games. The problem with Atlanta was that the Main Press Centre was too cramped, the communications system was inadequate in a number of key areas during the Games, and the transportation of media to Games venues did not work well. Gratton noted the Samaranch comment that 'the media are the last [or final] judges of the Games'. The concerns of the media are not merely with the success of the athletic carnival; they are also wrote about how well the city infrastructure works. Athens also learnt this lesson and profited from Sydney's experience. Richard Palfreyman, who had been the group manager, media relations at

SOCOG, played a prominent role in the Athens Main Press Centre.

A possible third factor — which is more difficult to document — relates to the obvious enjoyment of the Australian community for the Games and the party-like atmosphere that was created around the live sites and in television programs such as Roy and H.G.'s *The Dream*. Journalists do not work in total isolation and it would be surprising if they were not influenced to write more positively because they too enjoyed the event.

Milton Cockburn, a senior journalist with the *Sydney Morning Herald* who joined the SOCOG media department in 1997, wrote an interesting article as to why the host city media had such a negative attitude to the Games in general and to SOCOG in particular in the years leading up to 2000.[61] He posed the following questions. How could *Herald* readers be so convinced that the Games were going to be a disaster when the organisation of the Olympic Games was so excellent? How did the newspapers get it so wrong?

Cockburn believed that the Olympic reporters, who followed the Olympics day in and day out, lacked an appreciation of the huge scale and complexity of the project. As a result there were very few efforts to 'paint on a broad canvas' with journalists focusing on smaller and more manageable issues. There was also a tendency for journalists to hunt in a pack and become SOCOG-centric, failing to scrutinise other Olympic agencies. Some of the newspaper campaigns were naïve, such as the *Herald* campaign advocating public SOCOG Board meetings. This long-running campaign overlooked the fact was SOCOG was a commercial organisation and if it had been open to public scrutiny the 'real decision-making' would have moved elsewhere. Some of the newspaper criticism was based on misinformation. There was, for example, the controversy over 'oversized tickets' resulting in headlines such as 'Olympic tickets too big to fit in turnstiles'. However, as Cockburn noted, there were no turnstiles at the larger Olympic venues.[62]

Prominent Australian expatriate Clive James suggested that 'everything SOCOG did was regarded as its merest duty whereas everything it did wrong was a calamity' — perhaps, he could have added, a national calamity. Media attitudes were framed by a public nervousness about whether Australia could properly organise such an event. This attitude may have reflected the Australian 'tall poppy syndrome', which might explain the popularity of the long-running television series, *The Games*, which brilliantly parodied the organising committee as bumbling and incompetent. It also provided the Australian public with a ready-made scapegoat should Australia become the laughing stock of the world, as many feared, because of its poor organisation of the Games. The scriptwriters of *The Games* acknowledged this possibility when they arranged for the cast of the fictional organising committee to fly out of Sydney in the final episode, just before the Games began, so that they would not be around to 'face the music'.

The media criticism of SOCOG and the Sydney Games only subsided in June 2000, when the public enthusiasm for the torch relay broke the cycle of negativity. The daily litany of SOCOG faults were replaced by the good news stories of the triumphal progress of the torch progress, the character of the torch-bearers and the growing excitement of the community in the coming of the Games.

Cockburn's argument may explain the resurgence of media negativity from 2001 (see chapters 2 and 4). Because it was difficult to comprehend the larger picture of Olympic outcomes, journalists focused rather more on the immediate and the tangible — such as the lack of activity at Sydney Olympic Park in 2001 and 2002 — and did not consider other issues such as the steady growth in convention tourism (see Chapter 4), the international transfer of Australian expertise, and the success of Australian business in gaining Beijing contracts and other post-Games success stories (see Chapter 5).

Cockburn reflected on what he had 'learnt from this exercise' and suggested a number of recommendations for media management by an organising committee. Although his recommendations relate to the pre-Games period, they provide sage advice for those involved in the organisation of the post-Games environment:

> First, and most obviously, is the need for public affairs specialists in all large companies and organisations. No organisation can rely on the goodwill of journalists to get its messages across. An organisation must learn to make all of its announcements and the release of all information in a strategic fashion ...
>
> Second, is the vital importance of chasing down incorrect stories that appear in the media ...
>
> Third, while it is important to cultivate and maintain co-

operative and friendly relationships with the media don't assume that will stand you in good stead at all times ...

Fourth, it is not always necessary to respond to every article that appears in newspapers ...

Finally, keep asking yourself the question: can this information now be made public?

Chapters 2 and 4 demonstrate that there is a continuing need for Olympic leadership and careful and authoritative comment in the years after the event has been staged.

Conclusions

Politicians and civic leaders overstated the extent of cultural and community change generated by an Olympic Games. The civic booster rhetoric is short-lived and any sense of community cohesion does not last long, as Games euphoria evaporates. An Olympic Games does not change identity and culture in any significant and continuing manner. The prominence of Aborigines in the opening ceremony did not lead to any greater public interest in Aboriginal life, nor did it advance reconciliation in any significant way.

The re-branding of Australia internationally was a more successful exercise in that it appeared to generate greater interest in the country. The opening ceremony and *Brand Australia* were carefully constructed to add to the depth and diversity of popular images of the country. The extent that it enhanced tourism and boosted exports in the short or long term are discussed in the next two chapters.

Reflecting on the Barcelona 1992 Olympic Games Moragas *et al* noted that cities tend to overstate the benefits of the Games to promote a country's international image.

> There is a belief by Olympics hosts that holding a Games represents an opportunity to enhance one's image abroad. While this is not necessarily true, or is true to a much less extent than believed, it is nonetheless a compelling motivation for cities and countries to take on such a challenging and expensive feat of hosting an Olympic Games.[63]

Such a comment is equally applicable to the expectations relating to identity and culture as a result of the Sydney 2000 Olympic Games.

It is tempting to suggest that the failure of the Cultural Olympiad suggests that the sports and arts communities do not mix in Australia and that the arts communities resent the popularity and generous funding of sport. The fallacy of this argument is that some of leading artistic talent of the country did contribute to the success of the opening ceremony. The more likely explanation of failure of the Cultural Olympiad was that the Australian arts communities recognised that the Sydney Cultural Olympiad was a second or even third-tier cultural festival and was grossly under-funded as well.

Chapter 4

BUSINESS AND ECONOMIC OUTCOMES

There is ample evidence in this chapter and in Chapter 6 that Sydney Olympic authorities gave priority to 'business and economic benefits' rather than sporting, cultural and environmental ones. The rewards for investment in business benefits were, perhaps, both more tangible and compelling. As a result there was much greater planning for and funding of economic outcomes by the NSW Government, the Federal Government and the Australian Tourist Commission (ATC).

In the years immediately after the 2000 Games, Sydney received a glowing report card for its marketing programs and for its positive business and economic outcomes more generally. IOC member Dick Pound wrote in 2001 that 'never before' have the goals of Olympic marketing been 'met more successfully than in the Sydney 2000 Olympic Games'. He added that Sydney's successful marketing provided 'a benchmark for the future of the Olympic Games and the Olympic Movement'.[1]

IOC Marketing Director Michael R. Payne praised in particular Sydney's innovative program to promote a tourist legacy through a range of unprecedented programs that were in place before and after the Games. Payne contended that the Sydney model should be emulated by future cities:

> Australia is the first Olympic host nation to take full advantage
> of the Games to vigorously pursue tourism for the benefit of the
> whole country. It's something we've never seen take place to this
> level before, and it's a model that we would like to see carried
> forward to future Olympic Games in Athens and beyond.[2]

Tourism scholar Ray Spurr added that Australia was 'probably the first Olympic host to target tourism in any serious way'.[3]

Olympic scholar Holger Preuss reiterated Payne's view that Sydney's tourism legacy was likely to be a positive one and added that Sydney had identified a potential legacy windfall. Preuss added that Olympic cities in the past had not fully appreciated the value of a tourism legacy:

> It seems that in the case of Australia the tourism legacy was positive and has to be considered as a potential giant if the Games effect can leverage the tourism effect. Looking at the size of revenues expected from post-Olympic tourism in Australia, it is interesting to note that the tourism legacy is only mentioned along with other potential legacies.[4]

Tourism scholar Laurence Chalip concurred with this view. He pointed out that tourism constituted 44.6 per cent of the projected economic impact from the Sydney 2000 Olympic Games making tourism the largest single factor. He added that:

> The Australian experience suggests that there are huge gains in the market position of the host city and country as a consequence of hosting the Games. Awareness and interest in the destination are elevated. The challenge is to maintain and build on that awareness and interest.[5]

When Sydney made its bid for the Olympic Games, tourism did not feature as a significant outcome. Ray Spurr, who was then an official in the Commonwealth Department of the Arts, Sport and Tourism recalled that when 'we were consulted' about the bid with a view to obtaining Commonwealth funding the case was made on the grounds of sport rather than tourism.[6]

However, by 1995 the ATC had begun to target Olympic tourists[7] and studies completed in succeeding years were more positive about a tourism legacy. Arthur Andersen and the Centre for Regional Economic Analysis (CREA) at the University of Tasmania, for instance, in a study released in January 1999, estimated that the Sydney Olympic Games could generate up to $6.5 billion in direct economic activity for the Australian economy, with most of the economic benefits ($5.1 billion) confined to NSW. The study was based on the projected impact of the Games over a 12-year period from 1994–2006. Its other forecasts included an additional $2.7 billion in exports; the creation of 117,000 full and part-time jobs, with 90,000 of these jobs generated in NSW during the Games; and an increase in the Australian Gross Domestic Product (GDP) by around 1.2 per cent because of Games-related activity. Almost half — 44.6 per cent — of this predicted increase would occur because of additional 1.6 million tourists — with approximately 93 per cent of these tourists expected to come after the Games, though there would be a smaller 7 per cent increase during the Games. The study suggested that the Olympic Games could cushion Australia from the worst ravages of the Asian financial crisis of the late 1990s.[8]

Issues in assessing the Games' economic legacy

Although the Australian economy was a mature one, the domestic economy within Australia was relatively small. The Games represented an opportunity to address two key target sectors of the economy. An increase in international tourism and the greater export of service-based activities in the Asia-Pacific region would stimulate the economy (see Chapter 5).

A number of specific questions can be posed. Has Sydney's glowing economic report card in 2001 and 2002 been sustained in later years? Have the projected outcomes been realised? Have positive business and economic outcomes outweighed any negative ones?

There is also the question of identifying and isolating the Olympic tourist factor. How much of the increase in 2001 inbound tourism, for instance, was a result, direct or indirect, of the Olympic Games and efforts to leverage the Games? Or did the increase in tourism in 2001 occur because of other factors, such as the value of the Australian dollar, which plunged to under 50 cents — reaching a low point of 47.75 — in relation to the United States dollar?

Another issue worth consideration is whether the public or private sector provides the funds to increase tourism, and which sector benefits more in return. Chalip noted that government provided much of the funding to leverage tourism and added that 'the possibility remains that public investments to promote leveraging constitute an income transfer from taxpayers to the travel and hospitality providers'.[9] The issues of winners and losers in the host community, and whether positive (and) negative economic impacts are shared equally across the community will will be discussed further in Chapter 9.

Economic planning: the budget as a political document

An Olympic budget is a highly political document which has to be sold to the host community. It is likely to obtain greater acceptance if a surplus is predicted from the outset and if the expenses to the city are offset by tangible benefits. It is quite common for figures to be adjusted, since there is always some debate about what should be counted in the Olympic budget and what should not. Preuss has noted that the figures produced by some organising committees were 'incomprehensible', so that the true financial picture was obscured and hidden from the public in a welter of inaccessible figures.

Preuss reported an interesting example of the reporting of Seoul's 1988 Olympic budget. He described the farcical situation in which the surplus recorded by the organising committee for the Seoul 1988 Olympic Games varied from $US89.5 million to $US686 million. This situation occurred because the organising committee wanted the Games recognised as 'the most profitable ever staged in the history of the modern Olympics' but did not want to have to pay additional revenue to the IOC because of the size of its profit. As a result the organising committee did not include the sale of the village, estimated at more than $US389, in the official surplus. With a smaller surplus of $US192 million, the Seoul organising committee paid the IOC only $US2 million.[10]

There are many other indirect Olympic costs that are not included in the Olympic budget for a variety of reasons. Such expenditure is siphoned off into other budgets, such as public works. The expensive remediation of Homebush Bay and the rail link to Homebush Bay, for instance, were not counted in the Olympic budget because the state government contended that they were projects that would have been undertaken with or without the Games. The Olympic Games merely speeded up the allocation of public funds to these projects. However, the Games could not have taken place without such capital works.

The NSW Government also took advantage of the Games to complete three 'big ticket' items, which were not included in the official Games costs listed above. The three projects were:

$2 billion	Sydney Airport upgrade
$700 million	Eastern Distributor (a road link between the city and the eastern suburbs)
$320 million	Improvement of the Sydney CBD

While the upgrade of the airport was beneficial for the citizens of NSW in general, there were rumblings from regional NSW that there was too much spending on the city at the expense of country interests.

There are also hidden costs that do not become apparent until after the Games. Urban planning scholar Glen Searle noted that the NSW Government achieved the $1.6 billion required for state capital spending on the Olympics in part by delaying capital spending on non-Olympic budgets such as health and education. This amounted to a siphoning off of funding from core community budgets to pay for the Games. Table 4.1 demonstrates a remarkable increase in the recreation and culture budget for the three years from 1996–97 to 1998–99 over the three previous years and a significant decline in the health and education budget.[1]

Table 4.1 NSW Government capital expenditure changes by three-year periods in selected sectors.

Sector	% change from 1996–97 to 1998–99 over 1993–94 to 1995–96	% change from 2000–01 to 2002–03 over 1996–97 to 1998–99
Recreation and culture	144.2	−65.1
Health	1.6	7.7
Education	−18.1	40.5

While it was clear that health and education spending recovered in the three years after the Games, when spending on recreation and culture was dramatically cut, it is unclear whether the health and education budgets simply returned to their pre-1996 levels or whether the losses sustained in health and education over three years were recouped.

Continuing post-Games costs are not included in any Olympic budget, since organising committees are wound up soon after the Games. The management of Olympic venues, which are not self-sufficient, can become a continuing drain on the resources of a city or a state for years and even decades (see below).

The costs of the Games

The Australian Government estimated that the total cost of staging the Sydney 2000 Olympic Games was $3.5 billion, of which approximately two-thirds (65.7 per cent) were paid for by the public sector. This represented 0.06% of the country's GDP in 1990-2000.[12] The 2002 report of PricewaterhouseCoopers on the business and economic benefits of the Games, commissioned by the NSW Department of State and Regional Development, nominated a lower expenditure figure of $3 billion of which $1.9 billion came from the public sector and $1.1 billion from the private sector.[13] The NSW Government contributed $1326.1 million and the federal government $493 million.

Direct costs were only part of the story. The federal government actually contributed a greater amount of $648 million in indirect costs mainly for defence and security (see below).

SOCOG

The *Official Report of the XXVII Olympiad*, published in 2001, stated that SOCOG's total net operating revenue was $2387 million and its total net operating expenditure was $2015.7 million — resulting in a small profit of $371.5 million.[14] However, 'legacy contributions' of $467.7 million turned this into a deficit of $96.2 million. The legacy contributions were:

- NSW Government construction contribution
  $255.3 million
  (new venues and rail costs)
- NSW Government construction contribution
  $106.0 million
  (The village and other competition venues)
- SPOC contribution
  $17.9 million
- Athlete legacy (paid to the AOC)
  $88.9 million

In the final report of OCA of 31 March 2002, a smaller deficit for SOCOG of $59.8 million was reported.[15]

Without the athlete legacy contribution to the AOC of $88.5 million (which was adjusted upwards to $88.9 million by OCA), SOCOG would have virtually balanced its books. (The athlete legacy contribution will be discussed further in Chapter 7). A significant proportion of a contingency fund of $140 million was also returned to the NSW Government — a figure calculated at $43.8 million in 2001 but $80.2 million in 2002.[16]

NSW Government

The NSW Government released a final report on its financial contribution, which it estimated to be $1326.1 million. Construction and capital works were reported to be $1185.7 million and running the event cost $793.4 million making a total of $1979.1 million. These costs were offset by the generation of an additional $653 million in tax revenue.[17]

The NSW Government also believed that it received many other benefits — both financial and non-financial — for its large investment: such as the business and economic benefits which were outlined in the 2002 report of PricewaterhouseCoopers (see below) and improved sporting infrastructure. A long list of legacy benefits, notably sports venues, provided another government justification for the costs incurred.

The final report of OCA acknowledged that there were some small ongoing Games costs. It noted that 'the estimated annual maintenance costs for the venues to which the NSW Government retains a commitment or shared responsibility is $11 million'. It's a relatively small figure but without an end date.[18]

Commonwealth Government

The Commonwealth Government contributed $493 million in direct costs with the largest allocations being for grants to the NSW Government of $175 million for Games facilities and $145 million for Olympic and Paralympic athlete preparation. However, there were substantial indirect costs of $648 million. These included 'Other costs (principally Defence)' of $481 million, 'Security and other costs absorbed by Commonwealth agencies' ($107 million) and 'Revenue foregone' ($60 million).[19]

However, the federal government staged 94 networking events at Games time, targeting the infrastructure, information technology, agribusiness, education and biotechnology markets. Such promotion was considered to be successful and the Federal Trade Minister, Mark Vaile, claimed the program generated $1 billion in new business and investment in Australia.[20]

The federal government also provided some indirect funding for Olympic-related activity when it gave $50 million to the Australian Tourist Commission in 1999 to help it capitalise on the staging of the Olympic Games. However, this followed a long tradition of Australian Government support for the tourism industry that began when Don

Chipp was appointed the first Federal Minister for Tourist Activities in 1966. The following year, the Holt Government established the Australian Tourist Commission and provided it with funding of $1.5 million. In 1993 the Keating Government provided $80 million over four years for international tourism marketing and regional tourism development.

Private sector

The principal contributions of the private sector related to the construction and management of Olympic venues, such as the Olympic stadium, the SuperDome and the Olympic Village. The state government provided some funds for venues such as the Olympic stadium but the bulk of the revenue came from private companies (see Chapter 6).

Defining Olympic benefits

OCA emphasised the economic benefits of the Games in 2002, identifying three specific areas:

- Promoting Sydney and NSW as attractive investment destinations, especially for regional headquarters of multinational corporations;
- Promoting Sydney and NSW as tourism and convention destinations;
- Working with Commonwealth Government departments and private sector sponsors to raise the profile of Sydney, NSW and Australia.[21]

The PWC report documented a wide range of 'business and economic benefits' resulting from the Sydney Games. These included a projected $3 billion in business outcomes (with $500,000 million already in place by 2002), the injection of over $6 billion in infrastructure developments in NSW and more than $1.2 billion of convention business for NSW between 1993 and 2007, over $6 billion in inbound tourism spending during 2001 and a greatly enhanced business profile for Sydney, NSW and Australia, which the report estimated was worth $6.1 billion in international exposure.

Given that PWC was commissioned to collate evidence on the 'business and economic benefits' of the Games, it excluded discussion of any possible negative outcomes, though it did acknowledge such possibilities. The report noted that:

> Prior to the Games there was some discussion of the potential of this type of Games related activity crowding-out other economic activity in the State, and possibly distorting labour and capital markets. In the period since the Games, there have been reports on the negative impacts of the high level of economic activity generated by the Games and the temporary difficulties experienced by specific businesses or centers (sic). These issues have been acknowledged but have not been examined within the scope of the study.[22]

There was also the need, noted in the PWC report, to sustain these benefits in the future: the 'great challenge for Sydney, New South Wales and Australia is to continue capitalising on the vast array of opportunities that the Games have delivered'.

Another issue noted by PWC was that Sydney's positive economic story had not been properly recognised by the Sydney and Australian public. The report noted the problem of public disenchantment with Olympic preparations in the lead-up to the Games, owing to a succession of negative media stories on topics such as the ticketing scandals, the fears of runaway housing prices, possible protests and traffic gridlock. It was puzzling, noted the authors of the PWC report, that a successful Games had failed to dispel the public scepticism about the wider benefits of the Games, including its positive economic achievements. PWC reported in 2002:

> The Australian public may still perceive the Games as a sporting and national triumph — great for Australia, great for Sydney, a community-building experience — but somehow a commercial flop with a legacy of crippled businesses, an oversupply of housing and hotels, and no enduring business benefit.[23]

This paradox will be considered later below and has been discussed in other chapters (See Chapters 2, 3 and 6).

Tourism outcomes

As discussed in the introduction to this chapter, Australia received much praise for its promotion of Olympic tourism from the world's tourism and sporting leaders when the IOC and the World Tourism Organisation hosted a conference on tourism and sport at Barcelona in February 2001. John Morse, the managing director of ATC declared at the conference that 'there's widespread recognition that Australia got it right on tourism and the Olympic Games and I have been quite surprised at the number of countries who are interested in Australia's work'.[24]

The attempt to access positive tourism outcomes in Australia was not surprising, given that by 2000 tourism had become an increasingly important export industry. Since the late 1970s, the number of overseas visitors had grown substantially with the largest number of tourists coming from Asia and North America. Tourism in 2005 was estimated to be worth more than 11 per cent of total export earnings and provided employment for almost 6 per cent of the workforce. Since international (inbound) tourism constitutes approximately one-quarter of the country's tourism industry, any increase in inbound tourism would boost the tourism industry.[25]

Spurr noted in 1999 that there has been insufficient research on the impact of tourism before, during and after an Olympic Games. He also argued that tourism marketing professionals have been guilty of 'excessive optimism' in their projections of tourism benefits for past Olympic Games and mega events.[26] Chalip added that research on Olympic tourism is still in its infancy and relatively imprecise. He noted that attempts to quantify the tourism impact after the 1984 Los Angeles Olympic Games and the 1988 Seoul Olympic Games produced quite 'contradictory' results. While there was no evidence of a tourism boost from the 1984 Los Angeles Olympic Games, several scholars estimated that there were from 640,000 to one million additional visitors to Seoul as a result of the 1988 Games. However, the Seoul Olympics coincided with a major opening up of the country's aviation industry, which in itself helped to boost tourist numbers. This development made it even more difficult to arrive at any cause-and-effect tourism relationship with the Games. The contradictory assessments of the Los Angeles and Seoul Olympics may be a product of different times and countries, but the varying results may also reflect the simplicity of the Olympic tourism model employed, which treated visitor numbers as an 'interrupted time series' and then modelled 'the effect of the Games'.

Chalip noted the study of Ritchie and Smith on the impact of tourism on the 1988 Calgary Winter Olympic Games, which suggested that the Games added to Calgary's 'salience and attractiveness', producing a short-term boost during and immediately after the Games. After that there was a rapid decline to the previous baseline, so any tourist effect was short-lived. Chalip argued that for a city to gain long-term benefits in international tourist markets it was necessary for the Games to be 'leveraged', for strategies to be 'put into place that are designed to exploit the effect of the Games, and then to build on that effect'.[27]

The 1992 Barcelona Olympic Games were the first occasion when the Games were leveraged, when the city developed a long-term Olympic tourism strategy which continued in the decade after the Games. Pere Duran, the general director of the *Turisme de Barcelona* consortium, wrote in 2004 that 'there can be no doubt that the Olympic Games mark a "before and after" as far as tourism in Barcelona is concerned'. He added that from 1990 to 2002 Barcelona enjoyed the 'most spectacular tourist growth in Europe'.[28] This included general visitors to the city and convention delegates as well as the arrival of cruise ships.

Duran dismissed the view — repeated in his opinion all too often — that the Games were the catalyst that enabled the city to expand its tourist capacity in an impressive fashion. Rather, he believed that the Games 'were the excuse, perhaps the incentive, for a general process of analysis of the city in general and in particular of its role as a tourist centre'. The Games were merely one part of bold tourism initiatives, which continued well after the Games, to capitalise on the natural and cultural assets of the city. The *Turisme de Barcelona* program was established in 1993 — one year after the Games — to coordinate and advance Barcelona's tourism strategies. It brought together all the public and private sector groups interested in tourism.[29] The consortium advanced from a generic promotion of the city as a tourist destination to a more sophisticated approach that included promotions aimed at specific market segments and catering to the demands of specific interest groups. Barcelona's tourism section was also fed by a succession of major cultural and international events: such as the Miró Year in 1993, the Gaudi year in 2002 and the Universal Forum of Culture in 2004.

So was there a direct or even indirect connection between the staging of the Games and a successful long-term promotion of the city? Were the Olympic Games a cause or catalyst for this spectacular growth

The kangaroo has long featured as the stock image of Australia. The 'Swaggy Chorus' performed under a giant wooden kangaroo prop in the 1931 film, Showgirl's Luck, which was one of Australia's first 'talkies' (National Film and South Archive).

in the city's tourism?

Spurr concurred with Duran's view that there is a danger in inferring (and overstating) an Olympic tourism factor because there were other factors involved. Spurr noted that:

> Barcelona's tourism success is attributed to a combination of factors: media coverage during the Olympics; Olympics-related investment in Barcelona's waterfront precinct, which has made the city more attractive to visitors; improved accommodation infrastructure; and a major boost to the confidence and entrepreneurship of Barcelona's tourist industry. Some or all

of these factors contributed to putting Barcelona, for the first time, on the list of city short-break destinations for European holiday-makers.[30]

The Olympic Games provided the opportunity to undertake a major project of urban infrastructure, notably the revitalisation of the Barcelona waterfront precinct. While the waterfront project had some importance for the staging of the Games — the Olympic Village was based there — it had far-greater and more long-term tourism benefits.

The above comments suggest that Olympic tourism is not a stand-alone factor and does not flow from an Olympic Games as a matter of course. A city needs to identify its marketable attributes to develop a sophisticated plan to attract tourists to the city on a continuing and long-term basis. Olympic tourists usually visit a city on a one-off basis, so an 'Olympic tourism' strategy works only when it is integrated into broader and longer-term tourism planning.

Leveraging tourism

It is abundantly clear that the Australian tourism industry, backed by the Australian Government, invested significantly in positive Olympic tourism outcomes. Sydney did more than emulate Barcelona's model: it took leveraging to a new level, as Michael Payne acknowledged. The ATC claimed in 2001 that 'no other host country has taken the opportunity to use the Games to promote the whole country's tourism image as well as the host city's. No other country has worked so closely with the Olympic partners to develop benefits from linking the tourism brand with their products and services.'[31] The opening ceremony and the tourism focus of the 1992 Olympic Games, by contrast, was more on the city of Barcelona and the contribution of the Catalan people than on Spain as a whole.

Australia set new benchmarks for its positive tourist promotion before, during and after the Games. The ATC, backed by Australian Government funding, developed an ambitious program to leverage Olympic tourism. It expanded its visiting journalist program from 1996 to 2000, when it increased the program's budget by $12 million, a move supported by a federal government grant of $US5 million. Under this program print and broadcast journalists were recruited to visit Australia to write stories about the country, with the ATC providing information and research. The ATC estimated that the visiting journalist program added $2.3 billion in media coverage internationally.[32]

Other ATC programs included greater servicing of the international media before and during the Games, providing them with background images, stories and facts to enhance media stories. The ATC also formed a partnership with some other government agencies to create and service the Sydney Media Centre for non-accredited media. The ATC tourism promotion also extended to sponsors, with the ATC doing joint advertorials with some sponsors to build images of Sydney and Australia in their advertising.

A central thrust of the ATC was to refine and improve what it defined as *Brand Australia* (see Chapter 3), the purpose of which was to provide greater depth and dimension to the stereotypical and time worn images of Australia and give international tourists greater incentives to visit the country. David Headon noted in 1996 that some of the traditional images of Australia were of an empty country full of kangaroos and traditional Aborigines standing on one leg with a spear in one hand.[33] Using various channels of communication, including film and the opening ceremony, *Brand Australia* depicted a more modern and technologically advanced, multicultural society; a country that had a distinctive character, with a laid-back sense of fun and one which had a rich Aboriginal culture. John Morse believed that the ATC accelerated the development of *Brand Australia* by ten years taking advantage of a ten-fold increase in international media in Australia.[34]

The ATC program also included a follow-up program after the Games, which researched the extent to which Olympic exposure had changed Australia's image internationally. Ninety joint advertising campaigns to promote 'holiday deals' were also launched immediately after the Games and there was an 'aggressive' direct-marketing campaign though the redevelopment of the ATC internet site. Finally there was the 'building of the lucrative Meetings, Incentive, Convention and Exhibition (MICE) sector' which blossomed during the Games year.[35]

Tourism before and during the Games

Australia experienced a small increase in pre-Games Olympic tourists with many teams basing themselves in the country to familiarise themselves with its climate and culture. The 2002 PWC study stated that the pre-Olympic training of more than 127 teams from 39 countries in NSW added $US43.2 million to the state economy.[36] In the immediate years before an Olympic Games there are always an increasing number of 'Olympic Family' and media visitors as well.

However, the actual number of Olympic tourists during the Games itself was relatively small. OCA stated that there were 110,000 Olympic-specific visitors to Sydney during September 2000, of which one third — 36,000 according to Preuss — were 'Olympic Family': athletes, officials, sponsors and so forth. So the number of Olympic-specific tourists (excluding the 'Olympic Family') amounted to approximately 74,000. In September 2000 there was only a small increase — of 53,000 — in the average September figures. Preuss regarded the low visitor figures for September 2000 as 'surprising'.[37]

While many in the Sydney hotel industry believed that they would make a 'killing', a majority of hotels reported disappointing figures for July, August and September 2000. This result occurred for a number of reasons. First of all, there were fewer tourists than anticipated. Secondly, SOCOG overestimated the number of rooms it needed, including function

There were few visitors or tourists evident on a weekday in 2005 along the vast Olympic Boulevard at Sydney Olympic Park. The photograph was taken in the late morning on 11 October 2005.

Although the occupancy rates for many Sydney hotels were below expectations before and during the Games, this has not been the post-Games experience of the Novotel and Ibis hotels at Sydney Olympic Park. A third hotel will be opened at the Park in 2008.

rooms. When SOCOG released many of its rooms in August and September it was too late to fill them, so hotels were 'flooded with [empty] rooms previously held by SOCOG and now released'. Thirdly, the prices charged by hotels had been pegged at 1997 rates, when prices were lower due to the Asian crisis. Finally, the popular and free live sites across the city drained the number of patrons from local bars, forcing some to reduce their hours (see Chapter 3).[38]

There are many examples in Olympic literature of small businesses, like Sydney's hotels, overestimating the tourist demand at Games time. Many incorrectly regard an Olympic Games as a commercial bonanza which will create increased demand, enabling more products to be sold at higher prices. This was the experience of many small businesses at the Atlanta 1996 Olympic Games that had closed up by the second week of the Games.[39] It is evident that an Olympic Games or mega events do not stimulate sport, entertainment and popular culture across the board. Taronga Park Zoo, located conveniently on the shore of Sydney Harbour, reported a surprising 300 per cent decline in attendances during the Olympic Games.[40] Regional tourism operators, to the nearby Blue Mountains for instance, reported negative growth in September. The Australian Hotels Association reported much better tourist support of regional tourism — to places such as the Blue

Mountains — during the 2003 Rugby World Cup, because international visitors stayed for a longer period than they did during the Olympics and there was more time for travel between matches (see Chapter 2). Other states reported poor tourism figures in the second half of 2000. The Fortland Hotel Property Trust for instance, which owns regional properties throughout Queensland, suffered a net loss of $4.67 million for the second six months of 2000. Room yields for Brisbane fell 1.9 per cent and Cairns dropped 0.9 per cent for the whole of 2000.[41]

Football world cups, which are staged over six weeks and are spread over more cities (and even countries) than an Olympic Games are less likely to be affected by 'big event blues' — a term coined by Bailey in 1997 to suggest that many of the usual business and holiday travellers will avoid the city because they assume that there will be 'disruption to normal travel activity' and increased prices.[42] Preuss noted that this fear of overcrowding even affects local residents who become 'runaways' — residents who leave the city and take a holiday elsewhere.[43]

As the discussion of the 2003 Rugby World Cup in Chapter 2 demonstrated, this event may have attracted almost as many rugby-specific tourists (leaving aside athletes and officials) as the Olympic Games. The 2003 Rugby World Cup attracted 64,296 international tourists to Australia but many of them stayed longer and were spread more evenly around the country. As a result, the NSW economy in particular and the Australian economy more generally received significant boosts.

The post-Games tourist legacy

Most Olympic tourism analysts identify the post-Games period as the most productive period for tourism. John Morse stated in 2001 that 'the amount of media exposure and interest the Games generated is unrivalled, and that will result in a significant increase in visitor numbers over the next ten years'.[44] While Preuss acknowledged that the low number of tourists at the time of the Games was surprising, he quoted longer-term predictions which claimed that there would be a substantial and lasting tourism impact from the Sydney 2000 Olympic Games. The Tourism Forecasting Council, for instance, estimated in 1998 that as a result of the international exposure from the Olympic Games there could be an additional 1.6 million tourists from 1997 to 2004, adding $2.9 million to the national economy.[45] Preuss believed that 'Olympic tourism legacy is largely positive because the media coverage increases the desire of potential tourists to visit the country after the Games due to a change in the perception'.[46] However, he added the caveat that such a positive legacy depends on how well the Games are leveraged.

Others tourism scholars, such as Spurr, have been more cautious in predicting any longer-term tourism revenue. He argued that 'there appears to be little evidence that hallmark events have lasting effects on tourist arrivals' and that the 'promotion' impact of an event is 'short-lived' given that 'marketing generally has time limited effects unless repeatedly reinforced'. Spurr added that there had been negative growth in Los Angeles in the Olympic year (1984) and that there was little discernible change from existing tourism trends in Seoul in 1988. He added that there had been significant tourism post-event declines after the staging of the America's Cup in Fremantle (1987), the Australian Bicentennial (1988) and the Brisbane World Expo (1988). Spurr believed that Barcelona's successful post-Games tourism may have been the 'exception to the rule'.[47]

However, one of the problems in assessing an Olympic tourism factor is the lack of an agreed methodology to identify whether there is a causal link between an Olympics and a tourism affect. To date such a link seems to be largely inferred, with Olympic tourist researchers assuming that the massive promotion of a country must result in increased tourism.

Preuss is one scholar who has attempted to elaborate how tourism works and has noted a number of channels of communication: the transfer of a city's image through the media, the promotion of the city through advertisements and the conveying of direct and personal impressions by the transfer of information by tourists to a third party. Preuss also noted that while a tourism industry can promote particular attributes and a brand for the city and a country, the industry does not control other channels of communication, particularly indirect ones. While Preuss explains how tourism works, he does not identify how an Olympic tourism factor can be extracted from other forms of tourism.

So did Sydney, unlike most previous cities, sustain a long-term boost in tourism, either as a direct or indirect consequence of the Olympic Games? Did the returns justify the sizeable investment in tourism? Did the Games add anything to the Australian tourism growth that had been recorded in the 1990s, when the industry reported an annual increase of 7 per cent in inbound tourism from 1993 to 1999? In fact, but for the Asian financial crisis of 1998, when a negative growth figure was recorded, the annual pre-Games increase would have been higher (see below).

Although tourism figures were disappointing in September 2000, and for the July-September quarter of 2000, there were some promising signs over the next 12 months. In the last quarter of 2000 Australia recorded an additional 189,000 visitors — an increase of 15 per cent over the comparative figures for 1999. The PWC report noted a 4.7 per cent increase in tourism figures for the first three quarters of 2001 compared to the equivalent period in 2000.[48]

It is ironic that, while the PWC report was published in February 2002, it was based on data collected in the period until the end of 2001. Thus its tourism research stopped some three months after September 2001, when the world was transfixed by the terrorist attack of 11 September in the United States, which had a detrimental effect on the world of international tourism. The climate for international tourism was made worse by ongoing terrorist attacks, such as the Bali bombing in 2002 and the outbreak of Severe Acute Respiratory Syndrome (SARS) in Asia in 2003. Tourism to Australia also became less attractive with the steady rise in the value of the Australian dollar, which had slumped to below half the US dollar in March 2001 but by 2003 had crept to over 70 cents in the US dollar; in early 2005 it was a few cents off the 80 cent mark. There was also a slowing down of the world economy from late 2000, which affected the markets of America and Japan — the two countries most prominent in Australian inbound tourism.

In the face of such a catastrophic set of global circumstances, the Australian tourism industry suffered an unprecedented three years of negative growth. After the figures were posted for 2002, Australian Tourist Export Council managing director Peter Shelley stated that 'Australia had never experienced two consecutive falls in annual arrivals'.[49] However, there was an even greater negative growth of –2.0 per cent in 2003 and without the boost from the 2003 Rugby World Cup such figures would have been much lower. It seemed that all the ATC investment and government seeding money had come to nought — at least in the short term — and the pre-Games tourism forecasts were more than excessively optimistic: they were seriously wrong. Table 4.2 (opposite page) summarises the tourism trends over 11 years.

In order to rescue the tourist industry the federal government announced a $235 million package in November 2003.[50]

Australia's three-year slump in international visitors ended in 2004, when Tourism Australia reported a dramatic recovery with more than 5 million overseas visitors and an almost 10 per cent increase over the previous 12 months. However, this good tourist figure for 2004 was achieved from a significantly reduced base of two-and-a-half years of declining numbers.[51] Nevertheless, positive tourism trends were also reported in the first months of 2005.

Table 4.2: International visitors to Australia, 1993–2004

Year	International visitors	Percentage increase (decline)
1993	2,996,200	15.1
1994	3,361,700	12.2
1995	3,725,800	10.8
1996	4,164,800	11.8
1997	4,317,900	3.7
*1998	4,167,200	(−3.5)
1999	4,459,500	7.0
2000	4,931,400	10.6
**2001	4,855,700	(−1.5)
**2002	4,841,200	(−0.3)
***2003	4,745,900	(−2.0)
2004	5,215,000	9.9,

Source: ABS, *Year Book Australia*, 2005

*Asian financial crisis
**Global terrorism
***SARS and a higher $A

The December 2004 forecasts for international visitors until 2013 were also more positive. Inbound tourism is predicted to be above 7 million in 2010 and to reach almost 9 million by 2013. However, these figures fell well short of predictions by the ATC in February 2001 that there would be strong growth in Australia's inbound tourism with an average of 7.8 per cent per annum from 2001 to 2010. The ATC had predicted in 2001 that there would be 10.2 million tourists, rather than the revised estimate of 7 million, by 2010.

The ATC's forecast was based on:

- a relatively fast economic recovery in Asian nations,
- a continuation of positive economic growth in Europe and North America,
- the depreciation of the Australian dollar against most major currencies,
- Australia's marketing efforts overseas, and
- the effect of the Sydney Olympics.[52]

It is difficult to detect any long-term Olympic tourism impact because the post-2003 tourist figures had been shaped by many other factors. In addition to the continuing presence of international terrorism, the recovery of the North American and European economies was more protracted than anticipated. The decline of the Australian dollar in 2001 was arrested in 2002 and the Australian dollar steadily appreciated in value from 2003.

Conventions

Chalip has noted that an Olympic Games has great potential to stimulate conference and convention business. This represents a 'high yield market' because convention delegates typically generate much greater daily spending than other leisure tourists. A 2001 study by the Sydney Convention and Visitors Bureau found that 'international convention delegates spend up to nine times more per day than the average international visitor to Australia'.[53] Conventions represent a specialised segment of the leisure market because convention delegates are easier to target. Convention destinations are also determined by bids which are decided by a handful of decision-makers. Chalip added that 'the mere fact that Sydney had won the right to host the Olympic Games helped Australian destinations to capture 'the ear of [convention] decision makers'.[54]

Although Barcelona failed to build a city convention centre — this being the only significant piece of tourism infrastructure still pending at the time of the Games in 1992 — the Games had a positive impact on the city's positioning in the business meeting sector and the city was able to establish its status as 'one of the world's major cities for conferences and conventions'. The Barcelona Convention Bureau recorded the impressive rise in convention business from 1990 to 2001,[55] as shown in Table 4.3.

Table 4.3 Number of convention meetings and delegates in Barcelona

	1990	1992	2000	2001
Number of meetings	373	310	1380	1345
Number of delegates	105,424	108,464	269,508	255,433

The Sydney Convention and Visitors Bureau (SCVB) was established in 1969 as a joint venture between the NSW Government and the tourism industry. Its objectives were to promote Sydney as a 'meeting, incentive, convention, exhibition and special event destination'. It is a non-profit organisation with 300 members including hotels, restaurants, attractions, venues, entertainment, professional conference organisers and other business tourism suppliers.

Sydney and Australia's success in accessing convention tourism was manifest before the Games. By 1999 the International Congress and Convention Association ranked Australia seventh and by 2001 fourth in the world in terms of international conventions and business meetings. Sydney jumped from 10th place in 1999 to 5th in 2000 for the number of conventions hosted by the city.

Sydney's results flowed on to some of the other capital cities of the country: Melbourne was ranked 15th in 2000, Adelaide 38th and Brisbane 51st — the strongest result recorded by any country. In Chalip's view, based on a review of industry analysts, Sydney was the premier convention and conference destination by 1999:

> By 1999, industry analysts were ranking Sydney as the number one conference and convention destination in the world, and Melbourne as number two. In the post-Olympic period, Australian cities have continued to enjoy an advantage in the marketplace that they did not have prior to the time Sydney won the right to host the Games.[56]

This modest sculpture in front of the Sydney Convention Centre at Darling Harbour, which features the Sydney Olympic logo, is the only reminder in the city that an Olympic Games was held there.

The annual reports of the SCVB, summarised in Table 4.4, demonstrate that the increase in convention business before 2000 continued afterwards.

Table 4.4 Conventions held in Sydney 1993-2005.

Year	Bids won	Delegates	Delegate days	$ Value
1993-94	26	45,625	290,700	205,400,000
1994-95	41	49,820	259,350	201,500.00
1995-96	29	29,625	149,494	114,600
1996-97	34	70,100	329,350	205,400,000
1997-98	24	28,450	144,050	111,564,470

Year	Bids won	Delegates	Delegate days	$ Value
1998-99	40	38,020	168,010	116,847,490
1999-00	30	35,850	176,000	121,045,345
2000-01	37	58,420	240,460	149,435,979
2001-02	32	29,600	131,110	143,225,858
2002-03	47	69,200	345,170	291,349,735
2003-04	45	49,455	213,075	191,864,758
2004-05	35	37,365	157,145	148,072,555

Note: A new system to establish the value of convention tourism was introduced in 2001.

It is interesting to note that the specialist convention tourism market recovered more quickly than the international tourist market. After a significant drop in convention delegates in 2001–02, the SCVB enjoyed a bumper and record year in 2002–03, though this was partly due to the staging of a Lions Club International event in Sydney that attracted approximately 25,000 people and was worth an estimated $91 million. Researchers from SCVB attribute the decline in the last two years to be due to greater competition for convention tourism from a number Asian cities.[57]

Sydney's vibrant conference and incentive market had a positive effect on the Novotel and Ibis hotels at Sydney Olympic Park, which have recorded their highest occupancy rates since the Olympic Games. On the third anniversary of the Games the Novotel recorded an average occupancy rate of 86.3 per cent and the hotel complex as a whole an average of 82.4 per cent. Mark Ronfeld, the manager of Accor, the owner of the hotels, stated in 2003: 'Sydney Olympic Park has really made its mark as one of the city's foremost business and conference venues, which has meant that our hotels are heavily booked year-round'.[58] This occurred because of an increasing number of events at the Park and a growing conference business trade in Sydney's western business region. It was announced by Accor in 2005 that the Sofitel, western Sydney's first five-star hotel, would be built at Sydney Olympic Park and would open in mid-2008. The cost of the 18 storey, 210 room hotel was in excess of $50 million.[59]

Based on the figures from 1993 to 2005 it appears that the 1993 prediction of an injection of $1.2 billion worth of convention business in the years to 2007 had almost been met by June 2005, with an increase of $1.07 billion since 1993. It is likely that some of this increase, as Chalip noted, can be attributed to the Olympic Games and associated tourism programs.

Other business benefits

Jones Lang LaSalle noted that the Olympic investment in telecommunications infrastructure is likely to have beneficial impacts:

> The successful handling of the telecommunications aspects of the Sydney Games, not only provided a major boost to the international credibility of the technology providers (co-ordinated by the national telco — Telstra), but also provided Sydney with a long-term inheritance in the form of significant extensions and enhancements to the City's fibre optic network. Telstra's Millenium (*sic*) network includes a total of 4,800 km of fibre optic cable, linking 105 locations but focused on a ring between the Sydney CBD and Olympic Park in the city's inner western suburbs. As a result of this investment, the Homebush Bay area is poised to become a focal point for the Internet Data Centres within Sydney.[60]

Conclusions

From the vantage point of 2005 it seems clear that the tourism marketing professionals were guilty of 'excessive optimism', overstating the importance of Olympic tourism in particular and underestimating the role of other global factors. The 1998 prediction of the Tourism Forecasting Council of an additional 1.6 million visitors from 1997 to 2004 has proven to be wide of the mark; there was actually a much more modest increase of 897,000 visitors in this period. It also cannot be assumed that the additional visitors came either directly or indirectly because of the Olympic Games, in fact international rugby fans helped boost Australia's tourist figures in 2003.

Nonetheless there were some success stories in terms of business and economic benefits. The Games themselves 'exceeded bid revenue targets for all marketing programs, including broadcast, sponsorship, ticketing end licensing'.[61] Convention tourism to Sydney was a strong performer before and after the Games and recovered relatively quickly from the worsening global tourist market after 2001. The vibrant convention market had a positive effect on hotel occupancy, particularly at Sydney Olympic Park, even though many city hotels recorded disappointing results during the Games. There is also the continuing success story of the export of Australian Olympic knowledge and expertise, the international employment of Australian experts and the winning of international contracts.

It is ironic that the there appears to have been a greater immediate tourism boost from the 2003 Rugby World Cup than from the Sydney 2000 Olympic Games, even though less money was spent by the tourism industry and the Australian Government in leveraging the 2003 event. However, the Rugby World Cup capitalised on the sporting and transport infrastructure set up for the Olympic Games and benefited from Olympic tourism promotion and the post-Olympic activities of the NSW Department for State and Regional Development.

An Olympic city can access a positive tourism legacy providing, as Duran had suggested, Olympic tourism is integrated into a longer-term plan to promote a city's tourism markets. It is possible that the Olympic Games did advance *Brand Australia* by ten years, as John Morse claimed, though it will take continuing promotion campaigns to capitalise on this. The decline in inbound tourism in 2002 and 2003 appears likely to be a temporary setback in what is otherwise a rising tourism market. The Sydney 2000 Olympic Games are certainly one factor in a long-term positive tourism outcome.

Although the business and economic indicators have not been as positive as the PWC report suggested in 2002, it is nevertheless paradoxical that the media and the public in general concentrated more on negative Olympic stories in 2001 and 2002. During these years there was much more focus on the obvious failings of Sydney Olympic Park (see Chapter 6) so that it was the major post-Olympic story in town. Some of the tangible and positive outcomes of the Olympic Games were largely ignored.

There are a number of likely explanations for this post-Games negativity. It accorded, first of all, with the public mood of forgetting — and even suppressing — the positive memories of the Games. It is also evident that dramatic photographs of an empty Sydney Olympic Park and stories about the mounting deficits of Olympic venues were far more newsworthy than dry economic data which indicated a positive legacy. It is also evident that much of the story of Australia's success in exporting its Olympic expertise and knowledge has been largely untold. This story is part of the subject of the next chapter.

Chapter 5

INTERNATIONAL INVESTMENT AND CONTRACTS

The precise dimensions of international Olympic outcomes are difficult to gauge for a number of reasons. First of all, the various outcomes are diverse and not easy to identify. They include investment in Australia by international companies, the winning of overseas contracts, the export of goods and personnel and the transfer of knowledge and expertise. A 2001 report by the Australian company, Jones Lang LaSalle, on Olympic impacts noted that 'the specific impact of the Olympics on regional economies [such as the Asia-Pacific region] is at best an imprecise exercise'.[1] Secondly, there is no one agency that collects information on the international dimensions of the Sydney Games. The material in this chapter has been assembled from diverse sources. Thirdly, some outcomes that could be attributed to the Games are intertwined with other non-Olympic factors. The Australian universities push towards China in particular and Asia in general is a long-standing process and has been driven by a range of factors. Finally, as the 2002 report of PricewaterhouseCoopers (PWC), on the economic and business benefits of the Sydney 2000 Olympic Games pointed out: 'no comparable data is available [from previous Games] with which to compare the export development and investment attraction performance of other Games to Sydney 2000'. This makes the effort to capture such international impacts even more worthwhile and challenging.

Holger Preuss is one of the few scholars to explore the international business benefits of an Olympic Games: he included a brief section on 'Exports and foreign investments' in his book of *The Economics of Staging the Olympics*.[2] However, because his focus is on the Games period and its immediate aftermath, he does not capture any longer-term developments. Business generated by Sydney-Beijing Olympic axis continues to grow in 2006 and the Olympic relationship between the two countries is now stronger than it was in 2001, when Beijing won the bid to host the Olympic Games. The PWC report predicted that the Sydney Olympic Games would provide a great boost for international investment, for the export of Australian business, expertise and knowledge and for a greater international business involvement in Australia. The report claimed that because the Games had generated up to '$6.1 billion worth of international publicity' there would be substantial benefits for Australian business and investment. It added that no other Games host city 'undertook systematically to leverage the international visibility of the host city and the host country, to the advantage of so many industry sectors'.[3] This occurred because of coordinated strategies involving both the public and private sectors during and after the Games which will be outlined below.

The economic indicators listed in the Olympic Games Global Impact (OGGI) Program include relatively few items that relate to international investment, possibly because an OGGI program is completed two years after an Olympic Games. Apart from some entries on tourism, the only other international economic indicators are:

- Rate of establishment of foreign organisations
- Hosting of international events

Education is also listed by OGGI but it is classified as a social rather than an economic indicator. It will be argued below that Australian tertiary institutions have achieved a financial as well as an educational legacy as a result of their Olympic involvement.

This chapter, then, will consider to what extent Australia achieved favourable international outcomes from the Games, whether the positive projections made in the PWC report have been realised, and whether such benefits are likely to continue. Did the Games lead to a better profile and recognition of Sydney and Australia in international business?

How can the international dimensions of the Games best be defined and measured? Can the worth of international investment be assessed? Is it possible to capture Sydney's positive international business outcomes so that they can be emulated by other Olympic cities?

Agencies involved in exploiting Olympic opportunities

The opportunities to showcase and market Australian business internationally were recognised soon after Sydney won its Olympic bid in 1993. Government and the private sector combined to develop a series of initiatives to maximise Games business benefits. They were implemented by government agencies, such as Austrade.

Other organisations were also involved. The Olympics Business Roundtable was a private sector led task force, which was established by the NSW Government in June 1995. It was chaired by Richard 'Dick' Warbuton, chairman of the Sydney Harbour Casino. The Roundtable developed a series of strategies and programs to 'positively position Australian business and industry internationally'.[4]

The Business Club Australia, which was a marketing initiative that emerged out of the Roundtable, was launched in September 1998. The concept was jointly developed by Austrade and the NSW Department of State and Regional Development (DSRD). The Club, which was run by Austrade, operated during the Olympic year as a business centre located at Darling Harbour near the Media Centre for unaccredited media, where it had access to a large catamaran moored there. The Club offered priority access to government services for business people visiting Australia, and was a convenient meeting place for Australian and international business persons. An important component of the Club was the development and management of a business data base. This Centre provided another place for exchange of information, and the media collection of business stories as well as networking.

Planning by the Roundtable also led to three other programs. Anthony Jeffrey of PWC developed the idea of the Australian Technology Showcase (ATS), which was established in 1998 by a dozen private sector Olympic sponsors along with PWC and Newport Capital and implemented by DSRD. ATS's aim was to highlight innovative and commercially attractive technologies developed in Australia and to enhance overseas distribution opportunities. PWC noted that by December 2001:

> The ATS had signed up some 300 technologies … it has now delivered at least $288 million (exceeding its $200 million target) in economic benefit on an original Government investment of $6 million; and it now serves as a national prototype for industry development/export promotion programs with a technology focus.[5]

Investment 2000 (I2000) was another initiative developed by DSRD in 1998, this time in conjunction with Westpac, Telstra and the federal government agency Invest Australia. Its objective was to market Australia internationally as a suitable regional business location for Asia and the Pacific. I2000 was considered another 'winner' by the PWC report as it attracted 45 investments worth $520 million leading to the creation of 1150 jobs.

The Olympic Business Information Services (OBIS) was a third successful initiative which was managed for the NSW ISO Ltd on behalf of DSRD. The objective of OBIS was to provide 'tender-related information' for Australian businesses registered on its data base, which included some 5000 Australian suppliers, of which 4000 were from NSW. OBIS facilitated over $300 million in Olympics-related contracts.

As is evident from these activities, the NSW Department of State and Regional Development was a key player in driving business opportunities before and after the Games. As the government department nominated to seek out the business benefits of the Games, DSRD had an important role in all the above programs and established its own Olympics Services Group on 1997. DRSD worked with NSW businesses, assisting them to gain sports infrastructure and service grants so as to gain leverage from the Games. It also developed follow-up policies to maximise long-term benefits from the staging of events such as the Olympic Games. The department continues to promote Sydney as a venue for major sporting events that have the potential to generate even more future business benefits.

There were many direct and indirect benefits from this sustained promotion of business benefits by DRSD and associated organisations. The process resulted in more focused trade missions overseas and provided a more coordinated showcasing of Australian business expertise. Many Australian firms improved their promotion and accessed more international tender opportunities. The programs catered effectively for business visitors, delegations and international company boards. There were also regional company successes since programs were developed for Olympic events outside Sydney, such as pre-Games training.

The PWC report estimated that the Games would generate some $3 billion in business outcomes — both domestic and international — including $600 million in new business investment. PWC reported from its 'early data' that Olympic suppliers had secured almost $2 million in new post-Games business and there was a likely additional $1.5 billion Games-related contracts in the future. PWC also reported that by June 2001 the Australian Sports International Program had attracted 90 members and generated $13 million in new exports 'with a further $100 million pending'.[6] These contracts covered areas such as stadium developments and seating; consultancy services, sponsorships and strategies; and technical equipment and management.

Although the ATS has received more funding and has expanded its operations since 2000, the Olympic Business Information Services ceased after the Games by early 2001 as did the I2000 program. The PWC report added its opinion that 'with the benefit of hindsight' the funding of ATS 'may have been cut too soon'.[7] Fortunately other institutions were created, such as the Sydney-Beijing Olympic Secretariat (see below), which continued the long-term promotion of positive international business outcomes.

Exporting Olympic expertise

The staging of the Sydney 2000 Olympic Games added much value to Australia's sporting and events management reputation. It proved that the country had the capacity and expertise to successfully organise an event of this magnitude. In addition, the outstanding achievements of the Australian team in 2000 (and in 2004), given Australia's population and resources, demonstrated yet again the effectiveness of the Australian sports system. Australian Olympic expertise has been a very successful export in many arenas, while the Australian sports system, along with Australian personnel, have been successful in Great Britain.

Athens 2004

There was less of a natural axis between Sydney and Athens than with Beijing and London as there were fewer economic and cultural ties between Australia and Greece, even though Sydney and Melbourne boast a large Greek-Australian population. There was also a degree of rivalry between the Games organisers of Sydney and Athens (see Chapter 2). Following Sydney was not an easy task for the Greeks, given that Sydney had established new Olympic benchmarks which were difficult to match. However, the Greeks were determined to stage and brand their own Games. David Humphries noted in the *Sydney Morning Herald* of 8 November 2000 that 'early media reports suggested that Australian suppliers may have been limited in their access to major contracts at the Athens Olympics, for reasons associated more with internal political conflicts than with the abilities of Australian suppliers'.

Despite this cautious assessment, there was a significant Australian presence in Athens from 2001 to 2004. Andrew Walsh, the director of the opening and closing ceremonies for the 2003 Rugby World Cup, was contracted to Jack Morton Worldwide to help produce the same ceremonies for the Athens Olympic Games.[8] Former NSW Police Commissioner Peter Ryan was appointed Chief Security Consultant for the Athens Games and Richard Palfreyman from Sydney's Main Press Centre was recruited to the Athens Main Press Centre more than a year before the Games to assist in media operations. David Richmond Consulting Pty Ltd was contracted to provide strategic advice for the president of ATHOC from February 2001 to August 2004.[9] Michael Knight, the former NSW Government Minister for the Olympics, was an advisor to ATHOC. There were also many other Australians who visited Athens regularly to provide specialist advice and undertake consultancies, such as Nickie Vance, who was an expert on doping control. Many Australians had the chance to become part of an Olympic and Games 'caravan', which after Athens travelled to Beijing, London, Doha, Melbourne and many other bid cities such as Paris and Rio de Janeiro.

The post-Games Olympic consultancy career of Jim Sloman demonstrates how rich, varied and long-lasting it can be. Sloman, who had been the group executive for Lend Lease Property Services for almost two-and-a-half decades and had developed skills as a site engineer and project manager, was persuaded by Michael Knight to become the operating officer of SOCOG in 1996. Sloman had as good a grasp of design and construction issues as anyone on the organising committee and also developed expertise on 'organisation and budget issues and how to handle people'.[10] When he accepted a post in SOCOG there was the risk that he would be unemployed after 2000. However, after the Sydney Games, Sloman formed a company, MI Associates, with two other SOCOG general managers, John Quayle and Peter Morris. His company won roles in the Athens and London Games and is likely to be engaged to assist Rio de Janeiro in its bid for the 2016 Olympic Games. MI Associates has also been involved with the Commonwealth Games, the Asian Games, the Pan American Games and the 2003 Rugby World Cup.

Australian companies won a surprisingly large number of contracts — 37 — related to the staging of the Athens 2004 Olympic Games. Bligh Voller Nield, for instance, won major contracts to undertake master planning for the Olympic sites and the Hellinikon Sports Complex as well as designing a number of other venues. Other contracts, by contrast, were small: Dot Dash was engaged to design wayfinding signage and Horne Associates to develop landscape design for the Olympic Village. Yet other contracts proved to be problematic, with one being cancelled at a late stage, resulting in litigation. Starena International, a company based at West Gosford, won a $5 million contract in April 2004 to provide plastic seats for the Olympic stadium. Starena had already won contracts in 2003 to provide another 30,000 seats for the beach volleyball and the tennis centres and for the equestrian facility.[11] Unfortunately, the Greek organisers cancelled Starena's contract for the Olympic stadium seating at a late stage, resulting in a substantial losses for the company.

Some of the positive business results were achieved because DSRD implemented a post-2000 Sydney Olympics program in conjunction with Austrade to organise seminars on the Athens 2004 Olympic Games.[12] Federal Minister for Trade Mark Vaile stated in April 2004 that 'Australian companies are providing merchandise, accommodation, sporting equipment and engineering, cleaning and training services for Athens 2004' which were 'worth more than $200,000 million'. Although this figure was much smaller than the Olympic contracts achieved in relation to the Beijing Olympic Games, Vaile pointed out that these contracts 'will more than quadruple Australia's current exports to Greece'.[13]

There were two significant Australian educational initiatives at Athens associated with the Games. TAFE GLOBAL, the international arm of TAFE NSW, which trained the Olympic workforce and volunteers for the Sydney Games, signed a contract to begin an eight-month project from November 2001 on training and recruiting for Olympic personnel. The University of Technology, Sydney, organised a successful program in 1999 and 2000 enabling 120 Greek students to gain educational and administrative experience which prepared them a role in the 2004 Athens Olympic Games (see below).

Beijing 2008

The relationship between Australia and China has grown in importance

Sandy Hollway AO stands by Wang Wei, secretary-general and vice-president of BOCOG, who is being interviewed at Stadia China 2004 (Eric Winton, DSRD).

since the 1970s and 1980s, when the Whitlam and Hawke governments recognised its value; successive governments have followed suit. The Olympic link between Sydney and Beijing developed naturally because the two cities operate in roughly similar time zones and have developed increasingly close cultural and economic ties. Although Beijing wants to stage its own Games — which reflect Chinese and Asian culture and priorities — there is an obvious Chinese readiness to look to the Sydney Olympic model, more so than any other. When the Chinese President, Hu Jintao, visited Sydney in October 2003 and inspected Sydney's Olympic facilities he issued an open invitation to 'come over and help us with [our] Olympics projects'.[14]

Australia's position as a potential supplier of Olympic services and expertise had been strengthened by its open support for the Beijing 2008 bid. The potential benefits of this support, and consequently an Olympic relationship between Australian cities and Beijing, were first recognised by the ACT Government. Drawing cleverly on its sister-city relationship with Beijing, the ACT Government initiated an intensive period of activity from late 2000 until China's successful bid in July

2001, supporting frequent visits to Beijing by the Canberra-based firm Endeavour Consulting, which was headed by China specialist Peter Phillips. This firm drew in Olympic experts who had been prominent in SOCOG such as Sandy Hollway (CEO), John Bowan (International Relations), Phil Tully (Planning and Technical Management) and Milton Cockburn (Media Relations).

Hollway, Bowan, Cockburn and Tully assisted Beijing to develop its successful 2008 Olympic bid, travelling to Beijing on numerous occasions to advise on the many aspects of the bid. Hollway was even with the Beijing team at Moscow, when the announcement was made that Beijing had been chosen as the 2008 Olympic city.

Austrade had already identified the great potential economic benefit to Australia from the Beijing 2008 Olympic Games, predicting that Beijing would spend the massive amount of $US30 billion on the Games: $US1.6 billion for the 37 venues; $US14 billion on the Beijing Olympic site, which would include cost of new offices, hotels, the Olympic village, and parkland; and another $US14 billion on a wide range of infrastructure costs including roads, railways, airport runways and telecommunications.[15] Beijing looked to Sydney and Australia, perhaps more than any other country, to service such needs.

The NSW Government was quick to recognise the value of the ACT's Olympic initiatives. It organised a number of missions to China, headed by the then Premier Bob Carr and including the former head of OCA, David Richmond. One objective of these visits, which were coordinated by Austrade Beijing, was to assist NSW companies to tender for major contracts in Beijing. DSRD implemented a post-2000 Sydney Olympic business program to promote the state's Olympic expertise overseas.

However, the establishment of the Sydney-Beijing Olympic Secretariat (SBOS) in February 2002 by the NSW Government proved the catalyst that enabled NSW business to capitalise on Beijing Olympic business opportunities. SBOS provided businesses many specific services which were augmented by the efforts of DSRD, Austrade and ACBC. The services included:

- Informal strategic advice and assistance,
- Independent and realistic assessment of opportunities,
- A specialised information resource, and
- Advice and assistance with the timing and composition of Trade

Missions and other Australian promotional activities in China to effectively respond to available opportunities.

SBOS, which is funded by DSRD, was initially located in the Premier's Department alongside the Major Venues and Rugby World Cup Co-ordination Units. After several months it moved to the Department of State and Regional Development. David Churches, its director, and Sandy Hollway, its senior advisor, are the key representatives of SBOS in Beijing. The strategy committee also includes David Richmond. Eric Winton was appointed the senior manager of SBOS, several months after its establishment, to run the office on a day-to-day basis. SBOS works closely with Austrade, the Department of Foreign Affairs and Trade, the Sydney Olympic Park Authority and the Australia China Business Council.

Hollway recalled in 2005 that SBOS represented the fusion of three separate developments. Firstly, the ACT Government and the Canberra-based Endeavour Consulting recognised the potential Olympic synergies between Australia and China. Secondly, there was the close relationship and mutual respect between the Sydney advisers to the Beijing 2008 bid team; a relationship which had developed during Beijing's bid period.

Australian firms, including Starena International, were prominent at Stadia China 2004 at Beijing (Eric Winton, DSRD).

Thirdly, the NSW Government came to a similar conclusion to the ACT Government about the potential value of the China connection. Robert Adby, the director general of OCA who oversaw the wrap-up of Games organisations in 2001, recognised the potential to export Olympic knowledge and services. He oversaw the creation of SBOS and chaired a steering committee that included Austrade, the Australia China Business Council and other bodies with an interest in business with China.

SBOS provided individual businesses with information and advice about how best to access the Chinese Olympic market, given that it was so different from the Australian market. SBOS became a conduit, enabling firms to gain information on the tendering process and forthcoming contract opportunities as well as access to key officials in the Beijing organising committee, government agencies and principal contractors. As a result, NSW businesses have achieved great success in securing Beijing Olympic contracts. The then NSW Treasurer, Michael Egan, reported the success of such endeavours in the NSW Legislative Council on 11 and 17 March 2004 when he stated that six New South Wales companies travelled to Beijing to promote their expertise in Olympic and sports infrastructure at Stadia China 2004 Beijing — China's leading sports infrastructure trade exhibition and conference — which ran from 16 to 18 February 2004.

Egan added that the results of this well-coordinated promotion had been impressive:

> For the Beijing 2008 Olympics, Bligh Voller Nield won the right to design the Beijing Aquatic Park, which will be the city's largest Olympic facility … The company was also appointed to undertake initial master planning for the Beijing Olympic Green, the major precinct for the 2008 Beijing Games …
>
> Some other Olympic project successes for New South Wales companies are as follows: Sydney architects group GSA won the design competition for the Beijing Shooting Centre; two Sydney specialists in transport planning, engineering and consulting, GHD and Parsons Brinckerhoff, provided Olympic-related advice to Beijing agencies — GHD, for example, also won a contract to design a major water supply pipeline to Beijing … [16]

The Sydney firm PTW Architects was another Australian business to gain significant design contracts, including contracts for the National

Swimming Centre, the Watercube and the Olympic Village in Beijing. Cox Architects and Planners were contracted to design the Olympic sailing facility at Qingdao. Parsons Brinckerhoff have been engaged to prepare the transportation plan for the Beijing Olympic Green, the venue for 13 sports at the Olympic Games. The BOCOG EMS Manual and the BOCOG Environmental Master Plan were jointly drafted by CH2M Hill Australia and BOCOG.

In the past decade Bligh Voller Nield has been prominent in the design of major Olympic and sporting infrastructure. The company designed Sydney's Olympic stadium as well as Melbourne's Telstra Dome. In 2003 it undertook the broadcast operational planning review for all venues used in the Rugby World Cup.[17] The firm has also won a number of other sporting contracts, including the design of a football stadium in Venice, Italy.

According to Hollway's February 2004 assessment, Australian firms have won about half the design contracts for venues for the 2008 Olympic Games. He added that 'Australian architects are also short listed for participation in all current venue tenders and these projects have a value in excess of two billion Australian dollars'.[18]

While Egan had been proud of Australian representation at the Stadia China 2004, Australia had an even larger presence at Stadia China 2005 held in Beijing from 18 to 20 January 2005, when it was represented by 30 firms with diverse Olympic expertise — the largest national presence of any country. A significant attraction of this growing Australian presence at Stadia China was the possibility of procuring contract opportunities beyond the Beijing Olympics, such as the Guangzhou Asian Games and the Shanghai World Expo in 2010.

SBOS has tapped into a rich export opportunity which arose almost two years after the Sydney 2000 Olympic Games, and after Beijing won its Olympic bid in July 2001. The decision to create SBOS, and the speedy and flexible way in which the organisation was set up, proved both imaginative and inspired. The export of Olympic knowledge and services from Sydney (and NSW) to Beijing continues to expand in 2005.

The Sydney-Beijing Olympic axis is an interesting example of new Olympic business opportunities that can emerge several years after an Olympic Games. It is highly unlikely that the NSW Olympic business outcomes would have been as impressive if individual businesses had had to make their own way in the Chinese market. This suggests that the value of setting up strategic post-Games organisations that target new Olympic opportunities.

It is impossible to place a precise value on the worth of the NSW Olympic export business with Beijing, because many companies are unwilling to divulge contract details. SBOS assists the operations of many NSW businesses in China but there are other firms which operate separately. Also, as Eric Winton noted, the Beijing project market is also continuously undergoing change. No agency has collected, let alone calculated, the total value of such business. However, the continuing interest and involvement of many NSW and Australian firms in Beijing suggest that the business is profitable and the export returns are probably substantial.

The success of Australian companies in winning prestigious Olympic contracts in China has generated further sports business. PTW Architects and Cox have designed a number of sports arenas and swimming pools in Asia. PTW has also been engaged to design a sports 'hub' in Iran.

London 2012

The announcement on 6 July 2005 that London had been chosen to stage the 2012 Olympic Games had significant implications for the continuing export of Australian sports and Olympic expertise. If the Olympic synergies between Sydney and Beijing were close, the Olympic links between Sydney and London may prove to be even more significant. Britain and Australia have had a long and enduring sporting relationship which has been strengthened during the last decade.

An increasing British interest in Australian sport occurred for a number of reasons. In the decades after the establishment of the Australian Institute of Sport (AIS) in 1981, the Australian sports system became one of the most successful and internationally acclaimed. The AIS was backed up by improved Australian performances in all sports including Olympic sports in the 1990s. Without a well-developed sports system, British sports lagged behind many countries, including Australia. From the early 1980s to the mid 1990s, it achieved less success at the Olympic and Commonwealth Games.

However, this changed with the establishment of the UK Sports Institute in 1996, which emulated the successful Australian institute. This institute had a commitment 'to drive the development of a world-class high-performance system in the UK', with funds provided by the National Lottery. Four regional institutes were established in England,

Northern Ireland, Scotland and Wales. Although the UK Sports Institute has been established for a relatively short time, there has already been an improvement in the British performance in the past two Olympic Games (see below). There is also a great irony in the increased success of the Australian sports export business to the motherland, given that many of its sports came to Australia with British settlers and so became part of Australia's British inheritance, and given that Australia as a former colony had long been a fertile market for all things British including culture, identity and manufactured goods.

Australia finished well ahead of England — though not ahead of the combined United Kingdom total — in the medal table in the 2002 Manchester Commonwealth Games despite the latter's home advantage. England has not headed Australia at the Commonwealth Games since the home Games at Edinburgh in 1986, when Australia finished third in the gold medal tally to Canada, though second in the overall medal tally. In 1994 and 1998 Australia achieved more medals than the total of four separate UK teams. However, it should be noted that by the 1990s the British focus had been rather more on European sport than the Commonwealth Games, which Australia continued to take more seriously than most of the other nations involved.

Tables 5.1 and 5.2 compare Australia's and Great Britain's performance in recent Olympic Games and Commonwealth Games.

Table 5.1 Medals achieved by Australia and Great Britain and the position in the unofficial medal table at four recent Olympic Games.

Gold-silver-bronze (total)
Position in the unofficial medal table

	1992	1996	2000	2004
Australia	7-9-11 (27) 7th	9-9-23 (41) 7th	16-25-17 (58) 4th	17-16-16 (49) 4th
Great Britain	5-3-12 (20) 13th	1-8-6 (15) 36th	11-10-7 (28) 10th	9-9-11 (29) 10th

Table 5.2 Medals achieved by Australia, England, Northern Ireland, Scotland and Wales, and the position in the unofficial medal table, at four recent Commonwealth Games.

		1986	1990	1994	1998	2002
Australia	Gold	40	52	87	80	82
	Silv.	46	54	52	60	62
	Br.	35	56	43	58	62
	Total	121	162	182	198	206
	Pos.	3rd	1st	1st	1st	1st
England	Gold	52	47	31	30	54
	Silv.	43	40	45	47	51
	Br.	49	42	49	53	50
	Total	144	129	125	130	155
	Pos.	1st	2nd	3rd	2nd	2nd
N. Ireland	Gold	2	1	5	2	2
	Silv.	4	3	2	1	2
	Br.	9	5	3	2	1
	Total	15	9	10	5	5
	Pos.	7th	13th	10th	13th	17th
Scotland	Gold	3	5	6	3	6
	Silv.	12	7	3	2	8
	Br.	18	10	11	7	16
	Total	33	22	20	12	30
	Pos.	6th	9th	7th	11th	9th
Wales	Gold	6	10	5	3	4
	Silv.	5	3	8	4	15
	Br.	11	12	6	8	12
	Total	22	25	19	15	31
	Pos.	5th	6th	9th	10th	11th
British total	Gold	63	63	47	44	66
	Silv	64	53	58	54	76
	Br.	87	69	69	70	231
	Total	214	185	174	162	221

A keen British interest in the Australian sports system was evident well before the Sydney 2000 Olympic Games. John Bloomfield, who published a book on this topic, noted that:

> Approximately 30 high profile Australians were contracted to UK sport [in recent years], some of the more notable being David Moffett (who was CEO of Sport England and who has recently moved to a similar position in the Welsh Rugby Union), Wilma Shakespear (CEO of the English Sports Institute), Rod Marsh (Director, English Cricket Academy), Ian Robson (CEO of Sport Scotland) and Bill Sweetenham (National Performance Director of Swimming). The Australian press has made much of this, some even suggesting that the 'defections' will continue for several years.[19]

Anne-Marie Harrison, former chief executive officer of the Sports Federation of Victoria, Australia, was appointed the first executive director of the Scottish Institute of Sport, which was launched in October 1998.

In the past decade Britain has followed some of the practices of the Australian sports system by establishing the UK Sports Institute, as noted above. With the government generously funding high-profile sport through a national lottery, a large amount of money is now spent on British sport — 'in some cases this is four times as much as Australia spends on the equivalent sport'. Bloomfield warned that this might pose a future threat to the continuing success of the Australian sports system. However, it remains to be seen whether money, coaching, superb facilities and professionalism are enough.[20] The Australian sports system has prospered not only because the funding of the government and the private sector are backed by the community, but also because there is a national determination to achieve success in sport.

There has been a continuing demand for Australian expertise in managing and bidding for large sporting events. The Manchester Commonwealth Games Committee recruited 60 former members of SOCOG to work on the staging of what proved a successful Games.[21] Jim Sloman's company, MI Associates, was involved in these 2002 Games.[22]

Sloman had been involved with the Rio de Janeiro bid for the 2012 Olympic Games, but after Rio failed to make the short list he was invited to join London's bid team by the bid chairman, Sebastian Coe. Sloman, and MI Associates, spent the next year overseeing London's strategy and 're-working some of the Games sites'.[23] It is likely that Sloman will continue to play a role in the 2012 London Olympic Games, though he is also keen to advance the cause of Rio de Janeiro to host the 2016

Olympic Games. MI Associates also have a substantial involvement in the 2007 Rio Pan American Games.

MI Associates and TFG International were two companies involved in the successful London bid. It is likely that an Australian role in the London 2012 Olympic Games will increase in the next seven years. Even though there is a gap of 12 years between the Sydney and the London Olympics, the Sydney model continues to be valued in London. Affinity of language and culture represent other reasons why London will turn to Sydney rather than Athens and Beijing. It is unlikely that there will be any significant export of Greek Olympic expertise to London and whether Beijing wishes to market its Olympic expertise after 2008 remains to be seen.

Australian Olympic contractors have also won important contracts in London (as well as Athens and Beijing). Multiplex Constructions, which built Sydney's Olympic stadium, was a private company founded in Perth in 1962 by John Roberts. When the firm secured a £445 million design and construction contract to build a new Wembley, John Roberts, chairman of the Multiplex Group, noted that 'Multiplex has proven credentials in delivering some of the most complex and stunning developments on skylines the world over — with no more visible an example than Stadium Australia, which hosted the Sydney 2000 Olympics'. The Wembley project soured by 2004 when it became known that Multiplex faced problems with subcontractors, project delays and cost blowouts. By mid-2005 the Wembley crisis had led to the resignation of John Roberts as executive chairman of the Multiplex Group. Multiplex shares plummeted (the firm having gone public in 2003).[24] The company's affairs, and the disclosures of potential losses to shareholders, became the subject of an investigation by the Australian Securities and Investment Commission in 2005.[25]

An ABC *Four Corners* program entitled 'The Road to Wembley' of 5 September 2005 commented that the firm's troubled Wembley contract may not mark the end of the firm's Olympic contracts. It reported that Multiplex may seek construction contracts for the London 2012 Olympic Games and even bid to build another Olympic stadium. It remains to be seen whether Multiplex can overcome negative publicity in London resulting from its Wembley project.

BOARTES and the Capital Group, which are involved in major

events planning, secured contracts with the 2012 Paris Olympic bid organisation. BOARTES is yet another Australian company that has capitalised on its involvement in the Sydney 2000 Olympic Games. David Churches, who was a key figure in SBOS, had a senior technical advisory role with this Paris bid.

Asian and Commonwealth Games

The organising committee for the 2006 Asian Games at Doha, Qatar, have drawn significantly on Australian Games expertise. GHD, a Sydney-based engineering and project management company, won an international tender in 2001 to develop a masterplan for 78 programs, including the opening and closing ceremonies, accommodation, security, and transportation at Doha. The company put together a consortium which at its peak involved around 25 Australians ranging from Games officers Hollway and Churches, to architects such as Philip Cox, as well as cost-management, sport and other specialists. After GHD produced a comprehensive masterplan in 2003, the company's local office in Doha won work to design and supervise the construction of the main stadium at Doha with the support at the concept stage from Australian architects Cox Richardson and PTW. More recently MI Associates have been intensively involved in operational planning for the Doha Games, so there are many Australian Olympic experts working in Doha.

David Atkins, the artistic director of the opening ceremony for the Sydney Games, expressed disappointment when he failed to secure the contract for the Melbourne 2006 Commonwealth Games opening and closing ceremonies. When the contract was awarded to the US-based company Jack Morton Worldwide in September 2003, Atkins considered it a manifestation of the 'cultural cringe'.

However, Atkins achieved an even bigger financial prize when he was appointed the director of the opening and closing ceremonies for the 2006 Doha Asian Games. His budget to stage these events — $60 million — was roughly equivalent to what was spent at the Sydney Games and is double the $30 million available for the Commonwealth Games ceremonies. Atkins assembled a core group of about 12 — mostly Australians — in mid-April 2005. The Doha ceremonies team swelled to 50 by June 2005 and will number 200 by Games time.[26]

The Melbourne Commonwealth Games budget for the opening

ceremony, however, proved to be too conservative. By 2005, it was reported that the budget had blown out to $40 million, with the federal government funding the $10 million increase. It was also reported at the time that Nigel Triffit and Andrew Walsh from the Sydney 2000 ceremonies team had been drafted to the Melbourne 2006 ceremonies team. Former Sydney Theatre Company director, Wayne Harrison, was chosen to direct the closing ceremony.[27]

The demand for Australian Games expertise will not end in 2006. Given that India has had limited experience in staging Asian and Commonwealth Games — the Asian Games have been held in India only twice, in 1951 and 1982, and the Commonwealth Games not at all — the 2010 New Delhi Commonwealth Games provide yet another opportunity for Australian companies to win business. Although India has lagged a long way behind the other Asian sporting powers of China, Japan and South Korea for some decades, New Delhi seems increasingly committed to the hosting of international sports events and the development of a future bid for the Olympic Games. By mid-2005 SBOS had broadened its promotional outreach to target events such as the 2010 New Delhi Commonwealth Games and the 2010 Guangzhou Asian Games.

Knowledge management and knowledge transfer

One important SOCOG legacy was the development of an information and knowledge culture that grew out of its collection and management policies. SOCOG began with a well-established corporate library that had been inherited from the Sydney Olympic Bid Company. As SOCOG grew there was the challenge to better coordinate information flows, so in 1997 it was decided to develop a broader system for sharing information. A project team, which included personnel from the Lotus Consulting team, was employed to consult on the design of the system and to help implement it. On 30 June 1997 the internal Sydney 2000 Games Information system — known as 'Athena' after the Greek goddess of wisdom — began operation, as did a call centre extract, so that SOCOG had achieved a sophisticated level of information management. By October 2000 the Sydney Games Information system included 39,983 documents.

One of the legacies of SOCOG's innovative information management was a formal agreement between the IOC and SOCOG — with the IOC paying a reported $5 million for SOCOG's files[28] — to pass on knowledge on 'how we did it here' for future Olympic cities. The program, which became known as Transfer of Know How (TOK), represented the first attempt of an Olympic city to develop a management guide for future Olympic cities.[29] However, as the Sydney files of TOK related to the specific operations of its organising committee, there was also a need for a more generic system for the transfer of knowledge from one organising committee to the next.

To address this issue, the Olympic Games Knowledge Services (OGKS) was formed OGKS was launched by IOC President Jacques Rogge in February 2002 as a joint initiative with Monash Ed, a company of Monash University in the state of Victoria, Australia. OGKS was entrusted by the IOC to be its exclusive knowledge management services company, in collaboration with its shareholder, Monash University, to create a program to capture and document the knowledge gained by an organising committee and transfer it to the next Olympic city. Headed by Craig McLatchey, a former secretary general of the AOC and SOCOG board member who took up this position in December 2001, OGKS was based in Lausanne. OGKS made use of internet and data management expertise to create a range of educational, management and consulting services to Olympic Games organising committees and candidate cities. The partnership with Monash Ed ceased on 12 August 2004 when the IOC acquired the shares previously held by Monash University.

The OGKS model has inspired similar programs of knowledge transfer for other global sporting festivals, such as World Cups and Commonwealth Games, and Event Knowledge Services (EKS) was launched on 18 August 2004. EKS, also headed by McLatchey, provided 'know-how' to a range of global event owners and organisers, such as the Rugby World Cup and the Commonwealth Games. The EKS Knowledge Centre is a 'sophisticated web-enabled Extranet which delivers, to the desktops of event owners and organisers anywhere in the world, information required to effectively plan and implement every key aspect of a major event'.[30] The creation of EKS is important as it enables the global sports movement to benefit from initiatives that have been developed and refined by the IOC. Although EKS is a private company, it undertakes work for OGKS, which operates under the IOC umbrella.

The Olympic Games Global Impact Program (OGGI) was a separate project, set up in February 2002, to measure the specific impacts of a particular Olympic Games over an 11-year period (see Chapter 1). The operation of OGGI enabled each Olympic city to draw on previous expertise so that it no longer had to 'reinvent the wheel'. OGGI has been designed to provide the IOC with greater measurement and understanding of Olympic impacts to enable it to better manage future Games. The OGGI analysis provides a constructive way to plan to avoid problems such as gigantism and white elephants.

Tertiary education

A study by Cashman and Toohey, which was published in 2002, documented the contribution of the higher education sector to the Sydney 2000 Olympic Games and determined that it was more comprehensive than at any previous Games. A majority of the country's 45 universities had some involvement in the Olympic Games. Brendan Lynch, SOCOG Program Manager for Volunteer Recruitment, summarised the variety of involvement:

> First, universities and TAFE recruited and trained many specialist volunteers. Second, some staff were seconded — or took leave of absence to achieve the same end — to institutions organising the event. Third, TAFE provided general training for 110,000 staff and contractors. Fourth, training and accommodation facilities were provided by various universities. Fifth, research and conferences were organised by individuals and units at various higher education institutions. Sixth, some higher education institutions established special Olympic centres or units to maximise the benefit from the Olympic Games. Other institutions nominated a university liaison officer to coordinate Olympic programs.[31]

The study estimated that approximately 2000 staff and 20,000 students had some involvement in the Olympic Games and 22 memorandums of agreements were signed between various higher education institutions and with other organisations involved in the Olympics — 12 with SOCOG, seven with SOBO, two with the AOC and one with the NSW Government.[32] *University Business* (USA) stated that 'the Olympic Games

The Olympic Studies Room at the UTS Library contains many records from the Sydney 2000 Olympic Games.

in Sydney saw unprecedented involvement from the higher education sector'. *The Times* Higher Education Supplement (UK) reported that 'from designing the Olympic site to keeping it Olympic-free, from illuminating the 100,000 capacity stadium to predicting visitor numbers, academics — in their thousands — are getting involved in what one describes as "the biggest peacetime event in Australia". And they are advancing research and developing new insights in the process.'[33]

TAFE NSW played a significant training role in both the Olympic and Paralympic Games. This was the first time that one organisation had been selected to provide the training services for both the Olympic and Paralympic Games employees and volunteers. Approximately 110,000 persons were trained at 42 competition and non-competition venues in Sydney, Adelaide, Brisbane, Canberra and Melbourne.[34] The role played by TAFE NSW was summarised in the *Official Report of the XXVII Olympiad*:

> The training sponsor, TAFE NSW, played a significant role

in Games training, providing training consultants to design, develop and deliver training; training materials and ten training videos; editing of materials and training rooms and equipment.

Some 62,000 staff received Games orientation training, 130,000 received venue training and 65,000 received job specific training.

Training materials were developed first for the Olympic Games and then customised for the Paralympic Games. One orientation training guide was produced covering both Games.[35]

Tertiary educational outcomes

The coordinators of Olympic programs from 25 Australian tertiary institutions (more than half the tertiary institutions in the country) responded to the survey conducted by Cashman and Toohey. They found that the outcomes achieved were lower than expectations of the coordinators in all four categories surveyed. Table 5.3 compares expectations with outcomes in terms of importance.

Table 5.3

	Expectations	Outcomes
Community service	3.9	3.24
Staff/stud. opportunities	4.16	3.1
Financial gain	2.16	2.14
Promotion of institution	3.95	2.76

Note: Scores out of 5 (5=very important 1=no importance).

Cashman and Toohey concluded that this result occurred because a majority of institutions failed to adequately define the aims and expectations of their Olympic involvement and, as a result, there were 'no discernible or clear-cut results'. In addition, with no process to 'ratify or properly evaluate their involvement after the Olympic Games' many institutions were left 'flying blind'.[36]

There were, however, a number of institutions that enjoyed ongoing benefits after the Games. Melbourne's Monash University had a relatively modest Olympic involvement: it provided a small number of interns, and the cost of its Olympic involvement was reported to be only $18,000. However, because of its role as a leading education exporter

— with a network of campuses in Malaysia and South Africa and with involvements in centres in Germany, Italy, the UK and USA — Monash was able to secure a commercial contract with the IOC to set up OGKS (see above). Paul Ramler, deputy chairman of Monash University and chairman of Monash Ed, stated that 'working internationally with internationally recognised institutions, such as the IOC, and future organising committees, is consistent with our long term objectives'.[37] However, this partnership ended in 2004.

TAFE NSW has achieved ongoing benefit from its acclaimed training role in the Sydney 2000 Olympic and Paralympic Games. It played a prominent training role in the Athens 2004 Olympic Games. TAFE GLOBAL Pty Ltd — TAFE NSW's international marketing arm — gained an initial eight-month contract in November 2001 to provide planning and curriculum advice for the Athens 2004 Olympic Games. The contract was extended several times, so the TAFE involvement

Some senior technical staff from Greece's largest telecommunications company, OTE, undergo Games orientation training (TAFE GLOBAL).

with ATHOC lasted until after the Games, to December 2004. The combined worth of the contracts totalled $4.5 million, and four senior TAFE personnel were based in Athens for periods from one to three years. TAFE also secured contracts with two Greek sponsors — OTE, the parent telecommunications company and COSMOTE, the mobile phone company, to develop training plans and curricula. In contrast to the Sydney Games, in which TAFE was the sole trainer, in Greece TAFE worked with a local partner, the PRC/ITG Management House, which provided logistical and translation support.

TAFE GLOBAL has gained continuing international benefit due to its involvement with other Games, winning training contracts for the All-Africa Games and the Asian Games. The company's close contact with federal and state government agencies, as a result of TAFE NSW's training role in 2000, helped TAFE GLOBAL secure a small training contract for the All-Africa Games, held in Nigeria in 2003. DFAT, which helped initiate this contract, funded TAFE's costs in establishing this program. The company also secured a small contract for the Asian Games, to be held at Doha in 2006, to develop a training plan for the Games. TAFE GLOBAL was one of three companies short-listed in 2005 to secure a contract to organise training for these Games.

TAFE GLOBAL has the credentials to play a similar role for the Beijing 2008 Olympic Games and has had discussions with the Beijing Organising Committee for the Olympic Games (BOCOG). However, it has found the China Olympic market to be more difficult to access for a variety of bureaucratic and political reasons.

TAFE GLOBAL did not bid for the 2006 Melbourne Commonwealth Games, though it did advise a Victorian TAFE consortium. Although the rights to be the official trainers were won by another TAFE, Holmesglen TAFE, this decision demonstrated an acceptance that volunteers for all Games should be properly trained by tertiary-trained experts who should also develop an overall training masterplan. The organisers of future Games will continue to turn to TAFE NSW because of its proven training record. This is an important ongoing legacy of the Sydney Games.

Peter Holden and Helen Kebby from TAFE GLOBAL, who were based in Athens for one-and-a-half years and one year respectively, believe that the company has benefited in two major ways. Firstly, the training contracts won, particularly in Athens, were profitable for the company.

Secondly, the company has developed valuable links and closer working ties with federal and state government agencies, such as DFAT and the NSW Department of State and Regional Development. TAFE NSW also developed mutually beneficial partnerships with organisations as diverse as the Road Traffic Authority (RTA) and AusHealth. DFAT's awareness of TAFE NSW's ongoing training role was the prime reason for the contract with the All-Africa Games.[38]

A unique educational initiative was organised at the University of Technology, Sydney when 120 Greek students were recruited to undertake a master's degree in sport management and to gain practical experience working for SOCOG. The idea was proposed to UTS and SOCOG by Dimitris Gargalianos from the physical education department at Democritos University of Thrace. The proposal was submitted to the Hellenic Ministry of Sport which funded a number of scholarships.

One objective of the program was that the graduates would return to Greece with skills and experience that would allow them to contribute significantly to the organisation of the Athens 2004 Olympic Games. Both the IOC and ATHOC benefited, as the program 'advanced the IOC's Olympic education agenda in an innovative way and ensured that tacit Olympic knowledge would be transferred to ATHOC through the students who would be employed there'.[39]

UTS benefited from an additional 120 students in its master's program in 1999 and 2000 and the enhancement of its relationships with public bodies, such as SOCOG and ATHOC. The success of this program not only advanced Olympic education, but also added to the status of UTS as an institution involved in international education. This reputation has been enhanced by teaching contracts with two Beijing tertiary institutions, Tsinghua University and Capital College, which will continue until 2008. The establishment of the Australian Centre for Olympic Studies in 2005 was another significant outcome of the UTS Olympic involvement, which began soon after September 1993, and demonstrated this institution's long-term commitment to Olympic research and education.

UNSW, another university in Sydney prominent in the Olympic Games, also achieved worthwhile post-Games outcomes. The Centre for Olympic Studies gained much positive publicity for UNSW through its research, and publications and by the organisation of three major

Helen Brownlee of the AOC launches the Australian Centre for Olympic Studies at the University of Technology, Sydney on 6 October 2005. She was prominent in the delivery of education programs in the years before the Games.

international conferences in 1999 and 2000. The centre also collaborated with the other three leading international Olympic centres at Barcelona, Lausanne and London (Canada). It also became a repository for Olympic archives, including some of material from SOCOG. However, UNSW decided to close its centre in 2004 (see Chapter 1). Fortunately, UNSW agreed to transfer the centre's archives to UTS where they became part of a successor centre, which was set up in 2005.

For coverage of school-based educational outcomes, see Chapter 9.

Conclusions

Although the *Official Report of the XXVIIth Olympiad* was not able to specify the precise dimensions of post-Games international outcomes — because it was published in 2001 — its general predictions have proven to be correct:

For Sydney, for New South Wales and Australia, the Sydney 2000 Olympic Games provided massive exposure and publicity to the world and in many cases a first or renewed awareness of Australia. The business opportunities identified and the networks established internationally, particularly with the many thousands of business people who visited Australia during and prior to the Games, will continue to provide opportunities into the future for Australian business and trade, particularly in the Asia-Pacific region where Australia has a growing status as a stable and developed country with benefits to offer the region and the rest of the world wanting to do business there.[40]

The international benefits of the Sydney 2000 Olympic Games represent a success story which has hitherto been largely untold and undocumented. Because the story has unfolded mostly after the Olympic caravan moved on from Sydney, and because it has taken place on so many diverse international fronts, it has not been appreciated or acknowledged in Australia or internationally.

Although it is impossible to establish the precise value of overseas contracts and investment, they appear to be substantial. They have been realised because the NSW Government in particularly and other agencies have actively promoted such outcomes. Whereas attempts to leverage inbound tourism failed in the first years of the Games (see Chapter 4) — largely because of factors beyond the control of the Australian tourism industry — the leveraging of international business was an unqualified success.

The developing relationship with Beijing and China confirms the positive assessments of the PWC report of 2002. Ongoing business with China has achieved worthwhile results although it is difficult to place any precise figure on its value. An impressive feature is that the business continues to grow and may extend to other mega events — such as the Asian Games and the World Expo in 2010 — even though the Sydney Olympics continue to recede in time.

The less well-known, but nevertheless important stories of knowledge management and knowledge transfer, and the success of a number of Australian tertiary institutions in using the Games to promote themselves internationally, demonstrate that education was an important economic as well as cultural product.

Chapter 6

THE FUTURE OF SYDNEY OLYMPIC PARK

Sydney Olympic Park is the jewel of the Sydney 2000 Olympic crown. At the time of the Games, it represented a proud statement of the city's Olympic vision. Compared to any previous Olympic precinct, the park was larger and had a greater array of sports venues with state-of-the-art facilities. The strategy of locating the majority of Olympic venues and the Olympic village in one precinct minimised the problem of travel for athletes, officials and media. In fact, Sydney 2000 was the first occasion when Olympic athletes were housed in one convenient location. In short, the Park provided a spectacular theatre for the Games.

Another striking feature of Sydney Olympic Park was that it was the site of the Green Games, the large-scale and costly transformation of a dirty and polluted environment to a purportedly clean and green post-industrial space. This transformation was Sydney's gift to the Olympic movement in that it enhanced the environment, a cause which had been adopted as the third dimension of Olympism in 1995. Homebush Bay underwent a 'profound physical and symbolic restructuring' which has led to a 'refashioning of [its] identity'.[1] This precinct, in the words of Olympic historian Harry Gordon, was transformed in the 1990s from 'an ugly wasteland ... into ... one of the world's great sporting and industrial parklands'.[2] Geographers Dunn and McGuirk added that 'the imagery of Homebush was altered': the landscape was no longer considered 'a dirty, polluted industrial zone' but a 'post-industrial, clean and green space of leisure and sport'.[3] However, some green scholars questioned whether the remediation process was properly done (see Chapter 8).

Because it was a site of such significance in 2000 and because it continues to bear an Olympic name, the future of Sydney Olympic Park is critical to the post-2000 reputation of the Games. While there are various Olympic venues scattered around the city and suburbs, these sites have little ongoing identification with the Olympic Games. The Sydney Convention and Exhibition Centre at Darling Harbour and the nearby Sydney Entertainment Centre, which were the respective venues

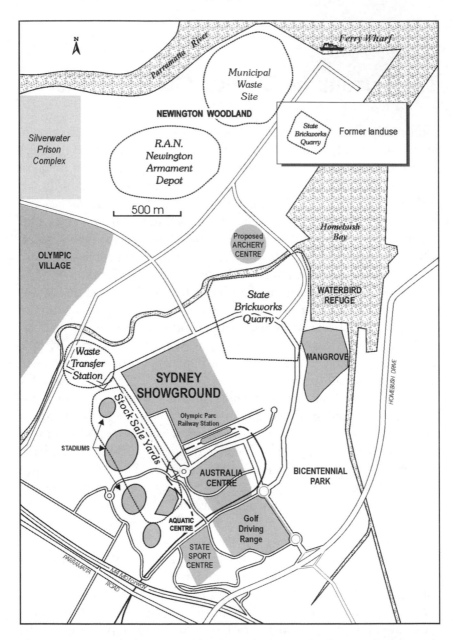

The past, present and future uses of Sydney Olympic Park. The Homebush Bay site has had a rich and varied history (Cartolab).

for boxing, fencing, judo, volleyball and weightlifting, have returned to their normal use and there is only one modest statue at Darling Harbour, which was Sydney's second most important Olympic precinct in 2000.

The Sydney Olympic grand plan diverged from that employed by Barcelona, which chose to decentralise its Olympic venues. Barcelona opted for four precincts rather than one, in order to spread the benefit of the Games to different areas of city:

> The underlying philosophy of the Barcelona Olympic Project ensured that the Games were decentralised. The idea of concentrating all installations in an Olympic Park — as had been the case in Seoul — was immediately rejected. Barcelona decided to share the Games with as many subsidiary host cities as possible.[4]

Four Olympic areas were selected at Barcelona. First there was the established precinct of Montjuïc, which already had a stadium (1936) and a swimming pool (1972). Next there was the existing sports precinct of Diagonal, which had the largest concentration of private sports facilities in the city. Two other areas, the Parc de Mar and the Vall d'Hebron, were chosen because there were insufficient sports facilities there.[5] So there was a conscious decision in Barcelona to spread of the city's sports amenities around, thereby increasing public access to sport.

Why then did Sydney opt for a more centralised Olympic precinct? Why did Sydney create a sporting precinct in which almost every venue was new? Barcelona, like some previous Olympic cities, built fewer new sports facilities than Sydney. The opening and closing ceremonies took place at an upgraded stadium at Montjuïc, which had been built in 1936 and renovated in 1972.

The main reason for Sydney's strategy was that the facilities of the existing sports precinct of Moore Park in Sydney's eastern suburbs were considered inadequate, because each of the existing stadia at Moore Park catered for only about 40,000 spectators though there were plans in place to add to the capacity of the stadia there (see below). Sports facilities were needed most in the west of the city, where the population had spread. Homebush Bay, it was frequently stated, was at the geographical heartland of Sydney's population. There was the added attraction that Homebush Bay was a large urban site considered suitable for sporting and recreational development. Urban planning scholar Glen Searle believed that the attraction of new world-class sporting facilities helped the Olympic bid 'secure public support' for the Games.[6]

Another issue that dictated the choice of Homebush Bay was that the citizens who lived near Moore Park and the adjacent Centennial Park had previously rejected the proposal of an Olympic precinct in their backyard. When the NSW State Government planned to submit an Olympic bid in the early 1970s for the 1988 Olympic Games, the consultants proposed the building of the Olympic stadium in the Centennial and Moore Park area. Following a storm of public protest in 1970 and 1971, an enquiry identified Homebush Bay as an alternative site.[7] It was later nominated as the future home of the Royal Agricultural Show, which moved from Moore Park to Homebush Bay where it opened in 1998 in a more spacious and modern environment.

Some events took place outside the Homebush area. Moore Park and the eastern suburbs sports precinct, though, were largely neglected as Olympic venues, and the Sydney Football Stadium (now Aussie Stadium) was allocated only a handful of football matches. However, some of the cycling road events tracked through the eastern suburbs, as did the marathon before heading to Stadium Australia. Beach volleyball was held at Bondi Beach and Sydney Harbour was the site for the yachting and the first leg of the triathlon. While cycling was at Bankstown, rowing at Penrith, equestrian events at Horsley Park and a number of team sports in the Darling Harbour precinct, all the prestigious events were allocated to Sydney's west.

By creating this new focus for the city's sport and culture, the state government was creating a potential future conflict between the east and west of the city. If Sydney Olympic Park became the successful home of major sporting events, the existing stadia of Moore Park would be less viable and could even become redundant. Alternatively, if the eastern suburbs sports precinct effectively resisted this new challenge to its sporting status, it was likely that Sydney Olympic Park might struggle. It would also require a significant increase in post-Games sporting and entertainment activities to maintain both of these precincts at a viable level.

Homebush Bay

The promises of the Sydney Bid Company Ltd were linked to one very large urban project: the remediation of Homebush Bay and the creation of a sporting precinct there. The 760 hectares of Homebush Bay included some remnant woodlands, and its extensive wetlands were the home for a variety of mammals, reptiles, amphibians and birds. It had been the location variously of an armaments depot, abattoir and brickworks. The quarry site later became a feature of Millennium Park.

It was in the early twentieth century that the state government resumed Homebush Bay, principally so it could become the site of the state abattoir, which operated until the 1980s. It also became the site of the state brickworks. The navy occupied land in 1897 at Newington, to the west of Haslams Creek and over the next century used it for the storage of armaments. From the 1950s there was extensive dumping of household and industrial waste at Homebush, including toxic material in some sections of the site, which was unrecorded. It was also the site from the 1950s of a number of industrial and chemical plants that pumped their waste directly into Homebush Bay, Parramatta River and ultimately Sydney Harbour.[8]

Homebush Bay had been identified by the state government as a site for urban renewal from the 1970s. The closure of the abattoir in the late 1980s, along with the earlier cessation of the brickworks, made redevelopment possible. The State Sports Centre, which included facilities for basketball and other indoor sports, as well as a hockey field, was opened in the 1980s. It provided the venue for the taekwondo and table tennis competitions during the 2000 Games and was the only completed sporting venue at Sydney Olympic Park that pre-dated the 1991 bid. Bicentennial Park was opened in 1988 and a privately developed business complex, the Australia Centre, was also established in the 1980s.

The winning of Sydney's Olympic bid in 1991 accelerated the development of the sporting precinct at Homebush Bay which had been planned to occur gradually over 30 years. The Athletic Centre, which became the warm-up track for the Olympic stadium, and the Aquatic Centre were under construction at the time of the bid. The erection of these two venues was an added selling point both for

Sydney's bid and the commitment to sport at Homebush Bay.

Well in advance of the 2000 Games, Sydney was able to unveil a brand new sporting precinct flanked by the completed recreational parklands of Bicentennial Park. The Park's third precinct was the 420 hectares of wetlands that made up Millennium Park. Stage 1 was completed by 2000, with the final stage scheduled for completion in 2010. Millennium Park, which included the quarry, wetlands and a network of pedestrian and cycle paths, was the location of only one Olympic sport, archery.

The remediation of Homebush Bay and the related concept of the Green Games were attractive features of the bid because the environmental measures proposed were more ambitious than any previous Olympic Games and advanced the IOC's commitment to the environment as the third dimension of Olympism (see Chapter 8). Environmental issues also shaped the contours of Sydney Olympic Park: treated and capped waste formed the basis of the man-made hills of Olympic Park, since it was considered best to deal with the past problems on the site rather than exporting them elsewhere.

The creation of Sydney Olympic Park

While the NSW Government underwrote the operation of Sydney Olympic Park, it looked to the private sector to cover most of the costs of construction and the operation of large facilities, such as the Olympic stadium. Similarly, in other instances, when the government paid for the construction of a facility, such as the Aquatic Centre or the Tennis Centre, it sought to spread the financial load by handing over the operations of such facilities to private and public bodies, including local councils, sports associations and the NSW Department of Tourism, Sport and Recreation.

The Sydney International Aquatic Centre, which was opened in October 1994, has proven one of the most successful and enduring facilities opened at Sydney Olympic Park. The cost of construction was $150 million plus another $41.4 million for increased spectator seating and an Olympic overlay. When President Samaranch visited the centre before the Games he stated that this was 'the best swimming pool that I have seen in my life'.[9]

The path of champions at the entrance to the International Aquatic Centre adds to the symbolic significance of this venue.

The Sydney International Aquatic Centre has proven to be one of the most popular venues at the Park. From 1994 to 2003 the Aquatic Centre recorded 10 million visitors, making it Australia's second most popular sports facility after the Melbourne Cricket Ground. In 2002–03, the centre attracted over one million visitors — more than the 700,000 that visited Sydney Olympic Park during the Rugby World Cup.[10] Visitors to the centre include lap and recreational swimmers, spectators, tour parties, swimming schools, swimming squads and fitness centre members. It is significant that the patronage of this centre has increased in each of the past three years.

This figure of an athlete, attached to the top of the AMP tower in the city before and during the Games, found an appropriate home after the Games outside the Athletic Centre at Sydney Olympic Park.

Table 6.1 Attendances at the Aquatic Centre in recent years (from Aquatic Centre *Annual Reports*).

	2001–02	2002–03	2003–04
Event attendances	218,810	274,222	258,246
Tours, spectators	87,901	64,619	61,204
Recreational swimmers	371,144	353,058	352,351
Others	303,458	352,143	417,517
TOTAL	981,313	1,044,042	1,089,318

The success of the Aquatic Centre was based on two factors. Swimming is a major sport in Australia and the Aquatic Centre gave Sydney its 'first new competition venue for half a century' that catered for all aquatic sports: swimming, diving, water polo and synchronised swimming. The North Sydney Olympic Pool, which had been built in 1936, is an outdoor pool which was not heated until recently. The Olympic swimming trials, held over eight days in March and April 2004, attracted an impressive 53,387 spectators. The second attraction of the Aquatic Centre was that it was a multi-purpose sport-for-all venue suitable for elite competition, recreation and leisure. The facilities included an Olympic pool as well as a leisure pool with a hydroslide, whirlpool and spa pools. A training pool included a movable floor which could be adjusted for swimming lessons and aquarobics. These features meant that the centre met a need 'for a high quality leisure swimming venue in the sub-region around Homebush Bay'. During the Games, a temporary wing swelled the capacity of the Aquatic Centre to 17,500. With the removal of this temporary seating the venue's capacity was reduced to 8500 — large enough for the needs of competitive swimming in the city.

The Sydney International Athletic Centre, which also opened in 1994 (at a cost of $30 million), provided Sydney with a much needed international track and field facility. Before 1994, track and field relied on an older facility, the E.S. Marks Field in the eastern suburbs, which had been opened in 1948. Given that track and field meetings rarely attract more than 5000 spectators, the capacity of the Athletic Centre is appropriate for the needs of the sport: it includes grandstand seating for 5000 and grass embankments that can accommodate another 10,000. With its modern facilities and space, the Athletic Centre is ideally suited for international and national athletic events as well as local and school carnivals.

Although the Athletic Centre is a more modest venue than the Aquatic Centre and has limited appeal as a place for leisure, it has enjoyed a useful post-Games life as a place for school and junior athletic as well as national and even international carnivals. Attendance figures have also increased in the last three years.

Table 6.2 Attendances at the Athletic Centre in recent years (from Athletic Centre *Annual Reports*).

	2001–02	2002–03	2003–04
Event spectators	157,881	163,607	181,045
General attendances	32,813	31,011	39,042
TOTAL	190,694	194,618	220,087

A critical factor in the success of both these centres was that they filled a gap in the city's sporting infrastructure and did not create competition with any existing venues in the eastern suburbs or the city itself. The Aquatic Centre was in fact managed by the eastern-suburbs based Sydney Cricket and Sports Ground Trust — an example of sporting cooperation between the east and the west.

The situation was quite different with the two largest stadia that dominate the skyline of Homebush Bay, the Olympic stadium — known initially as Stadium Australia and as Telstra Stadium from 2002 — and the SuperDome. With their larger capacities and more modern facilities, both venues represented a potential threat to the existing venues in the eastern suburbs and the city. The Olympic stadium was in direct competition with the Sydney Cricket Ground and Aussie Stadium at Moore Park. The SuperDome posed a threat to the Sydney Entertainment Centre, which was located in the southern section of the central business district, in that both facilities catered for indoor sports and general entertainment.

The Olympic stadium, which was the site of the opening and closing ceremonies, track and field and the football finals, was completed in 1999. It won a number of awards for its excellence and versatility due to the fact that it could be reconfigured for various sports. It was also acclaimed for its environmental features: water from the translucent polycarbonate roof is drained into underground tanks and recycled. The stadium was also the winner of a national energy award for its maximisation of natural light, and passive ventilation reduced power costs.

The bulk of the cost of the stadium ($710 million) was borne by a private consortium, Multiplex Constructions, with the state government contributing $124 million. Multiplex chose to fund the stadium though a public float of 30,000 units to raise $300 million. The float was then increased to 34,400 units to raise an extra $44 million. For this outlay each unit-holder received a gold pass which provided access to privileged seating for the Olympic Games and for sports events until 2030.[11] After the construction of the stadium, Multiplex handed it over to another private consortium, Stadium Australia Management, which operated the facility.

Sydney's original bid proposed a stadium of 80,000, but its capacity was increased to 110,000. It actually seated 115,600 during the Games, making it the largest stadium in Olympic history. The increased capacity occurred because of the need to cover the cost of the gold passes. However, a stadium of 80,000 was considered sufficient and more economically viable for Sydney's post-Games sporting needs, so the stadium was downsized after the Games. Most of the seating in two uncovered stands at north and south ends of the stadium were removed in 2001 and the stadium revamp was completed by 2003 when rooves were added at each end of the stadium, providing a continuous roof. The revised capacity for the stadium was 83,500.

The SuperDome, the site of basketball finals as well as artistic and trampoline gymnastics during the Games, was constructed as a multi-use indoor sports and entertainment arena, seating 21,000. This made it the largest indoor stadium in the southern hemisphere. Like much else that was created at Sydney Olympic Park, it has state-of-the-art facilities and many 'environmentally attractive features' including a rooftop solar power system. It was completed by September 1999 at a cost $197 million. The SuperDome was needed, it was contended, because the Sydney Entertainment Centre, which had opened in 1983 in the southern central business district of the city could seat only 10,000. The *Official Report of the XVII Olympiad*, published in 2001, predicted optimistically that the SuperDome had become 'the new heart of entertainment functions and conference servicing in Sydney'.[12] The SuperDome, like Stadium Australia, was privately managed.

The Sydney Showground was the site of seven Olympic sports (badminton, basketball, baseball, handball, rhythmic gymnastics, modern pentathlon and volleyball) and also housed the Main Press Centre. It is the site of an annual (largely agricultural) show held for approximately two weeks around Easter and run by the Royal Agricultural Society of NSW (RAS). The show had been held at Moore Park since 1817. The RAS was attracted to Homebush Bay because of the prospect of a larger venue, more modern facilities and improved transport access. The first show at Homebush opened on 3 April 1998 and it has been held there since. The RAS built and operated the pavilions and an oval.

The State Hockey Centre was completed in August 1998, one year before the scheduled date, at a cost of $15.5 million. It was on the site of a previous hockey field linked with the State Sports Centre and was the premier hockey venue in the State. The seating capacity of the field was augmented from 5000 to 15,000 during the Games.

The International Tennis Centre, which included a 10,000-seat amphitheatre style court, was the last venue completed at Sydney Olympic Park. The state government contributed $39 million to its cost, with an additional $7.1 million coming from Tennis NSW and Tennis Australia and $1.3 million from SOCOG. The venue has been managed by Tennis NSW, which moved its headquarters from White City in the eastern suburbs to Sydney Olympic Park. All major tennis tournaments in NSW are now played at this facility.

Sydney International Archery Park differed from all the previous facilities. Archery was staged in Millennium Park on an attractive 6.5 hectare site with the targets framed by mangrove wetlands. The $3 million park consists of a field and a multi-purpose pavilion, though a temporary stand of 4500 was erected at the time of the Games. It was dismantled soon after because the sport had no need for ongoing spectator facilities.

The Olympic Village consisted of approximately 850 houses and 350 apartments.[13] It was designed by a private consortium, Mirvac Lend Lease Village Consortium, at a cost of $590,000 million, with the NSW Government contributing $63.8 million. Mirvac financed construction of the village through the development and sale of land adjacent to the village. A number of village dwellings were sold to the public before the Games, though occupancy did not take place until after the Games. A unique feature of the village was the use of solar power; it became the largest solar powered suburb in Australia. After the Games the village became part of the suburb of Newington, with a population of 5000.

A key component of transport planning was the creation of a 5.3 km railway loop, which linked Olympic Park with the major suburban network and the creation of a below-ground railway station, just 400 metres from the entrance to the Olympic stadium. The system was set up so that trains could move 50,000 persons per hour to and from Olympic Park. The Olympic Park railway station, which featured an attractively designed roof which provided shelter, natural light and ventilation, won a prestigious architectural award. The length and width of Olympic Boulevard also provided ample space for bus transport to supplement the rail network.

The construction of Sydney Olympic Park ahead of schedule represented a triumph for David Richmond, director general of the

Olympic Co-ordination Authority (OCA), which had been established as a statutory body in 1995, consolidating the work of five government departments in a single more efficient authority. Richmond, a former senior public servant in health and author of the Richmond Report, was the 'quiet achiever' of Sydney's organising team. He turned around a construction program that was 'two years behind schedule' so that the 'entire building program' was 'completed in record time, 12 months before the Games'.[14] This enabled all the venues to be well tested beforehand. Richmond was aided by what Tony Webb described as a 'culture of collaboration' between government, industry and trade unions to achieve this massive construction program successfully. Agreements negotiated between these parties contributed to Sydney's trouble- and strike-free preparation.[15]

While Games officials took great pride in the development of a unique sporting precinct, some of the major venues struggled financially even before the Games. The public float to help pay for Stadium Australia failed to achieve its goals, with only half the units sold because there was no certainty about what sports would be staged at the stadium from 2000 to 2030.[16] While the stadium was full for a handful of international and finals football matches, it remained empty most of the time. As a result Stadium Australia reported a loss of $24 million in its first year, 1998-99, and a loss of $11 million in 1999-2000.

The SuperDome was the loser in its initial years in its competition with the Sydney Entertainment Centre. It soon became clear that the SuperDome was too large for its market and its location was less convenient for most indoor sport and entertainment events. The Sydney Entertainment Centre was also a relatively modern facility which offered a wide range of post-match entertainment whereas there was only a solitary hotel near the SuperDome. The SuperDome reported operating losses from its inception of an estimated to be $5 million per year.

Difficult days: the aftermath of the Games

The New South Wales Government created a post-Games authority, the Sydney Olympic Park Authority (SOPA), on 1 July 2001, to oversee Bicentennial Park, Sydney Olympic Park and Millennium Park. From that date the three parks became known as Sydney Olympic Park. The government provided SOPA with $50 million as seed money. SOPA's Mission Statement included the following:

> Sydney Olympic Park Authority will develop and manage Sydney Olympic Park, as a special place for sporting, both elite and non-elite, recreational, educational and business activities for the benefit of the community.
>
> Future development and management will be based on the principles of recognising the responsibility to preserve the Olympic legacy, of supporting stakeholders, of protecting and enhancing the environment, of maintaining high environmental and design values and while also generating an adequate financial return to reduce the dependency for ongoing funding.[17]

The nature of what constitutes 'the Olympic legacy' was not defined at the time, nor has it been since. Legacy in this instance, as is the case in Olympic discourse more generally, is taken to be a worthwhile and self-evident given.

During the Olympic and Paralympic Games, Sydney Olympic Park and its venues worked efficiently and smoothly. The wide, 1.5-kilometre long Olympic Boulevard — the spine of the Park — provided ample room for the largest crowds of up to 500,000 which came to the Park on peak days. The transportation plan, with its emphasis on public transport, worked well (see Chapter 8). The smooth operation of Sydney Olympic Park was one important reason why Sydney gained the ultimate accolade as the 'best ever Games'.

The Park has been transformed since 2000. The track from the Olympic stadium was removed and the stadium was reconfigured for sports such as football and cricket. Its capacity, as noted above, was reduced from 110,000 to 83,500 at a cost of $80 million. The symbolic marking of the Park, which pre-dated the Games, continued afterwards and represented an attempt to invest the precinct with greater significance. Most of the dwellings of the Olympic Village were sold off in the following years. Many other venues, such as the Aquatic Centre, have also been converted to a post-Games mode with reduced seating numbers.

If Homebush throbbed with life for the 16 days of the Olympic Games and another 11 days of the Paralympic Games, it resembled a ghost town in 2001 and 2002 and its vast expanses were frequently empty. With relatively few major events in the largest stadia, transport to the Park was sporadic, making it less accessible and attractive to the public.

In the two years after 2000 many in the local media dubbed Sydney Olympic Park a white elephant, suggesting that there had been insufficient planning for the post-Games future of the Park. 'The trouble' was, according to one journalist, that 'in the lead-up to the Games, there seemed little or no inclination to consider what sort of relationship Sydney would enjoy with the site once the event for which it was created was over'.[18]

In 2001 there was a chorus of local, interstate and international criticism claiming that Sydney had failed to capitalise on its Games success and maintain Olympic momentum. Former Victorian Premier Jeff Kennett suggested in August 2001 that Sydney had 'lost its fizz' and one year after the Games 'it's as though NSW is a flat bottle of beer'. Kennett added that:

> Sydney has failed to plan adequately for life after the Games … and was suffering from post-Olympic inertia …
>
> It's not that NSW hasn't built on the success of the Olympics. It didn't prepare prior to the Olympics for what it was going to do afterwards …
>
> … major infrastructure … trams, buses, trains, hotels, restaurants need long-term stimulus … you've got to keep feeding those things. Therefore major events … are major contributors to the level of activity and hype that occurs within the community …
>
> You're reducing the size of the stadium, but the big problem with the facilities at Homebush Bay is their location. They're too far from the [CBD]. If you look at Melbourne, all of our major facilities in real terms you can walk to from the CBD. In NSW it's a lack of sense of purpose, it's a lack of buzz … It's all on remote control. Nothing's changing. Nothing's growing. No-one's talking things up.[19]

Kennett's views could be partly discounted as those of a former premier from a rival state who had become a 'major-events impresario', and his criticism may have been motivated by the NSW Government's refusal to 'underwrite private-sector events'. However, Kennett's views received some endorsement from an unusual quarter. Ric Birch, the acclaimed director of the Sydney Olympic ceremonies, commented that:

> [Kennett] said what I thought was really essential [and that is that] governments are responsible for coming up with policies which increase the confidence of the population ... Jeff Kennett doesn't care about the buildings, the built environment. He knows that it's all about creating an emotion and a confidence ...
>
> I don't always agree with Jeff but on this particular point he's absolutely right ... He said you create an atmosphere in which the people are confident ... [Homebush Bay's] not to do with the buildings.[20]

Kennett and Birch stated the obvious: that Sydney Olympic Park needed

The view from the top of a bay marker, designed along the lines of a ziggurat, provides a panoramic view looking east.

more than its attractive built environment and unique landscape; it required public confidence in its worth. There was a need to 'feed' the Park with more events and to publicly answer the critics of the Park.

Equally damaging for the reputation of the Park was criticism by newly installed IOC President Jacques Rogge of the decision to downsize the Olympic stadium. Rogge declared in August 2001 that the Olympic stadium was a white elephant that had been built to that size 'against the advice of the IOC'. (It is ironic that Juan Antonio Samaranch, the previous president of the IOC, had been unstinting in his praise for the stadium, declaring it 'the most impressive stadium [that] I have seen in my life').[21] Rogge's comment thus 'stunned' Ken Edwards, the manager of Stadium Australia, and he implied that Rogge should have spoken up before the Games when he was head of the IOC's co-ordination committee for the Sydney 2000 Olympic Games.[22] Perhaps Edwards believed such IOC criticism was harsh because it occurred as a time when the facility was struggling.

David Richmond, the first chairman of the Board of the Sydney Olympic Park Authority, admitted at this time that there had been a lack of post-Games planning. He stated that OCA had 'commissioned preliminary studies on post-Games planning' in 1999. 'However, the real reason we didn't produce something by the end of 2000, to be very blunt, is that we were busy staging and managing the biggest event in the world.' Richmond added that 'he could not divert staff from live Olympic tasks to work on post-Games projects'.[23]

The state government retreated behind the mantra that Sydney Olympic Park was similar to another major urban project at Darling Harbour and would take time to gain public acceptance. Darling Harbour was created in 1988 when disused rail yards on the fringe of the central business district were converted into a precinct for entertainment, recreation and tourism. Initially Darling Harbour had been dismissed as a costly extravagance and a white elephant. However, within a decade the development gained acceptance from the Sydney public and visiting tourists.

Bob Carr warned in January 2001 that the challenge facing the Park would be 'measurably harder' than Darling Harbour because Sydney Olympic Park was removed from the city, but he added that 'we are going to develop a plan'.[24] Had a plan, and an authority to implement a plan, been in place in October 2000 there may have been less public criticism and greater public confidence in the future of the Park.

Symbolic marking

The symbolic marking of the park, both before and after the Games, was a continuing attempt to invest the park with significance. The relocation of the cauldron and the *Ignite* festival of 2001 (see Chapter 2) were attempts to rekindle public interest in the precinct. It was also linked to a campaign to improve the precinct's image, because many people even in 2003 continued to refer to it Homebush rather than Sydney Olympic Park. SOPA engaged the Write Communications Group in July 2003 to encourage the use of its formal name.[25]

Perhaps the most notable markers of the parklands are five geometric millennium bay markers — large contoured hills — which represent gateways and orientation points to the park. They have been described as ziggurats[26] — derived from the idea of Babylonian and Assyrian towers which featured an ascending pathway around the structure. The circular pathways are suitable for both pedestrians and cyclists who, once they have climbed the hill, are rewarded with commanding views of the Park. The ziggurats are another demonstration of the new clean and green landscape: as previously mentioned, buried beneath these sculptured hills are treated contaminated waste, reminders of a previous dirty and polluted landscape. Overhead powerlines, which dominated the landscape and were another reminder of Homebush Bay's industrial past, were buried in underground cables at a cost of $40 million.

Much of the symbolism of the Park relates to sport and the unique character of the Park as an Olympic landscape. The tree-lined Olympic Boulevard is flanked by 19 solar-powered lighting towers, with each one acknowledging previous Summer Olympic Games host cities. The main avenues of the Park are named after Australia's greatest Olympic and Paralympic athletes: Kevin Coombs, Sarah 'Fanny' Durack, Herb Elliott, Edwin Flack, Dawn Fraser, Shane Gould, Marjorie Jackson, Murray Rose and Shirley Strickland. 'Paths of Champions' were created at the Athletic Centre (for New South Wales athletes only) and the Aquatic Centre (which honoured Australian gold medallists, world champions and world-record holders) and added to the symbolic status of such venues. A 'forest of poles' at the archery park evokes the long sleek lines of arrows. The suburb of Newington, the former Olympic Village, features a monument which includes each of the names of the 2000 Australian Olympic team that stayed there.

Sydney's Kronos Hill is much more modest than the hill that overlooks ancient Olympia. The Sydney Hill has an elevation of only 13 metres.

Landscape architect James Weirick expressed disappointment that the urban design team retreated from 'a poetic ambition to invoke the gods of Olympia' at Olympic Park.[27] The only link with ancient Olympia is a Hill of Kronos, a reconstructed hillock on the western terminus of the main axis. Unlike the hill at ancient Olympia, which overlooks the whole site, Sydney's Hill of Kronos is much more modest.

The cauldron was removed and reconfigured by 2001 becoming an attractive sculpture in its own right (see Chapter 2). The relighting of the cauldron in 2001 and subsequently added to the symbolic significance of the Park (see Chapter 2). 'Games Memories', near the entrance of the Olympic stadium, honours volunteers (see Chapter 2). A sculpture of an athlete, which was attached at the top of a multi-storey building in the city — the AMP Centre Point Tower — was relocated to Olympic Park near the Athletic Centre.

Despite the many initiatives to enhance the symbolic status of the Park, SOPA authorities have been slow to promote Park tours or experiences for visitors who wish to re-connect with the Sydney Olympic Games. They have yet to define an attractive Sydney Olympic Park experience or tour, one of the problems being that the Park is so vast. However, The Telstra Stadium Explore Tour, which included a laser and sound show and video clips to create an Olympic atmosphere, was introduced in 2005. There is no museum for the Park as a whole — though a tennis museum opened at the International Tennis Centre in January 2005 — because the NSW former premier Bob Carr was strongly opposed to the idea of a museum, possibly because it represented an additional post-Games costs. However, the success of the Sydney Olympic Collection at the Powerhouse Museum has demonstrated that there is a continuing demand for Sydney Olympic information and that museums need not be expensive (see Chapter 2).

The improving status of the Park from 2003

The Olympic stadium and Sydney Olympic Park received a great boost from the 2003 Rugby World Cup (see Chapter 2). The event brought 700,000 visitors to the Park in October and November 2003, enabling Telstra Stadium to record a profit of $12.4 million for the final six months of 2003 after four years of deficits. The importance of this event cannot be overestimated: the success of this 'feeder event' countered negative publicity and restored public confidence in the Park. The staging of the Catholic World Youth Jubilee at Sydney Olympic Park in July 2008 is another prestigious 'feeder event' on the Park's calendar (see Chapter 2).

Whereas relatively few major sporting events were scheduled for the Olympic stadium in 2001 and 2002, more events and sports were added to its program in succeeding years. In 2002 there was an agreement in place to stage three Australian football matches at the stadium over each of the following seven years and a fourth match was added in 2003, when the Sydney Swans reached the finals, resulting in two crowds of over 70,000 in August and September. Interstate one-day cricket was played at the stadium from 2003, though Telstra Stadium lost a tussle with the Sydney Cricket and Sports Ground Trust in 2004 to gain the rights to stage international cricket matches. The New South Wales Cricket Association capitalised on the contest between east and west to extract concessions from the Sydney Cricket and Sports Ground Trust,

Sydney Olympic Park has abundant potential for recreation as well as sport.

which agreed to increase the capacity of the Sydney Cricket Ground from 40,000 to 55,000.

In March 2005 it was announced that the South Sydney Rugby League Club would play its home games for the next three seasons at Telstra Stadium rather than Aussie Stadium. Telstra Stadium provided the struggling club with a lifeline, as the reported annual guarantee of about $1.3 million enabled the club to stay afloat. Souths joined two other rugby league teams, Wests Tigers and the Canterbury Bulldogs, which also played some of their games at Telstra Stadium. While the average attendance at club games played by Souths was less than the league average of 14,800, it meant that there were regular rugby league games at the Park to supplement the occasional blockbusters, State of Origin and finals series matches as well as occasional international rugby and soccer matches.[28]

By 2005 there was the future prospect of more prestigious and revenue-earning matches in a wider range of codes. Two important soccer matches were staged in 2005: Australia versus Iraq on Easter

Saturday, 26 March, and the second leg of a vital qualifying match for the Socceroos, against Uruguay, on 16 November for the 2006 World Cup in Germany. Australia defeated Uruguay, ending a 32-year World Cup drought, in front of a full house with another 15,000 watching proceedings on a giant screen outside Telstra Stadium. (The equivalent qualifying match in 2001 for the 2002 World Cup, which was also against Uruguay, was staged at the Melbourne Cricket Ground).

There was the potential of another prize, pursued by Ken Edwards of Telstra Stadium, of securing future rugby matches of the NSW Waratahs, given that their contract with Aussie Stadium ended in 2006. The Waratahs played in the Super 12 competition — the Super 14 from 2006 — involving teams from Australia, New Zealand and South Africa.[29] The six home matches at Aussie Stadium usually attract crowds of around 30,000 for each match and should the Waratahs reach the semi-finals, which they did in 2005, there are potentially larger crowds.

The NSW rugby authorities followed the lead of the NSW Cricket Association, capitalising on the competition between Moore Park and Sydney Olympic Park. While NSW rugby authorities were pleased with the result — with matches shared between the two stadia and with an increase in the capacity of Aussie Stadium to 45,500 — 'neither Stadium received exactly the news that it wanted'. Although the compromise gave Telstra Stadium fewer matches than Edwards hoped for, there was the future prospect of some additional prestige rugby matches to supplement a handful of annual international matches: the Bledisloe Cup, the Tri-Nations tournament and tests against visiting touring sides. There was a ten-year agreement that any home final, pending the qualification of the Waratahs, would be played at Telstra Stadium from 2006. The agreement specified that one Super 14 match would be played at Telstra Stadium from 2009 and two from 2011.[30]

Park News, the newsletter of Sydney Olympic Park, reported in January 2004 that:

> More people than ever visited the Park [in 2003] with over 5.5 million visitors including over 900,000 to the Aquatic Centre; 750,000 to Bicentennial Park; 550,000 attending business events and 700,000 to the Rugby World Cup.

Increasingly Sydney Olympic Park relied on cultural and entertainment events to fill its calendar and make use of its many facilities and public space. It was the site of diverse events such as the 2004 and 2005 Sydney Festival, the World Youth Bridge Championships and the Jehovah's Witnesses held the Watch Tower Conference at the Olympic stadium from 11 to 14 December 2003. The Hillsong church now holds annual event at the Park making use the SuperDome, the Showground and the State Sports Centre, It has become an ideal venue for community events ranging from multicultural festivals and outdoor film to garden shows and children's events.

Planning for the Park's future

When a master plan for Sydney Olympic Park was finally adopted in May 2002, it provided another lifeline for Sydney Olympic Park. The plan recognised that the Park could not survive on sport and recreation alone and proposed greater residential and commercial development there.

A draft master plan for the park was published in February 2002 and adopted by the NSW Minister for Planning on 31 May 2002. It recommended the creation of a town centre near the railway station to house a residential population of 3000 and the establishment of small to medium offices to cater for a daily workforce of 10,000. The objective of this master plan was to attract people to Sydney Olympic Park on a permanent basis so as to help it attain greater self-sufficiency. A permanent population at the Park would result in greater public activity, more restaurants and shops and public meeting places and lead to a more regular train service.

The 2002 Master Plan represented a pragmatic shift in the thinking of the future of the Park by diversifying its character. Brian Newman, executive officer of SOPA, acknowledged this new direction in the 2002–03 *Annual Report* which stated that the Park 'is no longer a mono-experiential destination for world class sporting events, but rather, a place for living, working, learning and leisure'.[31] However, a hankering for sporting pre-eminence lingered in the Park's 2003–08 Corporate Plan, which stated its objective to 'build Sydney Olympic Park as Australia's premier sports destination'[32] — superior to its main rivals at Melbourne and Sydney's Moore Park.

Equally important to the master plan was the release of SOPA's 'Arts and Cultural Strategy 2005 to 2015', which was defined as one of the six key themes and economic platforms to 'underpin the development of Sydney Olympic Park into a multi-dimensional, economically sustainable township — the other five being sport; education; science and technology; health, recreation and wellbeing; and the environment. The arts and cultural strategy sought to take full advantage of the space and the unique natural and built environment of the Park. It is planned that the heritage listed buildings of the Newington Armoury site be developed as a 'significant arts and cultural site including exhibition and performance spaces, artist studios, artist residences and outdoor cultural festival spaces'. The Vernon Abattoir buildings, another heritage listed site that served as the Visitor Centre in the lead-up to the Games, will become a 'site for studios and office accommodation for arts organisations and workers in the urban core'. The building's theatrette will be used for arts and cultural activity.[33]

New life for the struggling SuperDome

The post-Games history of venues at Sydney Olympic Park remains a mixed one. While the aquatic, tennis and hockey centres are examples of venues that have had a successful post-Games life, and the future prospects of Telstra Stadium have improved, the SuperDome remained a troubled and controversial venue until 2004 having struggled as a sporting and an entertainment venue. In the four years since the Games, it was the loser to its city-based rival. The Sydney Kings basketball team played at the SuperDome in 2001 but moved back to the Sydney Entertainment Centre in the following year. It was clear from the start that the market was too small for two Sydney indoor 'entertainment centres'. In 2003–04 the SuperDome registered a pre-tax loss of $10.5 million and found it difficult to attract sufficient sporting and entertainment events to make it viable. On 30 June 2004 the Sydney SuperDome went into receivership.

In the month beforehand there was a 'spectacular spat' between the premier and the prominent former government civil servant Gerry Gleeson, chairman of the Sydney Harbour Foreshore Authority (SHFA) after Gleeson made a secret eleventh hour bid for the ill-fated SuperDome. Gleeson offered $23 million, which was almost three times the reported

$8 million offered by media mogul Kerry Packer's PBL for the SuperDome. Gleeson's bid was part of an ambitious plan to close down Haymarket's Sydney Entertainment Centre, which was run by the SHFA, transfer its live-venue functions to the SuperDome and redevelop the Entertainment Centre site to create more exhibition space at Darling Harbour.[34]

Premier Carr insisted Gleeson withdraw this offer, arguing that it was inappropriate for a public authority to buy a new entertainment venue and that it was not appropriate for the SHFA to 'own part of Olympic Park'. Carr added that the bid for the SuperDome should be left to market forces. This left the way open for Kerry Packer to purchase the SuperDome in September 2004.

With the support of Packer's PBL organisation the SuperDome has turned around its fortunes in the past 12 months with a mixed program of entertainment, culture and sport. In 2005 it featured a diverse range of programs such as 'Disney on Ice' (13–17 July), ARIA Awards (23 October), Taste of Chaos (29 October) and the Luciano Pavarotti farewell world tour (5 November 2005). While the Sydney Kings preferred to play in the city, another basketball team, the West Sydney Razorbacks based itself at Sydney Olympic Park, playing most of its home games at the State Sports Centre and several each year at the SuperDome. Netball tests between Australia and New Zealand in November 2004 and June 2005 have attracted record crowds for the sport of around 15,000. By May 2005 the US magazine *Pollstar*, which evaluates music venues for the concert industry, ranked the SuperDome as the sixth best venue in the world. David Humphreys, chief executive officer of the SuperDome, reported that *Venues Today* ranked the SuperDome as the premier international venue of its kind — with a spectator capacity of at least 15,000 — in terms of gross ticket sales.[35]

Unlike the 1956 Melbourne Olympic Games Village, the Sydney Olympic Village has not become a slum or a white elephant. The demountable units have been relocated and there was a strong demand for the village housing once they were put on the market in 1998 (see Chapter 9).

Conclusions: an assessment of Sydney Olympic Park

So what is the assessment of Sydney Olympic Park in 2006? Is it an

Olympic white elephant or an ongoing asset to the host community? Is it a testament to an Olympic vision and deserving of the Olympic name? Will it continue to be a drain on the taxpayers of New South Wales?

The future of Sydney Olympic Park is important for a number of reasons. It was a central plank of the 1993 bid promises that the Olympic Games would help Sydney create a unique precinct, in an area where it was most needed, that would advance sport, recreation and culture for the people of Sydney. The state government, on behalf of the taxpayers, invested massively in the Park. Since the host community contributed so much towards the success of the Games, it is entitled to anticipate worthwhile returns. Sydney Olympic Park initially struggled to realise its potential and it is now clear that there was insufficient planning for the post-Games use of a unique Olympic landscape. It is also likely that what happens at Sydney Olympic Park may affect the longer-term assessment of the Sydney 2000 Olympic Games.

It is also important to discuss the value of a centralised Olympic precinct because Beijing has emulated the Sydney's practice. However, Beijing will not create a brand-new precinct from scratch as Sydney did; rather it will develop the site that was used for the 1990 Asian Games. However, as was the case in Sydney, almost all of the Beijing Olympic venues in this area will be brand new.

The contrast between Sydney and some other Olympic cities, such as Seoul could not be greater, in terms of the post-Games use of major facilities. Very little has changed at Seoul's main stadium since 1988: the running track remains intact, the cauldron and even the flag poles have not been moved. The stadium has limited use and was unfortunately overlooked when the football World Cup was staged in Japan and Korea in 2002, when new venues were built. It provides very limited ongoing benefit for community of Seoul. This has not been the experience of Sydney's Olympic stadium.

Even so, the post-Games history of Sydney Olympic Park provides lessons — both positive and negative — on post-Games management of an important Olympic precinct. The chief executive of one sports venue stated that 'when the Olympics were finished everyone was burned out and tired' and 'by the time we got back to it, 12 months later, we lost a lot of momentum'. Brian Duffy, chief executive of Sydney Olympic Park Business Association, stated that 'we are a little critical of government for not having a master plan [in place earlier] for beyond the Olympics'.[36] The history of Sydney Olympic Park suggests the need for future Olympic cities to plan carefully beforehand for the post-Olympic outcomes of venues and precincts.

There have been more positive stories emanating out of Sydney Olympic Park since 2003. A number of sports have moved their bases to the Park. The International Tennis Centre has become the location of major tennis competitions in the state and the administration has moved there as well. The Australian Basketball Federation relocated its headquarters to Sydney Olympic Park in February 2003. The creation of Sports House in 2004 was an attempt to attract other sports to the Park. Although progress in promoting sports education at the Park has been modest, the Park has become a focal point for some programs in sports studies. The Department of Sport and Recreation located its head office at the Olympic Park Business Centre; the New South Wales Institute of Sport provides programs at the Park for 800 athletes, and the Australian College for Physical Education is located opposite the Aquatic Centre. It trains 360 students for careers in physical education, sports sciences and dance education. There has also been an expansion of education programs for primary and secondary schoolchildren at the Park (see Chapter 9).

The establishment in 2004 of Sport Knowledge Australia (SKA) at Sydney Olympic Park, which offers courses in sports science, sports management and coaching to senior sports managers in Australia and internationally, was an important educational development. Located at the former administration building at the abattoirs — the Visitor Centre at the time of the Games — SKA was supported by a federal government grant of $8.6 million for three years and jointly sponsored by the University of Sydney, the University of Technology, Sydney and the Sydney Olympic Park Authority.

The residential and business development of the Park, as outlined in the 2002 master plan, will make it more sustainable and community-friendly. Rather than becoming an obsolescent precinct, which would deteriorate over time, the Park has the potential to continue to showcase the Olympic ideals of sport, culture and the environment as well as addressing residential, commercial and entertainment needs. The symbolic marking in the Park is an example of best practice. The cauldron is now an attractive and accessible public sculpture that honours the medallists of 2000. The recognition of the volunteers, through the path of memories, was an important addition in 2002.

So was the decision to create a centralised purpose-built sporting precinct at Homebush Bay the best decision for Sydney's staging of the Olympic Games? The answer is probably yes, given the availability of land in Sydney and the particular sporting and community needs of the city. The increasing public patronage of Sydney Olympic Park and its sporting, recreational and cultural facilities demonstrate that there was a need for such a precinct. It is likely that a new focus on the Park as a multi-purpose landscape may sustain the possibility of a useful post-Games life; in time it might become a model to emulate for future Games cities. The precinct, like Darling Harbour, is likely to gain greater public support in the longer term.

Chapter 7

Sporting impacts

Sport is the first dimension of Olympism and is the primary stated purpose for the Olympic festival. However, it is clear that most organising committees are rather more concerned to pursue tangible economic and business benefits than sporting outcomes. While the benefits of sporting legacy are less self-evident than economic ones, they are important nonetheless. For any Games, five potential sporting outcomes can be identified. While some of these outcomes are linked, others are quite separate.

The first possible outcome is the prospect of an improved national performance at the Olympic Games. With the staging of a home Olympics, there is the incentive for local athletes to perform well in front of a home crowd. As a result, most countries hosting the Games enjoy a boost in the number of medals (see Table 7.1 below). This enhances the perceived success of the Games in the mind of the host community.

Another outcome is the prospect of more and better sports facilities in the host city and, sometimes, in neighbouring cities. If the venues are well planned and sustainable after the Games, they will leave a positive legacy. If such venues are surplus to a city's post-Games needs they will have a negative outcome, becoming white elephants and a continuing drain on the city's finances.

An Olympic Games, thirdly, has the potential to improve a country's sports system and programs for the delivery of sport. Because of the size of the Games, a city may create new partnerships with sports organisations, and these partnerships may be of long-term benefit. There is also the prospect of the better allocation of resources to sports associations.

Fourthly, there is a possibility that the staging of an Olympic Games may improve a city and country's programs of sports management and education, coaching and sports research, and add to its sports research base and infrastructure. Contemporary national sports systems increasingly depend on the latest sports science and research.

Finally many assert that an Olympic Games will encourage greater sports participation, and as a result improved health and fitness, among the community as a whole. It has been argued frequently that successful

168 The Bitter-Sweet Awakening

Olympic athletes become role models who inspire emulation in the general population. De Coubertin advocated both the encouragement of high profile sport as well as sport for all. He believed that elite and community sport are part of a continuum, with the success of each component dependent on the achievement of the other.

The sporting impacts listed in the Olympic Games Global Impact (OGGI) Program (see Chapter 1), begin with the issues of sports participation and school sport, suggesting that the IOC has a commitment to a broad-based sporting legacy. Olympic sports, records and medals are further down the list. The OGGI list of social indicators includes the following headings:

- Participation rates in sport
- Sports played
- School sports
- Available sports facilities
- Top-level sportsmen and women
- Results at the Olympic Games and world championships
- Media specialising in sport
- Sports broadcasting
- Official sports
- Judges and referees
- Drug testing
- Complaints and appeals
- Medals and national records
- Olympic records and world records

There are a number of questions that can be asked about the sporting outcomes of the 2000 Sydney Olympic Games. Were the five possible sporting outcomes pursued with equal determination resulting in positive outcomes across the board? Did the Olympic Games provide sport with a short-term or a longer-term boost? Was Sydney's and Australia's sporting legacy planned as carefully and funded as generously as the sustained program to leverage business and economic benefits?

The context of Australian sport

To understand the nature of sporting outcomes it is first necessary to consider the evolution of the Australian sporting system and how it operated in 1993. The past priorities and context of Australian sport helped frame the explicit and implicit sporting objectives that were part of Sydney's 1993 Olympic bid.

Australians have had a long love affair with the Olympic Games — the Summer Games in particular — and value them more than the people of many other countries. Australia has an established tradition of Olympic success, particularly in the pool, where it ranks second to the United States in terms of the number of Olympic swimming medals achieved.[1] Until the 1970s, the country's Olympic success had been based on natural talent, backed by some innovative coaching, particularly in swimming, because Australian Olympic officials were passionately committed to the amateur ideal. This situation altered in the 1970s when there were the beginnings of a professional sports system in 1973.[2] This process was accelerated in 1976 when Australia performed relatively poorly at the Montreal Olympic Games, achieving only one silver and four bronze medals. Australian Olympic athletes, particularly the swimmers, were no competition for the state-supported professional athletes particularly those from the German Democratic Republic (East Germany).

Although few Australians wanted to emulate the East German athlete assembly line and their reported use of drugs, amateurism was dead and buried in Australia by the end of the 1970s. The Commonwealth Government established the Australian Institute of Sport (AIS) at Canberra in 1981 — dubbed the 'gold medal factory' — where athletes had the best of facilities, coaching and support and could pursue athletic careers full-time as scholarship-supported professionals. It was a sports assembly line that had some similar features to the GDR but not others. The Australian system was less totalitarian and there was no systemic drug taking, though Australia was not immune from drug scandals.

Bob Ellicott, the federal Minister of Sport in 1981, believed that the AIS would continue to produce a stream of athletes who could compete successfully in international competition and benefit sport as a whole. He stated that 'the establishment of the AIS will not only affect the athletes at the top level, but also filter through to the grass roots'.[3] Ellicott gave credence to what became known as the 'trickle down' or 'demonstration' effect that excellence at the top inspires people at all levels of the sports system to greater participation. The operation of this effect after 2000 will be discussed below.

An interest in sports participation had long been a stated concern of Australian politicians. A National Fitness Act had been enacted in federal parliament in 1941 — significantly when Australia was at war — and led to programs aimed at encouraging greater youth fitness. During the term of the Whitlam Government (1972–75) greater attention was paid to sport and recreation than before and the first federal Sports Ministry was created in 1972. However, the major funding priority of this government was community recreation for all ages rather than high profile sport.

The Australian Sports Commission (ASC) was established in 1984 to complement the work of the AIS. While the AIS focused on the development of elite athletes, the ASC was more responsible for Australian sport as a whole: it was set up to provide 'a more coordinated approach to sports development in Australia'. Its primary functions were 'to maximise funding for sport from the private sector, to provide leadership in the development of Australia's performance in international sport, and to increase the level of participation in sport by the non-elite'.[4]

However, the pursuit of international sporting excellence is a costly one. Kieran Hogan and Kevin Norton calculated that the cost of each of the 25 gold and 115 other medals won by Australia between 1980 and 1996 was $37 million for each gold medal and $8 million for a medal of any other description.[5] The authors added that, even allowing for inflation, the funding for Australian elite athletes increased massively from $1.2 million in 1976 to $106 million in 1998. The authors noted that the quest for Olympic success had become so costly that there remained limited funds for sport for all and community sports programs. Hogan and Norton noted that 'Federal policy directs the bulk of the ASC budget to élite athlete programs' and that 'a smaller proportion goes towards community participation'.[6]

Since the late 1970s, the priorities of the Whitlam Government have been reversed. The Whitlam Government adopted a 'bottom-up approach', with greater funding of grass-roots sport, in the hope that it would improve both community participation and greater development of outstanding athletes. This system was largely abandoned in the late

1970s, by which time it had become clear that Australia was no longer achieving the extent of Olympic success that it had enjoyed in the past. The focus shifted from the late 1970s to a 'top-down' approach to identify and fund the most gifted athletes who had the best chance of achieving success in international sport.

Before the Games: predictions of sporting legacies

The creation of a sporting precinct was a central plank of the Sydney bid and was a core promise made to the people of Sydney. Implicit in the promise was that these state-of-art facilities would serve both for the Games themselves and for the people afterwards, particularly those of western Sydney. This region was chosen because the people there had insufficient sporting facilities compared to the population of eastern Sydney, who were serviced by the facilities of Moore Park. SOCOG referred to the Games as the 'Athletes' Games' thereby underlining the city's commitment to the sporting participants — the athletes.

In the Sydney Olympic Games Review Committee report to the Premier of NSW in 1999 the idea of a sporting legacy figured prominently along with other stated Olympic benefits, which included trade, tourism, investment and enhanced international recognition. This report identified two types on sporting outcomes: new and upgraded sporting facilities and increased participation in sport:

> An Olympic Games that is successfully staged and financially managed leaves a positive legacy for the host city in terms of new and upgraded sporting facilities and venues; new and improved infrastructure; enhanced international recognition; enhanced international reputation; increased tourism; new trade, investment and marketing opportunities; and increased participation in sport.[7]

In its final report to the NSW Government of 31 March 2001 OCA spelt out some specific sporting achievements resulting from the Sydney 2000 Olympic Games. The outcomes included the likelihood of increased sports participation:

Sport and Recreation

- The sporting community of NSW, particularly Western Sydney, has been left with a legacy of world class sporting facilities. It is anticipated the availability of these facilities will increase sport participation rates.

- Department staff gained valuable experience in providing services and facilities for elite athletes as a major international event.

- Disadvantaged youth have been given the opportunity to experience the Games and have shown a greater interest in participating in sport.

- Post Olympic programs have been developed to promote sport in the community.[8]

It is instructive to note that sports participation figured in three of the four claims. There was an assumption, discussed further below, that greater sports participation would flow as a matter of course with the creation of world-class facilities. It is also relevant to observe that the first listed outcome remained an anticipated rather than an achieved result in 2002. There was no documentation in this report that the achievements relating to community participation in sport had been realised.

The lead-up to the Games

As the Games approached, the interests of high profile and Olympic sport were guided shrewdly by John Coates, president of the Australian Olympic Committee (AOC) and the most powerful sports official in the country in the 1990s. The only lawyer to have led the Australian Olympic movement, he was 'tough minded', a 'realist' and an astute negotiator, who was invariably 'one step ahead' of his opponents in negotiations. Coates came well prepared to any meeting, often with a document or contract in his back pocket.[9]

Born in 1950, Coates was involved in the sport of rowing as a cox. He moved into administration at an early age, becoming an official on the Australian Olympic team in 1976. He served as the *chef de mission* and general manager at Seoul in 1988 and in the four following Summer Olympic Games. Coates was a member of the NSW Olympic Council and the Australian Olympic Federation (AOF) from 1980, becoming president of the AOC in 1990 — the AOF having changed its name to the AOC in 1990. He played a key role in Sydney's successful bid to stage the 2000 Olympic Games, having been previously involved in the Brisbane and Melbourne bids for the 1992 and 1996 Games respectively. He was awarded an AO (Officer of the Order of Australia) in 1995 for his services to sport and the Olympic movement and became a member of the IOC in 2001. Coates has been prominent in many Australian sporting organisations and is deputy chairman of the Australian Sports Commission. He became a member of the Council of the International Rowing Federation (FISA) in 1992.

Recognising the importance of an Olympic Games to secure the future of Australian Olympic sport, Coates, with the assistance of the AOC's legal counsel Simon Rofe, drafted a 31-page endorsement contract that sanctioned Sydney's bid for the 2000 Olympic Games. From the time that it was signed by the lord mayor of the City of Sydney and the premier

Archers practising on 12 October 2005. The targets are framed by mangroves and one of the five bay markers is behind them.

of the NSW Government on 1 May 1991, it left the AOC in a powerful bargaining position in control of the bid and organising committee and all aspects of the staging and financing the Games.[10]

As a result, when AOC President John Coates and Sydney Lord Mayor Frank Sartor signed the host city contract minutes after Sydney had won the bid on 21 September 1993, the contract dictated that 10 per cent of any profit should go to the AOC, 10 per cent to the IOC and 80 per cent 'for the general benefit of sport in the host country' — with the use of such funds to be spent at the discretion of the AOC.[11] Because it had the power of veto, the AOC effectively controlled the body that ran the Games and its budget. This left the NSW Goverment, which had the burden of funding the Games, without much control of its operations. This situation caused some conflict.

A crucial dinner at Sydney's Chinatown in 1996 — which became known as the 'Knight of the Long Prawns' — helped resolve the differences between the NSW Government and the AOC, which were destabilising Olympic preparations. Michael Knight, who had become the state's Minister for the Olympics in 1995, met with Coates (and Graham Richardson) at this dinner to negotiate a settlement. The agreement between these two Olympic heavyweights was quite crucial to the smooth running of the Games. At the end of the evening Coates had agreed to relinquish the AOC's right of veto over the budget plus its share of 90 per cent of the Games budget in return for a massive war chest for Australian sport of $75,000 million. The sum in question was adjusted upwards the next day to approximately $90 million when Coates reminded Knight that the agreement was in 1992 dollars so that the amount to be paid in 2000 needed to be adjusted for inflation.[12]

The AOC eventually received $88.9 million for an athlete legacy. This money was paid to the Australian Olympic Foundation.[13] With shrewd investment, the AOC ensured that its future Olympic programs would be well funded: both Athens in 2004 and Beijing in 2008. It was reported in the *Weekend Australian* of 30 April–1 May 2005 that 'the $90 million (*sic*) nest egg, controversially paid to the Australian Olympic Committee from the Sydney Games budgets, has grown strongly in the past year to provide a $112 million platform going into the Beijing Olympics'.

Coates achieved another win for Australian Olympic sport in March 1994 when he persuaded Prime Minister Keating to allocate $135 million (later supplemented by another $5 million) to provide the basis for a medal incentive scheme. This enabled the AOC, with the backing of the ASC, to develop a well-endowed Olympic Athlete Program — with a budget of almost $200 million — to prepare athletes for the 2000 Games and to help secure its target of 60 medals in 2000: 20 gold, 20 silver and 20 bronze. Under this scheme greater funds were allocated to sports with medal prospects while sports with little or no medal prospects and non-Olympic sports received reduced ASC funds compared to previous years.[14]

Another $231 million was allocated to the Sports Assistance Scheme, which covered expenses relating to Olympic and Paralympic sports, to attract and pay for the best international coaches and to introduce training scholarships. There was also a Talent Identification Program whereby some 100,000 schoolchildren were screened to assess their sporting potential. As a result some 1315 students were selected for elite training programs.[15] Lynn Embrey contended that the selection criteria was similar to that adopted in eastern bloc countries:

> The pyramid model of sports for all leading to limited elite development no longer applied. Rather, the inverted T model of the eastern bloc countries was adopted as a more efficient selection tool. In this model a large population sample is tested as early as possible to select children who meet specified anatomical, physiological, and genetic criteria. They then enter long years of training for excellence.[16]

However, in Australia the 'T model' was simply one of the pathways towards elite sports participation.

The war chest provided by Coates and the other Olympic programs put in place ensured that Australia achieved an outstanding athletic result in 2000 — virtually meeting the AOC's medal target. To ensure that there was no decline in the Australian Olympic performance after Sydney, Coates wasted no time and released a '2004 Olympic Medal Plan' shortly after the conclusion of the Sydney 2000 Paralympic Games.[17] The Australian performance at the Athens 2004 Olympic Games was exceptional in that Australia achieved a larger number of gold medals there than in Sydney, even though the total medal tally in 2004 was less than in 2000. Australia is the only recent host country to increase its gold medal tally in the Games subsequent to hosting. Table 7.1 shows the number of medals achieved by various countries before, during and after hosting the Olympics.

Table 7.1 Medals achieved by selected host countries before, after and at the time of the hosting the Games

Gold, silver and bronze medals (total)

	Two Games before hosting	The Games before hosting	Hosting year	Games after hosting	Two Games after hosting
Australia (Melbourne 1956)	2-6-5 (13)	6-2-3 (11)	13-8-14 (35)	8-8-6 (22)	6-2-10 (18)
USA (Los Angeles 1984)	34-35-25 (94)	DNA	83-61-30 (174)	36-31-27 (94)	37-34-37 (108)
South Korea (Seoul 1988)	6-6-7 (19)	6-6-7 (19)	12-10-11 (33)	12-5-12 (29)	7-15-5 (27)
Spain (Barcelona 1992)	1-2-2 (5)	1-1-2 (4)	13-7-2 (22)	5-6-6 (17)	3-3-5 (11)
USA (Atlanta 1996)	36-31-27 (94)	37-34-37 (108)	44-32-25 (101)	40-24-33 (97)	35-39-29 (103)
Australia (Sydney 2000)	7-9-11 (27)	9-9-23 (41)	16-25-17 (58)	17-16-16 (49)	NA

DNA = did not attend
NA = not applicable

In just 16 years, from 1988 to 2004, the size of the Australian Olympic team had almost doubled, making it the second largest team at the Athens 2004 Olympic Games. While China and Russia were much greater medal prospects than Australia in 2004, Australia had a significantly larger team than China (with 87 more athletes) and Russia (with 22 more). Australia also had 30 more athletes than another Olympic power, Germany, even though the Games were held in Europe. The success of a large number of Australian teams in qualifying for and medalling in the Olympic Games was another reason for the team's size. Table 7.2 compares the sizes of recent Australian Olympic teams with some other teams.

Table 7.2 Size of recent Australian Olympic teams, compared with some other large teams, from recent host cities.[18] (The ranking of each team in terms of its size against the other six teams in this list).

Country	1988 team size	1992 team size	1996 team size	2000 team size	2004 team size
Australia	255 (6th)	279 (5th)	417 (3rd)	671 (1st)	471 (2nd)
China	277 (5th)	245 (6th)	298 (6th)	271 (7th)	384 (5th)
*Germany	608 (1st)	463 (3rd)	465 (2nd)	422 (4th)	441 (4th)
**Soviet/Russia	482 (2nd)	472 (2nd)	388 (4th)	436 (3rd)	449 (3rd)
USA	443 (3rd)	537 (1st)	649 (1st)	586 (2nd)	534 (1st)
Spain	230 (7th)	418 (4th)	287 (7th)	321 (5th)	316 (6th)
South Korea	393 (4th)	226 (7th)	302 (5th)	281 (6th)	265 (7th)

*In 1988 there were two German teams: German Democratic Republic (East Germany) and Federal Republic of Germany (West Germany).
** Russia was part of the USSR team in 1988 and the Unified team in 1992 before competing as a separate team.

Coates and the Australian Olympic Committee targeted a top five finish in the Athens Games. The Australian team earned an even better result, finishing fourth. Table 7.3 shows the position on the unofficial medal table of the teams of recent host cities compared to the usual top five teams.

Table 7.3 Position on the unofficial medal table of the teams of recent host cities as well as other usual 'top five' teams.

Country	1988	1992	1996	2000	2004
Australia	10th	7th	7th	4th	4th
China	4th	4th	4th	2nd	2nd
Germany	3rd	3rd	3rd	3rd	6th
Soviet/Russia	1st	2nd	2nd	3rd	3rd
USA	2nd	1st	1st	1st	1st
Spain	6th	13th	13th	25th	20th
South Korea	7th	10th	10th	12th	9th

While the USA and Russia have usually occupied the top two positions in the past two decades, China has now joined the top three as a prolific medal-winner. Australia has moved steadily up the medal table since 1988, rising from tenth to fourth. Germany, which had ranked third in four successive Games from 1988, slipped back to sixth, two places behind Australia in 2004. After hosting the Games in 1988 South Korea, has mostly managed to achieve a top ten position. Spain, by contrast, has slipped down the medal table after it hosted the Games in 1992.

Sustainable sports facilities

It is interesting to note that Sydney's Olympic planners believed that the Games would leave the city with positive outcomes in terms of larger and better- equipped sporting venues. This was why Sydney organisers deliberately chose to construct 'few temporary venues', even though it was noted that by OCA that 'Games construction costs' would have been 'reduced' by so doing.[19] Permanent venues were preferred because it was contended that they would leave a post-Games legacy for the city's population. However, such a legacy would only be a positive one if the venues were sustainable and used by the community.

Chapter 6 has noted that the legacy of sports facilities at Sydney Olympic Park was a mixed one. The post-Games experience of the Park demonstrated that the creation of state-of-the-art facilities did not necessarily produce the desired legacy unless they were located in an appropriate place and targeted an achievable audience. It is also

Robin Bell gained a gold medal in the C1 slalom on 1 October 2005 at the world championship held at the Penrith Whitewater Stadium. This facility has undoubtedly encouraged Australian performance in this sport (Jeff Brown, Riverlands Visual Media).

abundantly clear that more and better facilities did not automatically generate greater usage and lead to more sports participation as a matter of course (see below).

Chapter 6 also noted that the post-Games history of facilities at Sydney Olympic Park followed three differing models. First, the character and location of the Aquatic and Athletic Centres serviced a sports demand. These venues gained an immediate and continuing public acceptance and have proved sustainable in the longer term. A public demand for the Olympic stadium, by contrast, was slow to develop after 2000 partly because the stadium was partially closed for some time while it was reconfigured. It is also clear that there was insufficient planning for sports to use this venue. However, there have been more sports events there since 2003 and the venue has gained greater public acceptance. The SuperDome, by contrast, proved difficult to market though its fortunes have improved from 2004.

The post-Games history of sports facilities in other parts of suburban Sydney demonstrated a similar mixed pattern. It is ironic that one of the most controversial Olympic venues (see Chapter 9), the beach volleyball stadium at Bondi Beach, had no negative post-Games outcomes because the temporary stadium was quickly dismantled in October 2000. Despite the fears of residents that the erection of the stadium would lead to environmental damage to the beach, it was returned to its previous state in October 2000 without any major problems. The local community also received some compensation from OCA in the form of some improvements to the Bondi Pavilion (see Chapter 9).

The Mountain Bike Course, which was part of and operated by Fairfield City Farm, also no longer exists. The seven-kilometre cross-country course was established in bushland on a 186 hectare working farm which offered many rural activities including sheep shearing, mustering and milking. The course cost only $100,000 to construct, though the cost of the Olympic overlay was $3.9 million. Insufficient use of the mountain bike course saw it close by 2002. However, Fairfield City Farm continues to operate successfully.

Children play at the Ryde Aquatic Leisure Centre in 2004 (Paul Hartmann, Centre Manager, RALC).

Like the Bondi Beach stadium, the temporary seating for 4500 at the Archery Centre was removed, though the Archery Centre continues its operations at Sydney Olympic Park. Neither beach volleyball nor archery required spectator facilities of this size in non-Olympic mode. This practice conforms to the current IOC policy that if there is no identified post-Games community use for sports facilities temporary facilities are preferable.

The privately owned Ryde Aquatic Leisure Centre (RALC), which was the site of the preliminary rounds of the water polo competition, was equally controversial as the beach volleyball stadium in the lead-up to the Games. Many residents objected to the lack of public consultation, the private nature of the new development and the use of designated public land. While the RALC was born in controversy, it has left a significant legacy for the Council and its community in the longer term with increased patronage in recent years (see Chapter 9).

The Penrith Whitewater course, the site of Olympic canoeing and kayaking events, is another self-supporting facility that has operated successfully in the post-Games period as a venue for national and international events and as a focus for community recreation. It is run by Penrith Whitewater Stadium Ltd, which was set up and is owned by Penrith City Council. As the only man-made whitewater course in the southern hemisphere, it has hosted many international and national championships since it opened, including three Slalom World Cups (1999, 2000 and 2003), the World Freestyle (Canoe) Event in January 2005 and the World Slalom Championships in October 2005, the latter involving up to 400 athletes from 80 countries. The most popular recreational activities include rafting, with 140,185 patrons recorded from 1999 until September 2005, and paddling, with 25,650 persons over the same period. Although the venue was reported to run at a small loss initially, its last two years (2003–04 and 2004–05) have proved profitable for the company.[20]

Most of the remainder of Olympic venues are publicly owned and have been a continuing drain on the NSW Government. There is a commitment by the government to maintain and support three struggling venues, the Sydney International Regatta Centre at Penrith, the Sydney International Equestrian Centre at Horsley Park and the Sydney International Shooting Centre at Cecil Park, but only for a period of five years from 1 July 2001.

The International Regatta Centre at Penrith Lakes was described by Australian gold medallist Clint Robinson 'as definitely one of the best in the world'.[21] However, the anticipated revenue for the venue in 2003–04 was only $520,000 which represented only a quarter of the running costs.[22]

The Sydney International Equestrian Centre, which is owned and operated by NSW Department of Sport and Recreation, has been described 'as the best showjumping facility in the world'.[23] However, the centre exists merely as a venue having no club attached to it or horses stabled there. The revenue generated in 2003–04 from 4185 riders and about 38,800 visitors was around $650,000 but this was well below costs; the state government guarantees an annual sum of $1.3 million. Sport and Recreation is negotiating with Racing NSW to lease it as a training facility.[24]

The Sydney International Shooting Centre is an 'extremely hi-tech venue' and in 2001 was described as 'the most sophisticated facility of its kind' in the world.[25] The Cecil Park Clay Target Club leases the site, but it is managed by Sport and Recreation, although the NSW Government took back the lease in 2004. Although the Centre was the site of a world cup event in 2003–04 and two new clubs used it for competition, the facility raised only $116,000, which was only about 10 per cent of its $1.1 million operating grant.[26]

Given the continuing losses incurred on these three facilities, the future of such venues remain problematic. This is also true of several other publicly owned Olympic facilities, for which the NSW Government shares responsibility with local councils. The Dunc Gray Velodrome, which is leased to Bankstown Council, and the Blacktown Olympic Centre, which caters for baseball, softball and athletics, are facilities of this type. While the Dunc Gray Velodrome has staged international cycling events since 2000, including world cup events, it has struggled to meet its costs. This is also true of the Blacktown Olympic Centre.

Improvement in the Olympic sports system

Another result of the 1996 agreement between Michael Knight and John Coates at the 'Knight of the Long Prawns' was the establishment of the SOCOG Sports Commission (SSC) on 5 June 1996, which was an autonomous body separate from the organising committee. The creation of the SSC effectively gave it control over all 'sports-related and sports-specific matters'. The SSC, rather than the SOCOG Board, thus had the 'power and the authority' to make a range of sporting decisions relating to sports competition, equipment, operations and relationships with local and international sports bodies and national Olympic committees. A significant feature of SSC was that it was run by people who had sports management expertise. The SSC included John Coates (chair), Craig McLatchey (secretary general of the AOC), Kevan Gosper (an Olympian and a senior IOC member) and two people from the SOCOG Board, Graham Richardson and Graham Lovett, who both had sports expertise. On the day of the agreement Coates described it as 'the most significant day in the history of the AOC' and 'an outstanding result for the Olympic movement in this country'.[27]

Bob Elphinston, SOCOG's manager for sport, recalled that there had been no 'similar structure' to the SSC at previous Olympic Games. While previous organising committees had set up sports sub-committees and liaised with the key sports stakeholders — such as the local sports bodies and the international sports federations — the Sydney model was unique in a number of respects. The SSC was an autonomous body 'having full control over all decisions relation to the organisation and conduct of sport and athletes'. Once its budget had been approved by the SOCOG Board, the SSC was able to allocate resources as it saw fit. The creation of the SSC was 'enshrined in legislation' which gave it 'quite significant powers'.[28]

SSC played two important roles in Sydney's Olympic sports program. It ensured that good sports decisions were made about venues and competitions and about the refinement of the Olympic sports program which takes place in the lead-up years to the Games. Secondly, the SSC was able to resist efforts to prune the sports program when SOCOG indulged in cost-cutting because of revenue shortfalls in the immediate years before the Games. Elphinston noted that there were some people in SOCOG who regarded the test events as a waste of time and money. However, the sports-minded personnel of the SSC were able to resist the cost-cutters.

A number of sports administrators and managers assessed that the SSC had a positive impact on the planning and delivery of sport in Sydney so that good sporting decisions were 'made quickly by people who possessed the appropriate expertise'. They concluded that sports delivery was given priority at Sydney, whereas this did not occur at previous Games until after the opening ceremony. In the lead-up years organising committees were more inclined to focus on what were seen as more pressing issues such as political maters, revenue raising, marketing and its relations with the IOC.[29]

The respondents stated that there were a number of key sports-related decisions made by the SSC that added to the success of the Sydney Games by:

> supporting the inclusion of the discipline canoe slalom and the construction of the new white water venue at Penrith, the inclusion of women's water polo, extra athlete spots for women's diving, shooting and indoor volleyball, the lengthening of the football competition schedule so that it began before the Opening Ceremony, and beach volleyball remaining at the Bondi venue despite vociferous local protest.[30]

The inclusion of women's water polo was a good sports decision because it extended the IOC's policy of gender equity in all sports. It was also a popular in Australia because it enabled the Australian team to win this event. One respondent in the Frawley and Toohey article on the SSC believed that had the decision had been left up to the SOCOG Board it may not have included women's water polo for budgetary reasons. The SSC ensured that 'the planning and delivery of sport' remained a central priority of the organising committee.

Sydney's SSC model has been emulated by the organising committees of Athens and Torino and it is likely that it will be implemented in some form in Beijing. However, Elphinston reported that efforts to develop a sports commission in Athens largely failed for political reasons.[31]

Olympic education and research

There are some interesting examples from previous Olympic Games of positive post-Olympic outcomes for youth sport, for sports education, research and management. The large surplus from the 1984 Los Angeles Olympic Games resulted in a substantial endowment of $US93.5 million for the Amateur Athletic Foundation of Los Angeles (AAFLA). The Foundation

Library, which opened in 1988, has become one of the leading international Olympic and sports libraries and with an ongoing program of digitisation has provided a great boost for Olympic education and research. Since 1985, the AAFLA has also invested over $100 million in youth sports in Southern California promoting sports participation and coaching education. The Sydney Games did not produce a surplus of this order and there has been no post-Games funding of junior sports, research and education.

The very attractive venue for wrestling and weightlifting at the 1992 Barcelona Olympic Games, designed by the prominent Barcelona architect Bofill, later became the National Institute for Physical Education of Catalonia after the Games. The Montjuïc precinct of the Barcelona Games now combines sport and physical education. Some programs of sports education and research have found a home at Sydney Olympic Park thereby replicating what has taken place at Barcelona (see Chapter 6).

Other chapters examine the involvement of tertiary institutions in the Sydney Olympic Games and assess educational outcomes (see Chapters 2 and 5). There is also a discussion of programs of Olympic education developed for schoolchildren and an assessment of their impacts (see Chapter 9).

Sports participation and sports for all

In the *Olympic Charter* there is a commitment both to high profile and to mass sport and the suggestion that they should complement each other. The Olympic motto, 'citius, altius, fortius' (faster, higher, stronger) provides a core rationale for high-profile sport. However, the *Charter* also identifies a wider purpose for sport when it states that 'the goal of Olympism is to place everywhere sport at the service of the harmonious development of man'. It adds that 'the practice of sport is a human right. Every individual must have the possibility of practising sport in accordance with his or her needs' and in a non-discriminatory fashion. So there is a commitment to the worth of sport for all and the wider benefits of sports participation.

Pierre de Coubertin himself recognised the value of mass participation and the close link between between high profile and mass sport. He believed that the revival of the Olympic Games would lead to greater physical fitness of youth. In a lecture in Paris in 1929 he stated that:

Young people enjoying rafting at the Penrith Whitewater course which caters to recreational as well as elite sports users (Matthew Newton Photography and Penrith Whitewater Ltd).

> For a hundred to engage in physical culture, fifty must engage in sport. For fifty to engage in sport, twenty must specialise. For twenty to specialise five must be capable of astonishing feats.[32]

Thus high profile and mass sport were part of a pyramid. De Coubertin believed that 'astonishing feats' of the specialists encouraged mass participation and that mass sport provided the recruits for high profile sport. The rhetoric that an Olympic Games will benefit the host community continues to be enunciated both explicitly and implicitly. It is often contended that new sporting facilities — such as at Sydney Olympic Park — will benefit the community as a whole. It is often stated that a 'trickle down' or 'demonstration' factor operates so that more average sportspersons are inspired to emulate the deeds of the stars.

De Coubertin further believed that all sport — whether high performance or mass sport — should have an educational and ethical basis. Ethics, he contended, represent a core element of the Olympic movement, which distinguishes it from the sports movement more generally. The ethical dimensions of the Olympic movement are important because they are the grounds on which the Olympic movement claims leadership of the international sports movement. Olympic ethics include a commitment to fair play, a respect for one's opponents, internationalism and non-doping. There is also a wider commitment to culture and the environment — the other two dimensions of Olympism. The IOC has endorsed de Coubertin's commitment to sport for all. The IOC is the patron of the World Congress on Sport for All, which has been held biennially since 1986. The IOC has also stated that the 'Sport for All' is a movement which 'aimed at realising the Olympic ideal'.[33]

However, Professor Hai Ren, director of the Olympic Research Centre at Beijing, has noted that in recent decades the gap between the contemporary Olympic Games and community sport seems to have widened. Elite sport has also become linked to work and the market, emphasising the value of monetary return for athletes. High-profile sport is increasingly driven by global media and sponsor interests with an emphasis on sport as entertainment and show business. Those who market elite sport have exhibited limited interest in junior sport and sports development — even though both provide the necessary feeder system for elite sport — and the promotion of mass sports and recreation.[34]

Since 1980, the elite sport that is on show at the time of the Olympic Games is more driven by professionalism and commercialism and by greater application of science and technology to stretch the bounds of human performance. Olympic high-profile sport has become organised more as a national business, because many countries believe that success at the Olympic Games is beneficial for national prestige. Increasingly countries equate the achievement of gold medals as proof of national vitality and worth.[35] As a result many countries invest significantly in high-profile sport.

There has been a paucity of studies on post-Games participation in sport and whether an Olympic Games provides a short or longer-term bounce for community participation in sport. Studies produced after 2000 on the 'trickle down effect' — the flow on effect from elite to community sport — have suggested that there were very little, if any, changes to sports participation at the community level, with the exception of a short-term bounce after 2000.[36]

Allan Coles, in a report of the Australian Sports Institute Study Group in 1975, made the interesting point that national sporting excellence can both encourage and even discourage sports participation:

> A causal connection between excellence at the top and breadth of participation cannot simply be assumed. Excellent performance cannot only serve to encourage but also to discourage popular participation according to the factors involved.[37]

Bloomfield amplified this point, noting that discouragement from sports participation may occur because Olympic athletes achieve a 'level of performance' which is seen as unattainable'.[38]

A paper was prepared for the Australian Bureau of Statistics (ABS), and published in November 2001, on 'The Impact of the Olympics on Participation in Australia'. It was sub-titled 'Trickle Down Effect, Discouragement Effect or No Effect?'[39] The study examined the quarterly ABS estimates on sport and sports participation from August 1998 to November 2000. The researchers noted a significant decline in participation rates in all categories from 59.5 per cent in August 1998 to 49 per cent in August 2000. However, they contended that the Olympic Games produced a small bounce from August to November 2000 with the participation rate improving to 51 per cent. The largest jump was in the 18-24 age group (62.9 to 70.0 per cent) and the 35-44 age group (49.3 to 54.0 per cent). The study concluded that there was no evidence of any discouragement effect.

While this study may suggest that there was some short-term lift in sports participation, there is no evidence of any longer-term effect. Veal and Toohey have looked at the impact of the Sydney Games over a longer time frame, using data covering the period from before 2000 to 2002. Their central concern is to analyse the possible operation of a 'trickle down' factor and sports participation before and after the Sydney 2000 Olympic Games. However, they note that the design of available measuring instruments has changed at key times and to such an extent that it is impossible to make any informed assessment about the possible operation of a trickle down factor and any impact of the Olympic Games on mass sports participation. The authors add that this 'scant regard' for the development of appropriate methodology suggests either that government and other agencies are not seriously concerned about such issues or they are simply incompetent.[40]

Veal and Toohey conclude that there was no evidence of an identifiable Olympic effect on sports participation after the Games. While there was a growth in participation in some Olympic sports from

1999–2000 to 2001–02, there was decline in others. More impressive growth rates were recorded, surprisingly, in 21 non-Olympic sports — perhaps suggesting a negative or discouragement Olympic effect. The authors also note that when the *Official Report of the Games of the XXVIIth Olympiad* was published in 2001 there was no mention of sport in the legacy section, suggesting that it was a low priority issue. (However, the final OCA report in 2002 did include sporting legacy — see above).

The Veal and Toohey study has questioned the argument made in the ABS article for a small post-Games sports participation boost. They rightly contend that there were no adequate tools of measurement and their more extensive research suggests an opposite conclusion. It seems then that the research case for a boost for sports participation after the Sydney Olympic Games either cannot be made or has yet to be made. It also seems clear that if the issue of sports participation and community involvement in Olympic sports are deemed an important legacy of an Olympic Games, that more effort needs to be made to develop adequate measuring tools.

Hogan and Norton have also questioned whether there is any correlation between the national success of elite athletes and participation in sport over a long period. They compared Australian sports participation rates between 1975 and 2000 'when Australia enjoyed an enormous and unparalleled rise in international sporting success'. While such sporting achievements may have led to increased national pride, a growth of international sports tourism and enhanced sports infrastructure, there was a reported growth in adult sedentariness and a decline in active sports participation, which does not include spectating. In Australia, like the United States, there have been reports that the proportions of overweight and obese children are increasing.[41]

Conclusions

Australian Olympic sport benefited from the astute leadership of John Coates, who ensured that the Games would generate a future war chest to maintain Australia's outstanding Olympic sporting traditions. Through the efforts of Coates and the AOC, Australia experienced great success at the Sydney and Athens Olympic Games and a similar performance is likely at Beijing in 2008. However, Coates also played an important role in the establishment of SSC, thereby ensuring that the Olympic sports program was given priority in 2000 and that good sports decisions would be made be made by those with sports management expertise. The success of the SSC model has inspired emulation in future Games cities.

The legacies of sports venues, by contrast, has been mixed one, as noted in this chapter and the previous ones. There was less planning and funding for their post-Games use and for sports development than for other legacy concerns such as the maintenance of the Australian elite sports system and for business and economic benefits.

It has yet to be proven that the Olympic Games provided any short- or longer-term bounce in sports participation of the community at large. In fact the opposite may have occurred in that the achievements of professional athletes may have discouraged less talented sports participants. Research has questioned whether a trickle down or demonstration effect operates.

Hogan and Norton contended that the trickle down argument has been used by countries such as Australia to justify increased government funding on elite sport. Veal and Toohey have argued that because measurement of sports participation is so imprecise, bid cities can make unrealistic and unsupported claims about the anticipated community sporting benefits of an Olympic Games when public support is needed to secure IOC votes. They quote an astonishingly precise but dubious Chinese claim of 1992, one year before the unsuccessful Beijing bid for the 2000 Games, that 'the proportion of the population who participate in sports activities on a regular basis will rise from 34.9 per cent to over 40 per cent because of the [winning and staging of the] Games'. Veal and Toohey believed that that a statement made in connection with the London bid for the 2012 Olympic Games on the impact of the Games on the 'Government's sport and physical activity objectives' is more realistic and honest:

> There is little evidence that hosting events has a significant influence on participation. As the majority of people experienced hosted events via TV, it is difficult to separate the impact of winning international competitions from that of hosting ... international success does not appear to have a lasting effect on participation.[42]

If the IOC is seriously concerned to encourage greater sports participation and the development of school and junior sport, it will need to provide greater incentives for bid cities to measure and encourage greater sports participation for the community as a whole in the host country.

Chapter 8

THE GREEN GAMES AND THEIR OUTCOMES

The idea of 'sustainable sport' is relatively new both in 'sport and environmental circles'.[1] Although environmentalism has been prominent as a global social movement for more than three decades, its application to sport has only occurred in recent times. The Sydney Games were prominent in elevating the idea of sustainable sport both in Australia and globally.

The idea of the Green Games was an important selling point of the Sydney 2000 Olympic bid because it coincided with a move by the IOC to recognise the environment as a core principle of Olympism in the 1990s. The IOC was influenced by the greater global prominence of environmental strategies since the Brundtland Report of 1987, which first espoused the idea of sustainable development. The United Nations Conference on Environment and Development at Rio de Janeiro in 1992 — which

A large artificial and walled hill, built along the lines of a sarcophagus, was a major site for treated contaminants.

became known as the Earth Summit — brought together government, industry and the community to further advance global environmental agendas. The IOC made a submission to the Earth Summit.

The IOC added an environmental clause to the *Olympic Charter* in 1991, which stated that 'the IOC sees to it that the Olympic Games are held in conditions which demonstrate a responsible concern for environmental issues'.[2] An environment theme was added to the bid manual to encourage aspiring Olympic cities to include it in their plans. The environment was confirmed as the third dimension of Olympism in 1995, after sport and culture, and the Sport and Environment Commission was created at the same time. So the time was ripe for a Green Games proposal.

Extravagant claims were made by the Sydney bid team, at the time of the bid, about the impact of the Green Games. Bruce Baird, the minister responsible for the bid, claimed that 'no other event at the beginning of the 21st century will have a greater impact on protecting the environment than the 2000 Olympic Games in Sydney'.[3] In a similar vein, Rod McGeoch, the chief executive of Sydney's bid team, stated that 'the Environmental Guidelines [see below] would make Sydney's Olympic plan a prime example of ecologically sustainable development in the 21st century'.[4] Associate Professor Deo Prasad from the SOLARCH group at the University of New South Wales, who had a long involvement in Environmental Sustainable Development (ESD) and the built environment, adopted a more cautious stance in 1996 when he stated that 'the task of delivering these promises may seem astounding considering the commercial realities of developing large infrastructure projects' of 'such magnitude and visibility'.[5]

Greenpeace Australia (hereafter Greenpeace) was prominent in the development of the Green Games concept and later claimed that it had 'conceived the idea of the Green Olympics'.[6] A Greenpeace design for the Olympic Village in July 1992 was one of five submissions selected to undergo further refinement. In partnership with some of the other preferred firms, Greenpeace was involved in final version of the village design.[7] Following the competition, 'Greenpeace was invited to help develop the *Environmental Guidelines* for the Sydney Olympic Games' which were incorporated into the bid. The *Guidelines* contained 'a detailed range of commitments in the areas of planning and construction, energy and water conservation, waste avoidance and minimisation, air, water and soil quality, and protection of significant natural and cultural environments'. After Sydney won the bid, the *Guidelines* were enacted into law by the NSW Government.[8]

It appears that the phrase 'the Green Games' was coined by the media. It was a compelling and popular tag even though it was an imprecise term that later created problems for the local Olympic authorities, as noted below.[9] The Green Games were undoubtedly one of the reasons — though probably not the main reason — why Sydney narrowly defeated Beijing in 1993 for the right to stage the Games. President Samaranch stated that Sydney 'won partly because of the consideration given to environmental matters'.[10] The Green Games achieved much publicity internationally from the time of the bid.

While the local media talked up the Green Games in 1993 and the environmental issues featured prominently in the initial years of preparation, Sydney's Olympic organisers progressively realised that the lofty environmental agendas of 1993 were difficult and costly to realise given the tight seven-year Olympic timetable. Journalist Murray Hogarth noted in 1997 that 'politicians and Games organisers have been running away from the "Green Games" tag' ever since Sydney won the bid. Michael Knight, after becoming the Minister for the Olympics in 1995, preferred the phrase 'the greenest Games in history' or 'an environmentally friendly Games' while Richard Palfreyman, from SOCOG media relations, preferred 'a small "g" green Games'. (Green Games have been capitalised in this chapter because this was how they usually appeared in the Australian media).[11]

Palfreyman dismissed the phrase 'the Green Games' as a 'dreadful term' blaming the media for its invention. SOCOG's 'preferred tag', he added, was the 'Athletes' Games'.[12] Australian Broadcasting Corporation Olympics reporter Kevin Wilde believed that the term 'Green Games' came a distant second or even third as the likely tag for the Sydney Games, after the 'Athletes' Games' and the 'Millennium Games'.[13] This was certainly the case in Sydney and Australia but probably less true internationally.

So why was there this retreat from the Green Games in the three or four years before the Games? Why did Palfreyman refer to this tag as dreadful? Perhaps it was because SOCOG realised that the idea of the Green Games was open-ended, leading to unrealistic green expectations.

(Frank Hubbard, James Hardie Industries).

Practical concerns, as Darryl Luscombe of Greenpeace noted, shaped the decision-making of OCA, which was influenced rather more by construction deadlines than a 'true desire to solve the [environmental] problem' — this being the major concern of Greenpeace and other green groups. In the lead-up years to the Games SOCOG discovered that the Green Games exposed it to continuing criticism because, as Palfreyman put it, 'a bad environment story is always a good story'.[14] He alluded to another problem linked to the idea of the Green Games when he complained in 1997 that 'we are finding ourselves caught up in the wider debate about the environment'.[15] The phrase 'the Green Games' also elevated the environment to a status equal to sport, thereby implying that the promotion of environmental agendas were as important as sporting ones. Prasad made a similar point when he noted that a commitment to the Green Games enabled green groups to continually raise the green bar.[16] In retrospect, those who promoted such an idealistic environmental platform in 1993 may have been naïve to talk up the environment, thereby raising expectations about the delivery of such a wide range of environmental promises. They certainly did not anticipate the problems associated with the realisation of the Green Games.

It was also hardly surprising that green groups attempted to widen the agendas of the Green Games, as an official association with the Olympic Games provided a rare opportunity to promote environmental agendas to a wider public. Naturally, green groups raised issues not only about the environment of the Olympic precinct — the venues where the Games would be staged and the Olympic Village — but also about surrounding areas. Greenpeace expressed concern when it found 50 drums of dioxin in June 1997, some with gaping and rusted holes, at north Newington, adjacent to the Olympic construction site, though three kilometres from the main stadium.[17] There was also debate about the dioxin in Homebush Bay. Palfreyman complained about alarmist headlines about Homebush Bay that appeared in the *Sydney Morning Herald* — 'Dioxin in Homebush Bay hits Games Site'. He pointed out that Homebush Bay was a few kilometres from the main stadium and wryly added that there were no swimming events scheduled there.[18] Such a response did not satisfy green groups who believed that it was important to deal with environmental problems properly at Sydney Olympic Park as a whole rather than simply in its sports precinct. OCA did not address this problem because it was outside its jurisdiction, and the

NSW Government shelved the issue of dioxin in Homebush Bay because it was considered too difficult and costly.

Despite SOCOG's retreat from the Green Games by 1997, it continued to promote the idea of an environmental legacy. It produced a 25-minute video in 1998 — *Our Environment: Our Olympic Legacy* — which documented its ambitious environmental initiatives and described them as the city's 'Olympic legacy'.[19] The presentation confirmed that the environment was an 'integral component' of the city's Olympic bid and that the environmental measures represented new and smarter practices that would result in a worthwhile environmental legacy. SOCOG CEO Sandy Hollway hoped that Sydney would be remembered for 'our innovations and achievements in the environment'.

However, the goals of the Green Games were progressively relegated to the sidelines in 1999 and 2000 as the city focused on the primary task of staging the athletic event. SOCOG had more immediate problems to deal with, particularly after Games preparations were set back by Olympic scandals after November 1998, mostly arising from the Salt Lake City Olympic bid. The local media focused on a succession of local controversies, such as the ticketing fiasco, the marching band controversy and the allegations of corruption made against Australian IOC member Phil Coles. The Green Games slipped from public debate and has never really resurfaced — before and after the Games — as an important issue in the Olympic city even though the idea of the Green Games continues to be of great interest for future Olympic cities as well as the IOC.

There have been widely divergent assessments of the Green Games. The *Official Report of the XXVII Olympiad* stated that 'the environment record of the Sydney 2000 organisations was one of the shining achievements of the Sydney 2000 Olympic Games'. As a result the IOC has adopted Sydney's *Environmental Guidelines* as its future benchmark.[20] Green groups, by contrast, have given the Green Games a mixed report card, itemising successes in some areas but failures in others, as described below. Some critics from the green left have dismissed the Green Games as a 'green wash', a superficial and temporary rinse which gave an appearance of being green and disguised the lack of substantial environmental substance.

How have the Green Games been evaluated and assessed? Have there been positive environmental outcomes both for sport in Australia and for the environment more generally? Did the Green

Games change public attitudes to the environment and promote environmental education? Did Sydney provide a worthwhile environmental model for future Olympic cities? All of these issues, as well as the issue of transport, will be considered in this chapter.

The Green Games in the 1993 bid

Sydney's green promises were more ambitious and wide-ranging than any previous Games. There had been some green initiatives at the 1994 Lillehammer Winter Olympic Games, but they were relatively limited when compared with Sydney's. Lillehammer's green programs included an ambitious waste management policy, the establishment of environmental specifications for the suppliers of goods and services, and some energy-saving techniques. The green measures at Atlanta in 1996 and Nagano in 1998 were relatively modest. There were significant claims of green innovation at Atlanta 'but there was little evidence of this during the Games'. The only exception was a 300KW photovoltaic system on the aquatic centre roof.[21]

Prasad has described the wide range of Sydney's green promises, noting that they included:

> specific calls for consideration of issues such as energy conservation, use of renewable energy, passive solar buildings, appropriate material selection, density of developments, and appliance and equipment selections. The main areas included issues such as conservation of species (flora and fauna, and people and their environment), conservation of resources (including water, energy, waste materials, open space and top soil) and pollution control (air, noise, light, water, soil and waste).[22]

He added the interesting comment that 'it is not clear whether the broad range of "green" issues and their implications were fully understood' by the Sydney organisers or for that matter by the IOC. Prasad suggested that the following issues had not been adequately canvassed. What was a justifiable cost to realise the Green Games? How was environmental success to be measured? How green was green enough? What benchmarks should be employed to evaluate the Green Games?[23]

Greenpeace noted another unique feature of the Green Games, suggesting that 'no other city has attempted to incorporate environmental protection into all stages of the planning and development of its Olympic site in the way that Sydney has'. Sydney had taken a greater risk than any previous city:

> to make its environmental commitments public in the form of official *Environmental Guidelines* as part of its bid and prior to the construction of the Olympic site. These Guidelines allow organisations such as Greenpeace, companies tendering for Olympic contracts, local communities and the general public to know exactly what these commitments are up front. Sydney will be held accountable to these Guidelines in September 2000.[24]

One important innovation of OCA was its Environmental Tender Specification document, which required tenders to include 'environment management systems'. As a result industry was encouraged to develop environmentally sustainable development solutions.

So Sydney's commitment to the Green Games was not only broad-ranging but also very public. It was a high-risk strategy because SOCOG and OCA could be held — and were held — accountable for environmental successes and failures.

Green groups and the Green Games

A unique feature of the Green Games was that many green groups were involved with the planning, monitoring and assessment from its inception. Every Australian green lobby welcomed the idea of the Green Games because it provided them with a unique opportunity to publicise green agendas. However, green groups such as Greenpeace had ambivalent relationships with SOCOG and OCA because they were both supporters and critics. Greenpeace recognised that on balance it was better to be part of an ambitious green proposal than to remain aloof. From 1995 Greenpeace published a public report on the progress of Olympic environmental commitments every 100 days.

The proposal to remediate Homebush Bay tested Greenpeace's resolve because it was a 'contentious' issue. Greenpeace was aware that 'it was a bold and important decision to construct the main Olympic venues in an area that was recognised as being heavily contaminated by past industrial practices'. However, Greenpeace added that 'the vision of restoring the Homebush Bay site from one of virtual neglect to a showcase for the world is one to be encouraged'.[25]

In 1999 and 2000 the relationship between Greenpeace and the OCA became increasingly strained as OCA became more concerned with meeting its athletic deadlines than with environmental commitments. Greenpeace even resorted to court action in 1999 when OCA installed the refrigerant HCFC 123, an ozone-depleting chemical, for the air-conditioning of the SuperDome.[26]

The Green Games were closely monitored and evaluated by a number of other agencies. Green Games Watch 2000 (GGW 2000), which was established in 1995, was a coalition of five environmental groups: the Australian Conservation Foundation, National Parks Association of NSW Inc., National Toxics Network, Nature Conservation Council of NSW and the Total Environment Centre. GGW 2000 was created as an arms-length body to play the role of an independent watchdog and monitor the environmental commitments. It was funded by the Australian and NSW governments with each providing $80,000 per annum; it also received support from Environment Australia and OCA. GGW 2000 ceased operating after the Games.

GGW 2000 submitted annual critical reviews of OCA's progress in implementing the *Environmental Guidelines*. OCA in turn responded to these reviews, thereby initiating a debate between the two organisations. GGW 2000 also circulated two to three newsletters each year and produced an educational booklet for high school students informing them 'about the processes and issues involved in the "greening" of the Games'. These were some of GGW 2000's strategies to encourage 'community awareness and participation' and more 'debate about ecologically sustained development'.[27]

The Earth Council, which was also commissioned to report to OCA on environmental progress, was a product of the 1992 Earth Summit at Rio de Janeiro, and its mission was 'to support and empower people in building a more secure, equitable and sustainable future'. Maurice Strong, who was described by Michael Knight as 'the founding father of the Earth Summit'[28] and who was the chairman of the Earth Council, was a senior figure in the United Nations. He was considered 'one of the most respected international figures on environmental matters'. The Earth Council submitted its first review to OCA on 23 July 1997.

Many other green groups were drawn into the debate on the Green Games. Ian Kiernan, chairman of Clean Up Australia — a national non-profit organisation — was involved in the environmental committee that framed the bid and was a member of OCA's Environmental Advisory Panel. However, he resigned from this committee when he was disappointed with its commitment to water and waste programs.

Transport

Sydney, like other contemporary Olympic cities, faced a significant transport challenge, as projections estimated an increase of 80 per cent in rail travel and 50 per cent in bus traffic during the Games. The record of the Sydney rail system attracted much media criticism in the 1990s with frequent reports of late trains and derailments, with 30 reported rail derailments in 1999 alone. Six people were killed in a train crash at Glenbrook, in Sydney's Blue Mountains, in 1999. A new generation train, known as the millennium train, had been intended for release in 1998 and 1999 but because of operational and mechanical problems its introduction was delayed until 2002.

Many in the media regarded Sydney rail as a transport service in a dangerous state of repair. Few would disagree with the comment of NSW MP Peter Debnam, who became the state opposition leader in 2005, that Sydney's transport was 'unplanned, congested and suffocated due to a bad public transportation policy for many decades'. The public was also sceptical about whether the Games would improve Sydney's transport. A survey conducted in February 2000 found that 60 per cent believed that 'traffic congestion would not show improvement or be worse after the Games'.[29]

One objective of Sydney's transport planning for the Olympic Games was to avoid the traffic problems experienced in Atlanta. A post-mortem after the Atlanta Games concluded that Atlanta's transport problems stemmed from the reliance on volunteer bus drivers who were unfamiliar with the city.

Some of the major Sydney transport plans were linked to the Green Games, though transport scholar Professor John Black noted that the *Environmental Guidelines* relating to transport were 'not very onerous'.[30] The two most important were as follows:

L. Transport

Sydney is committed to:

3. Public transport being the only means by which spectators will be able to directly access events at major Olympic sites;

4. Satellite car-parking venues being established so people can transfer to trains, buses and ferries for access to Olympic sites.

The principal Olympic transport initiative, the rail loop at Homebush Bay — which linked Sydney Olympic Park to the existing rail network — was built to encourage travel by public transport to Sydney Olympic Park.

The Olympic Roads and Transport Authority (ORTA) was established in March 1997 to 'plan, coordinate and deliver integrated road and transport services' for both the Olympic and Paralympic Games. ORTA was headed by Ron Christie, regarded as 'Sydney's most experienced transport executive'. Bob Leece became its CEO in 2000 when Christie became coordinator of the NSW rail system.[31] Christie devised strategies, such as restricted operations for goods trains from 1 am to 5 am, to reduce the strain on the rail network during the Games.

Monitoring the Green Games

The differing assessments of green groups added to the debate on the Green Games in the Olympic city. While GGW 2000 was critical of green progress on many fronts, Maurice Strong of the Earth Council consistently rated the Green Games more positively. Ian Kiernan of Clean Up Australia brought another perspective to the debate, as noted above.

Greenpeace did more than simply report on the Green Games. In June 1997, Greenpeace took non-violent direct action to publicise its dissatisfaction the clean-up of Homebush Bay when it raided the Olympic site. Greenpeace activists donned protective gear to secure 50 barrels of dioxin that were found at Newington, two kilometres from the main Olympic precinct. The waste containing chloro-benzenes, had been progressively uncovered during remediation works and since mid-1997 had been stored at north Newington within a specially constructed clay-lined holding area under orange plastic sheets. Residents living near this area were alarmed when some of the plastic sheets blew into drains leaving the waste mounds uncovered. This Greenpeace intervention achieved maximum publicity in the popular press.

Greenpeace makes safe barrels of dioxin waste near Olympic site, Homebush Bay (Greenpeace/Barry).

A year before this event, Greenpeace activists dug up recently laid lengths of PVC pipeline at the Olympic site on the grounds that such chlorine-based products were unhelpful to the environment. (Polyvinyl chloride is considered one of the worst forms of plastic from an environmental health perspective). These actions also resulted in wide publicity both for Greenpeace and the Green Games.[32]

The relationship between green groups such as Greenpeace and OCA was often problematic, as Darryl Luscombe noted. Many of OCA's environmental policies, while well intentioned, were shaped by pragmatism and driven by Olympic deadlines. Luscombe acknowledged, however, that OCA 'have continued to engage with community groups in an apparently genuine desire to resolve the problem'.[33]

Assessing the Green Games

Green groups were generally disappointed with Sydney's environmental achievements compared to bid promises and to environmental best practice, regarding the Green Games an opportunity that had been partly lost. The management of GGW 2000 was critical when OCA developed a second and weakened version of the *Environmental Guidelines* that 'made them easier to work with, and blocked the adoption of targets to quantify success and failure'.[34] It was further noted by representatives of this group that 'without a system of clear benchmarks, grading for accurate assessment became very difficult so that the *Guidelines* became "motherhood statements"'.

The first report of GGW 2000 in 1997 — a 41-page document — rated the Green Games just five out of ten. While there were positive comments about energy conservation, the report noted the issue of pollution was a 'major weakness' and developments in waste, water and air quality had emerged as 'problem areas'.[35]

Greenpeace's detailed report of 15 August 2000 presented Sydney 2000 with a bronze medal and awarded the Green Games a 'C' — 'just 6 out of 10','noting that environmental performance had taken a 'turn for the worse' from September 1999 as the Games approached. While Greenpeace and GGW 2000 conceded that there were some wins for the environment, there were also significant losses.

Greenpeace canvassed every aspect of the Green Games, with scores ranging from 'A' (excellent) to 'F' (failure). The categories where the Green Games rated best were in renewable energy, transport, water recycling and biodiversity. Toxic remediation, the presence of PVC and refrigeration and cooling rated relatively poorly. The toxic remediation of Homebush Bay — perhaps the core platform of the Green Games — received an 'A-' as a 'world-class attempt' but received a 'D' for the clean up of the Olympic site by the OCA and an 'F' for the clean up of Homebush Bay and the old Union Carbide site by the NSW Government.[36] Table 8.1 shows the marks the Green Games received in each category.

As the Games drew closer green groups believed that there was too much environmental expediency (Frank Hubbard, James Hardie Industries).

Table 8.1 Greenpeace Olympics Report Card August 2000

SUBJECT	MARK	COMMENTS	SUBJECT	MARK	COMMENT
OLYMPIC PLAYERS			**TRANSPORT**		
IOC	Incomplete	Attendance problems	First car-free Olympics	A	Great effort
Minister for the Olympics	D	Absent	Train line expansion	A	Excellent
SOCOG	C+	Broke under pressure	Airport to Sydney train link	A	Leaping ahead
OCA	C	Reluctant participant	Olympic car fleet - Holden	F	Total failure
Overall Players' Score	C	Leadership lacking	Solar buggies	A	Nice touch
KEY ENVIRONMENTAL AREAS			Natural gas buses	D	Missed opportunity
Environmental Guidelines	A	Shows real commitment	City transport during Games	B-	Could do more
			Promoting bicycle use	C	More effort needed
RENEWABLE ENERGY			**BIODIVERSITY**		
Solar energy in the Olympic Athletes' Village	A+	Excellent work	Protection for endangered green and golden bell frog	A-	Stick with it
Energy efficiency and environmental design in Athletes' Village and Olympic venues	A+	Did your homework	Australian plantation timber and FSC timber use in Athletes' village	C	Good start
Solar panels on Olympic venues(SuperDome, Regatta Centre, Olympic Plaza lights, Entertainment Centre)	B+	Good effort	Dunc Gray Velodrome Bankstown	F	Unnecessary failure
			Saving Newington remnant forest	B-	Well done
Green power use by organisers	B	Mixed results	Recycled timber in Olympic venues	C	Mixed result
Green power use during Games	A	Excellent	**REFRIGERATION AND COOLING**		
Olympic Hotels - Ibis and Novotel	A	Well done	Air conditioning in Olympic venues	F	Biggest on-site failure
Millennium Park solar system	A	Creative thinking	Refrigeration in Olympic venues	D	Token effort to mask failure
Solar Media Village	C+	Reluctant effort	Olympic sponsor Coca-Cola	A-	Giant leap ahead for the environment
Solar Thermal Power Station	F	Gave up to easily	Olympic sponsor Samsung	C+	Late effort
TOXIC REMEDIATION			Olympic sponsor McDonald's	D-	Poor effort
Treatment of highly toxic dioxin waste found on the Olympic site by OCA	A-	World-class attempt	Temporary venues and equipment	F	No effort
Clean up of Homebush Bay and old Union Carbide site by NSW Government	F	Missed assignment and deadline and broke promises	**WATER**		
Clean up of Olympic site by OCA	D	Could have done more	Olympic water recycling system	A-	Leading the way
Clean up of old ICI (now Orica) factory at Rhodes Peninsula	F	Limited effort	Hotel (Ibis and Novotel)	B+	Good try
Elimination or reduction of PVC at Olympic site	C-	Should have tried harder	Dual water system in the Athletes' Village	B+	Thinking ahead
Elimination or reduction of PVC in Athletes' Village	A-	Good try	Aquatic Centre swimming pools	B+	Just short of perfect
Temporary marquees during Games	F	Missed opportunity	**OTHER**		
WASTE			Bondi Beach volleyball stadium	F	Unnecessary failure
Games-time waste and recycling plan	?	High hopes	Modular housing in the Athletes' Village	A	Above and beyond assignment
Games-time packaging & utensils	A?	Great possibilities	Environment Pavilion	F	Shocking failure
Streets Ice Cream (Unilever)	F	No effort	Worm farms	B+	Creative initiative
Lidcombe Liquid Waste facility	F	Report to the principal	Olympic Torch	A	Nice touch
Sewage treatment	B	Great initiative	Auditing of Environmental Work	D-	Shoddy attempt
Construction waste recycling at Village and on site	B+	Well done	OVERALL GRADE	C	Taken a turn for the worse since September 1999

GGW 2000 made a similar assessment to that of Greenpeace echoing the theme of green wins and losses:

> The main green wins include public transport access, solar power applications, good building material selection, recycling of construction waste, progressive tendering policies, energy and water conservation and wetland restoration. The main green losses include the failure of most Olympic sponsors to go green, poor quality Olympic merchandising, environmentally destructive refrigerant selection, loss of biodiversity in some projects, failure to clean up contaminated Homebush Bay sediments in time for the Games and the lack of transparency and effective public communication by OCA (Olympic Coordination Authority) and SOCOG (Sydney Organising Committee for the Olympic Games).[37]

Eight tons of phthalate toxic sludge and heavy metal contaminants are removed from Homebush Bay on 15 October 1998 and returned to the old ICI Homebush chemical factory (Greenpeace/Piccone).

Despite such criticisms, GGW 2000 noted that 'environment groups have used lobbying and media coverage to expose problems [that] they have found'. They realised that the failings of the Green Games were newsworthy and had potential educational benefit.

The Earth Council rated the Green Games more positively. Its 1997 report card stated that OCA had made 'impressive strides thus far' and was 'well on target to meet the vast majority of commitments'. 'Overall', it added, 'OCA deserves strong commendation'. The Earth Council rated OCA's progress to meeting its ESD commitments on 11 broad criteria — including facility planning and construction, energy and water conservation, transportation, protection of significant natural and cultural environments, waste minimisation and the treatment of toxic wastes — with an average score of eight out of ten. There was no category in which the Games scored lower than seven.

However, even the Earth Council acknowledged some areas where there was room for improvement, such as 'OCA's relation with environment groups', which had not developed into a 'constructive relationship'. There was also the equivocal stance of OCA on the use of PVCs.[38]

Jeff Angel, chairperson of GGW 2000, believed that the higher scores of the Earth Council occurred because of the:

> Earth Council's desire to make the bureaucracy 'feel good' and GGW's [2000] desire to see the Games achieve a legacy of high standard design, practices and skills for which there will be an ongoing market and use. A robust lasting legacy requires high benchmarks and strict standards to meet the 21st century environmental crisis.[39]

Several years before the IOC introduced OGGI, to capture environmental impacts, as well as social and economic indicators, Sydney's green groups made a thorough and detailed analysis of the strengths and weaknesses of the Green Games and publicised the results. Table 8.1 then, is just one example that demonstrates how seriously green groups, such as Greenpeace, monitored every aspect of the Green Games.

There were several groups who were very critical of the Green Games. The green left attack on the Green Games focused in particular on the remediation of Homebush Bay. Sharon Beder, who published an article in 1994 on 'Sydney's toxic Green Olympics', complained in 1997 that the media had failed to report on the contamination of the site before 1993. She also noted that there had been no environmental impact study before 1993 so that there was no assessment of the potential risk of using the site for the Olympic Games. She was highly critical of Richard Palfreyman's claim at the 1997 Green Games conference at the University of New South Wales that Homebush Bay had been properly remediated:

> Why does Richard Palfeyman refer to remediation in terms of world-class standards and leading edge, when it is a cheap, dirty, quick and convenient option? ... It is covering up the problem or putting a frame round its edges.[40]

Members of the green left — who defined themselves as dark green as compared to liberal environmentalists, whom they regarded as light green — were sceptical of the 'on-site treatment' at Homebush Bay. They regarded the 'bank vault' system of containment and monitoring of untreated toxic waste as the least safe method of dealing with the problem of this formerly degraded site, because there was the possibility of leachate leakages contaminating soil, ground-water and waterways.[41] Dark-green environmentalists believed that the natural environment had intrinsic worth in its own right, and they felt that light-green environmentalists regarded the environment more as an economic resource which could be used to advance social and political agendas. Members of the green left dismissed Sydney's Olympic environmental measures as opportunistic and subservient to sporting agendas.

Helen Lenskyj concurred with Beder's criticism of the adequacy of the remediation of Homebush Bay. She believed that the Sydney Games would become known as the 'Green Wash Games' because they represented a 'public relations exercise in which governments and corporations engage to generate an environmentally friendly image, while, behind the façade, conditions fail to measure up to current standards of best practice'.[42] However, Lenskyj conceded that there were some positive elements to the Green Games. She noted that 'the IOC acted in an uncharacteristically progressive manner in establishing environmental guidelines for bid and host cities'. She added that 'except for the predictable corporate environmentalist perspective, these provisions are comprehensive and proactive, at least on paper'. She noted that all the Australian green groups gave credit to OCA's genuine achievements

— as presumably she did as well — in the areas of 'renewable energy, transport, and biodiversity'. However, she added that 'OCA's secrey and lack of transparency in decision making' was also a major shortcoming of the Green Games.[43]

Criticism also came from sources other than the green left. Although German scholar Holger Preuss was upbeat about Sydney's economic legacy (see Chapter 4), he was less positive about Sydney's environmental achievement. He quoted Greenpeace's 'C' evaluation of the Green Games and added that 'the irony of locating the Olympics on a toxic waste site has fuelled scepticism around the world about the validity of the Green Games image'.[44]

The environmental legacy for Sydney

Despite the limited delivery of the Green Games, Prasad believed that the environmental legacy was significant. Writing in 1999 he stated that:

> The Games are clearly acting as an agent for change in a number of ways. The introduction of 'green' criteria in building projects has helped bring a change in thinking which should be a legacy. The IOC is now adopting the environment as a key factor in decision-making about future Games. The release of information about processes, environmental strategies/ guidelines, benchmarks, and environmental measurement and reporting will be of great value to the professions and industry. The Games will have left a better-informed community about environmental issues.[45]

However, he added that the effectiveness of the remediation of Homebush Bay, the centrepiece of the Green Games, will only be known in the longer term. It may be 30 years before an assessment can be made.

In the absence of any specific post-Games studies it is difficult to assess whether or not, and to what extent, the Green Games acted as an agent for social change. However, it would be surprising if the vigorous debate on the Green Games did not have some impact and make the Australian public more aware of the link between sport and the environment and of environmental best practice — such as recycling, energy management and waste and water recycling — and environmental negatives such as the presence of dioxin, PVCs and oxone-depleting chemicals.

Did the Olympic Village encourage other communities to make greater use of green energy? Did the village provide a model which was emulated by local governments around the country? Did the Games boost the export of Australian environmental technology? Deo Prasad and Mark Snow of SOLARCH at UNSW wrote in 2000 that 'knowledge gained from the solar village thus far has already facilitated a rapid increase in the number of developments proposing to integrate solar energy'. The same authors added in 2004 that the solar innovations at the Olympic village 'are capturing the imagination of individual homeowners through government support programmes such as the PV (photo voltaic) rebate programme'.[46]

Transport outcomes for Sydney

After the Games there were nothing but plaudits for the smooth transport operations. Although he was critical of many aspects of the Olympic Games, Greens MP Ian Cohen commented that the 'public transport ran effectively and safely in an unprecedented manner'. Independent NSW MP, Clover Moore, who became Sydney's lord mayor in 2004, stated that 'residential amenity of many inner-city streets improved during the Games. It was the very opposite of what I feared.' The local and international press echoed these positive assessments. The *Washington Post* of 22 September 2000 quoted Dick Pound, who 'lauded the transport system here [in Sydney]'. Oliver Holt in the *Times* of London of 2 October 2000 stated that 'Sydney staged (the Games) almost flawlessly. The transport system coped admirably.'[47]

Almost 29.5 million passenger trips were recorded during the days of the Olympic Games compared with the 13.8 million under normal circumstances. CityRail achieved a new record ticket sales figure, 465,892, for the final day of the Games. The system worked without any publicised hitch — through there was a train derailment on the last full day of competition near Flemington rail yards, which was perilously close to the Olympic track. However, this train was not in service and carried no passengers. A bus crisis before the Games, which began as an organisational problem but became an industrial one as drivers expressed their dissatisfaction with the conditions of work, was averted

The attractive Olympic Park railway station, conveniently located near the Olympic stadium, provides easy access to the Park for large numbers of people.

only shortly before the Games. With the huge numbers of people opting to travel by public transport, there was less traffic on Sydney roads. During the Games traffic was reduced by 15 per cent and 24 per cent in peak periods.[48]

Why did Sydney's Olympic transport work so well? ORTA believed that it was a case of 'good planning, good weather and good luck, coupled with great public cooperation and quick thinking and hard work when things went wrong'.[49] It also helped that event starting and finishing times were outside of the weekday peak traffic periods. Free public transport for volunteers and holidays for students and many businesses reduced the strain on the transport system, and ORTA had developed successful communication strategies policies to better manage travel demand. Its media spokesperson, based at the transport management centre in the technology park at Redfern, offered daily advice for the travelling public. The reduction of goods rail traffic during the Games reduced the risk of rail disruption because previous derailments of the past year involved goods trains.

Sydney's Olympic geography was another factor that assisted with Olympic travel management. As the athlete and media villages were located close to Sydney Olympic Park, athletes and media were required to undertake only limited travel by coach. With Sydney Olympic Park's wide boulevard and many open spaces, it could accommodate crowds of up to 500,000, and people could move around it without overcrowding and delays. Volunteers played an important role expertly managing (and humouring) the orderly crowds waiting in long lines for trains from Sydney Olympic Park station.

Black identified a number of positive Olympic transport legacies in regard to transport policies. Firstly, the Games demonstrated the value of an integrated ticketing approach that included transport and venue entry. He added, secondly, that transport systems were enhanced by the emerging technology of an 'intelligent transport system' that included on-board, in-trip and pre-trip information relating to fares, smart tickets, timetables and the next departure or arrival. Black expressed disappointment in 2005 that the NSW transport bureaucracy had not advanced this concept further. A third legacy he identified was the value of improved communication with all transport users, as had occurred during the Games. Finally, Sydney's transport organisers gained valuable experience in developing appropriate transport policies for future mega events.

However, it is abundantly clear that the Games did not lead to any significant improvement in Sydney's transport system after the Games. In the years after the Games the familiar complaints about Sydney's rail and road transport re-emerged; there were rail delays, derailments and other deficiencies and road congestion and pollution. Sydney is still struggling to find solutions to its transport problems. The Cross City Tunnel opened in 2005 and the Western Sydney Orbital is under construction — both of which relate to improved car movement. A first section of the Chatswood to Parramatta rail link, which is scheduled to be opened in 2008, will alleviate but not solve the city's transport problems.

It is also unlikely that the emphasis on public transport during the Olympic Games led to any major change in commuter behaviour, other than to encourage people to travel to Sydney Olympic Park by public transport when a major sporting or cultural event was held there. Because such events were intermittent, public transport to Sydney Olympic Park remains irregular. The creation of a residential population at the Sydney Olympic Park will improve future public transport (see Chapter 6).

Why didn't Sydney use the Games to solve or at least improve its chronic transport system? Transport initiatives were high on the list of Athens Olympic agendas. The organisers of the 2004 Athens Olympic Games created a new underground railway system to alleviate city traffic congestion, built a new airport and established a better link road between the airport and the city.

The majority of Sydney's Olympic funding was spent on sport, and to a lesser extent, on the environment, rather than on transport. The creation of a modern sporting precinct at Homebush Bay was the city's big-ticket item and there simply was insufficient finance to tackle other city problems.

Why did Sydney opt to spend more money on sport rather than solving Sydney's transport problems or dealing with other issues such as the city's dwindling water supplies? Was an opportunity missed to improve Sydney's ailing transport system? There are two answers to this question. The creation of a super sports precinct was a more attractive proposition to the host community and was considered the best way of selling the Games to the Sydney public. Improvements in public transport, the better the supply of water and a decrease in pollution, simply did not have the same public appeal.

However, there is an even more fundamental answer. Solving Sydney's transport was and is a long-term and costly undertaking. It could hardly be achieved in a decade let alone during a tight Olympic timetable. Funds were simply not available both for the organisation of an international sporting festival and a major overhaul of Sydney's transport.

It is also likely that the transport improvements at Athens alleviated rather than solved the city's transport and pollution problems. At best the Olympic-related transport changes dealt with some of the worst transport problems. They will work in the longer term only if they are integrated into longer-term transport plans.

The environmental legacy for the Olympic movement

The Green Games were imperfectly realised in Sydney and attracted much criticism. The effectiveness of the remediation of Homebush Bay will not be fully known for decades. It was also true that SOCOG retreated from the idea of the Green Games well before 2000. It seemed that the high hopes for the Green Games had been dissipated by 2000 although the idea continued to attract attention internationally. After 2000 there has been limited discussion in Australia of the Green Games and it seems that Sydney's flawed environmental legacy has been forgotten.

However, Sydney did advance the Green Games and produced some significant outcomes. Although Greenpeace, like the other green groups, was highly critical of the Green Games in the years before the Games, Greenpeace rated them positively in 2000 and afterwards. Asked in August 2000 whether Sydney's Olympic Games were the 'first Green Games', a spokesman for Greenpeace responded that they were, despite some 'green failures'.[50] Greenpeace presented a tougher set of updated environmental Olympic guidelines to the IOC on 20 September 2000, based on the lessons learned from Sydney's experience as well as new environmental concerns such as the banning of genetically modified food. Greenpeace developed a generic guide to sustainable events, which it believed to be relevant for Olympic-bid cities and event organisers.[51]

A second important outcome was that the Green Games were a very public and democratic exercise. GGW 2000 proved to be a fiercely independent and conscientious watchdog group. Eventually its robust stance may have proved too much for the federal government, which withdrew the government's funding ten months before the Games. While the federal opposition claimed that this was a case of 'sour grapes', Senator Hill gave the lame excuse that as the facilities had been completed there was no further role for GGW 2000.[52]

The most important outcome was that the prominence of the Green Games emboldened the IOC to direct future bid cities to take the environmental seriously. As a result Athens included major environmental initiatives in its bid, including the improvement of its transport system by the construction of a subway system and the reduction of pollution. Similarly Beijing placed a high premium on the reduction of the city's pollution and is extending its subway system.

Despite SOCOG's reluctance to use the phrase 'the Green Games', the term has now become an accepted part of the Olympic Games. The Australian Government's Department of the Environment and Heritage had no qualms in extolling the Green Games in 2004 when it suggested that the organisers of the Sydney 2000 Games had been 'acclaimed for their unprecedented commitment to environmental excellence in planning and staging the events'.[53]

BOCOG defined the 'Green Olympics' as one of the 'Three Themes of Beijing 2008 Olympic Games'. Its environmental objectives are very broad:

> The main concepts of Green Olympics are to build an ecologically balanced city and create a pleasant environment for the 2008 Olympic Games; to minimise negative impact of Olympics on environment, in line with the sustainable development ideas of protecting environment and resources, and ecological balance; and to implement education programs throughout the preparation and staging phases of the Olympics in order to raise the environmental awareness of the whole society and encourage the public to play an active role in the actions aimed at ecological environmental improvement.[54]

Conclusions

What then are the lessons of Sydney's Green Games for future bid and Olympic cities? Greenpeace believed that there were eight main lessons:

- Environmental issues must be tackled before the construction begins;
- environmental commitments must be made public and passed into law;
- keep written track of what's happening;
- require an external and independent evaluation of environmental aspects;
- organisers must ensure the best environmental systems and materials are used throughout the project;

- contract environmentally-conscious companies and experts to implement the use of environmental technologies;

- public consultation is a must;

- ensure that the key players — athletes, public, media, sponsors — are aware of the environmental issues related to the project.[55]

Sydney's problem was that it promised environmental achievements on many fronts and raised the expectations of green groups and the community in general. Its green program was so ambitious that it left the Green Games open to criticism. Given the IOC's commitment to the environment and that the Green Games have come to stay, it might be more circumspect to target specific green initiatives — such as a particular improvement in transport infrastructure — which are achievable rather than promising the world.

A positive lesson from the Sydney Games was the public and democratic character of much of the Green Games in that green groups were invited to monitor and to report to (and even to criticise) OCA. In this way green issues were publicly debated in the Olympic city. Perhaps this green scrutiny was too much for OCA because even the compliant and generally supportive Earth Council criticised OCA's secrecy and lack of transparency in decision making, stating that 'it had not always acted early enough to communicate its plans and to provide the public with timely and complete information' and that 'recent highly publicised clashes with environmental groups [in 1997] are a symptom of a poorly functioning relationship which has at its heart frustration over inadequate communication and transparency'.

Although the Green Games were only partially realised, the Sydney Olympic Games did establish new environmental benchmarks. The continuing public debate on Green Games advanced the notion of sustainable sport and made the general public more aware of green issues and groups. Another outcome of the Sydney Olympic Games is that the environment has been placed more firmly on the IOC agenda and all future bid cities now need to address green issues more seriously.

Landscape architect Professor James Weirick questioned whether the Olympic Games would lead to 'any marked improvement in Sydney's ongoing environmental problems: air and water quality and lack of biodiversity'.[56] He could have added transport to this list and questioned whether the Games provided positive outcomes for Sydney's ailing public transport system. However, it is not possible for a mere sporting event, no matter how prestigious, to address and solve a wide range of long-standing urban problems which require complex and costly solutions. The Olympic Games are not a panacea that can solve a wide range of urban problems, though it is possible that they can alleviate some specific problems.

Chapter 9

THE HOST COMMUNITY — WINNERS OR LOSERS?

In his study of the unsuccessful Cape Town bid for the 2004 Olympic Games, Harry Hiller suggested that the prevailing view 'among all elite sectors' was that the 'Olympics would be good for the city' though such a view was not necessarily shared by the 'grass-roots'.[1] He rightly stressed that the primary impetus for any Olympic bid came from civic leaders and business interests rather than the host community at large because the former defined the potential benefits and had most to gain from the staging of an Olympic Games. However, the support of the host community is crucial to the success of a mega sporting event so a city's leaders need to legitimate a bid in the eyes of the host public.

Holger Preuss identified five groups of potential winners from the hosting of an Olympic Games. Local politicians are the first likely beneficiaries in that they can use the event to attract external resources to their city, alter its budget priorities and undertake major infrastructure change. A major sporting event provides an opportunity for civic boosterism and political grandstanding. Preuss suggested that the construction industry — and the business community more generally — which builds new hotels, venues, roads and housing, is the second winner. Since many Olympic developments result in improvements and even gentrification of parts of a city, high-income groups represent a third winner. Tourists — and the tourist industry — are the fourth group to benefit because of enhanced promotional opportunities. Finally, Preuss argued that the general population of a city will benefit 'from the general upswing in economic activity produced by the improvements to the urban infrastructure and, consequently, to the image of the city'.[2]

Preuss thus agreed with Hiller that politicians and the business elites were the most likely winners from the hosting of an Olympic Games providing that the Games are successfully organised. It is significant that the host city's general population comes last in Preuss's list of winners. While business groups anticipate specific and tangible benefits, the only reward for the majority of the host community are benefits that are shared by all five winners.

As noted in earlier chapters, city leaders usually make specific promises to the community to legitimise a mega event, making it appear more attractive to ensure the continuing support of the host community from the time of the bid to the staging of the event. The promise of an attractive sports precinct in Sydney's western suburbs helped sell the Sydney Olympic Games to the community (see Chapters 6 and 8).

Critics of the Olympic Games, such as Helen Lenskyj have a more pessimistic view about the impacts of an Olympic Games on a host community. She argued that Olympic 'legacy benefits accrue to the already privileged sectors of the population' with the disadvantaged bearing a disproportionate share of the burden.[3] She added that the cost of funding a major sporting event skews a city's budget, making less money available for housing, health, welfare and other social programs.

The range of community impacts

The costs and benefits of an Olympic Games to the host community can be considered both in terms of short and long-term impacts. During the preparation period and the staging of the Games, specific groups and communities are affected, such as people living close to Olympic venues or Olympic construction. There are also disadvantaged groups who may be forced either to pay higher rents or face eviction from their accommodation. The management of disaffected groups, who may oppose specific Olympic developments or the staging of the event itself, is a related issue. There is also the question of whether the groups which have to shoulder Olympic burdens are adequately compensated.

A broader issue relates to the management of anti-Olympic lobby groups, which surface in most cities at the time of the bid, in the lead-up years and during the Games themselves. The handling of anti-Olympic lobbies is a sensitive issue for Olympic organisers. Public protest at the time of a bid or the staging of the Games can generate adverse international publicity which will damage a city's Olympic reputation.

Equally important is the assessment of longer-term benefits and burdens to the host community. Does an Olympic Games result in higher prices and rents and, if so, are they temporary or longstanding? Does the staging of an Olympic Games improve life for the majority of citizens or does it exacerbate social inequities in an Olympic city? Are the promises made to the community by civic leaders to justify the event realised?

The IOC, in recent years, has expressed an interest in ensuring long-term community benefits as a result of the staging of the Olympic Games. The Olympic Games Global Impact (OGGI) program included the following categories in its list of social indicators that relate to this topic:

- Public consultation and participation

- Pressure groups

- Community centres and associations

- Public referendums connected with the Olympic Games

- Deferment and abandonment of public policies

- Consultation with specific groups

There are many issues that can be canvassed further relating to the host community and the Olympic Games. Much of the literature to date has focused on public support (or opposition) to the staging of an Olympic Games and the involvement of the community in the lead-up and Games period. Less has been written on whether host communities continue to be affected, either beneficially or adversely, in the years after the Games.

Management of the host community: opposition groups

Although there was robust criticism of SOCOG in the host city in the seven years before the Games, which partly reflected a public nervousness about the ability of SOCOG to properly organise the Games (see Chapter 3), there was limited opposition to the Olympic Games during this time. There was also an absence of damaging protests at the time of the Games.

One of the first organised Olympic opposition groups was the Olympic Impact Coalition (OIC), which was formed in February 2000. It represented an eclectic group of over 30 community organisations that were concerned with indigenous, environmental, anti-poverty, housing, human rights and related issues and held public meetings and organised protests. OIC received support from two NSW Greens parliamentarians, Lee Rhiannon and Ian Cohen. At a meeting on 14 May 2000 OIC changed its name to the Anti-Olympic Alliance (AOA) — thereby making its stance clearer — and set about developing a protest timetable.[4] PISSOFF — People Ingeniously Subverting the Sydney Olympic Farce — was another group but it largely confined its activities to the internet and had a low profile.[5] AOA and PISSOFF disappeared after the Games.

The Toronto anti-Olympic coalition, Bread Not Circuses. was by contrast much better organised, more publicly visible and more enduring than any of the Sydney anti-Olympic organisations. Like AOA, Bread Not Circuses was a coalition of green, welfare and left interests that argued that money should be spent on necessities, typified by 'bread', rather than on luxury sporting festivals which were dismissed as 'circuses'. It was founded years, rather than months, before the various bids proposed by Canadian cities, had a national profile and a continuing life as an anti-Olympic organisation. Bread Not Circuses actively opposed the Toronto bid for the 1996 and 2008 Summer Olympic Games and then shifted its attention to the successful Vancouver bid for the 2010 Winter Games.[6]

The Bread Not Circuses coalition developed sophisticated campaigns to advance its cause both in Canada and the Olympic community generally. In 1990 it even sent representatives to Tokyo, where the IOC chose Atlanta for the 1996 Olympic Games, with Toronto coming third. Such was the coalition's high profile that it was invited to brief the IOC technical commission in March 2001 on homelessness and housing in Toronto only months before the decision was made on the Olympic city for 2008.

Michael Shapcott, who founded the coalition in 1989, was its initial driving force. Based at the University of Toronto's Centre for Urban and Community Studies, he became prominent as a housing and social justice advocate, who founded numerous organisations involved in the issues of housing, homelessness and disaster relief. Shapcott, who has been less prominent in Bread Not Circuses in the past decade, was the New Democratic Party candidate for Toronto Centre for the Canadian Parliament. He finished second on the ballot attracting about one-quarter of the vote.

Another Toronto academic, Helen Lenskyj, has become the professional face of the anti-Olympic cause in Canada in the past decade, although she has no organisational base of her own.[7] Lenskyj has written two Olympic books and numerous articles that document the negative legacy of an Olympic Games on a community. She was involved both in Toronto's unsuccessful bid for the 2008 Summer Olympic Games and Vancouver's successful bid for the 2010 Winter Olympic Games.

The lack of public protest in Sydney surprised Lenskyj, who closely monitored Olympic disaffection from a variety of green, left and Aboriginal groups. She anticipated that a public protest on the opening day of the Games would attract 30,000 protesters. Because she believed that such action would be 'violently suppressed by the police', she made the prediction before the Games that 'I expect there will be violence, there may even be fatalities'.[8]

The only large-scale protests to occur in September 2000 took place in Melbourne. When the Asia-Pacific Summit of the World Economic Forum met there from 11 to 13 September 2000, 10,000 demonstrators took to the streets. There were rowdy scenes on the second day when police charged the protesters, resulting in some 200 injured. The Western Australian premier Richard Court was trapped in his car for some time and his vehicle was damaged.[9] By contrast, there were no similar protests against another global movement, the Olympic Games, in Sydney a few days later. There was instead a remarkable outpouring of public enthusiasm when the torch relay arrived in Sydney, several days before the Games. The only Aboriginal demonstration (which was authorised) consisted of a peaceful tent embassy of 150 persons at Victoria Park near the University of Sydney.

The few small protests in Sydney in the days before and during the Games were uneventful and attracted no media interest. Lenskyj noted that the AOA organised a protest of 200 members when the torch relay passed Newtown on 14 September, the day before the Games. I happened to be an observer in the torch-bearer's bus as it passed Newtown — having carried the torch for 500 metres at nearby Enmore Park — and the AOA crowd looked more like 20 than 200. Five hundred Aborigines marched from Redfern to the Tent Embassy, then to Hyde Park and Prime Minister Howard's Sydney office, but this protest was as much about Howard's policies as about the staging of the Olympic Games.[10]

Lenskyj argued that the failure of an Olympic protest to materialise and the absence of violence occurred because of the 'power of the

Olympic industry' to ensure the 'uncritical support from a generally docile mass media' and SOCOG's ability to capitalise on the divisions within Aboriginal communities.[11] However, there are other possible explanations for the universal public support for the Games. One is that Aborigines were given more reasons to support than to oppose the Games; another factor was SOCOG's inclusive attitude, and finally there was the status of Cathy Freeman as Australia's best track and field prospect.

Aborigines

The issue of Australia's indigenous communities was a sensitive political issue for the local Olympic organisers. It was linked to other human rights issues that attracted the interest of the international media. There was the possibility of demonstrations by indigenous people and arrests during the Games — which would have attracted international media attention — as had occurred at the time of the Brisbane 1982 Commonwealth Games. Although the Queensland Government allowed one protest march four days before the Games — and around 3000 people marched — 'illegal Aboriginal protest activity continued relentlessly throughout the duration of the Games'. Aborigines defied the *Commonwealth Games Act,* which enabled police to detain 'unauthorised people' in the vicinity of Games sites and venues, which had been passed months before the Games.[12] However, in Sydney, there was a significant risk for Aborigines that any demonstration against the Olympic Games that detracted from the event might unleash a sizeable backlash from the non-indigenous majority.

While all Australian political parties recognised that Aborigines were worse off materially, educationally and health-wise than the rest of the community, there was disagreement among politicians and the community about what policies were appropriate to deal with the situation. While some favoured an official apology to Aborigines, reconciliation and a commitment to land rights — which had been the subject of two High Court decisions in the 1990s — others, such as Prime Minister Howard, preferred what he called 'practical reconciliation', a focus on improving Aboriginal health and their social and material life. Aboriginal communities were divided about whether to use the Games to highlight their predicament to the world or whether to support the Games, particularly because some high-profile Aborigines were members of the Australian Olympic team.

Realising the sensitivity of indigenous issues, the bid committee

Gary Ella, program manager in SOCOG's Aboriginal and Torres Strait Islander Relations Unit, speaks at a UNSW forum on Sydney Aboriginal People and the Olympics on 22 October 1999.

included some prominent Aborigines in the Olympic bid process from its inception. SOCOG recruited a number of Aboriginal athletes and established an Aboriginal and Torres Strait Islander Relations Unit to deal directly with Aboriginal leaders and communities. The unit had a staff of four with former rugby international Gary Ella as the program manager. Indigenous issues also featured prominently in the cultural presentation of Australia in the opening ceremony and the cultural program, which began with *The Festival of the Dreaming* (see Chapter 3). The Games logo incorporated a boomerang in its design even though it was, as Aboriginal Darren Godwell noted, appropriated by a non-indigenous artist, like so many other Aboriginal symbols.

Were indigenous Australians winners or losers as a result of their active participation in the Olympic Games and their unwillingness to protest? Were the Olympic Games beneficial or detrimental for Aborigines and Torres Strait Islanders?

Although the Games may have promoted a greater awareness of Aboriginal culture, there was, as Marcia Langton noted, no increased engagement with Aboriginal life by the non-indigenous majority. Godwell argued that indigenous representation in the Olympic Games conformed to 'the representation of indigenous peoples in the Australian public domain [and] is consistent with an underlying avoidance' of complex questions relating to race relations.[13] It was as if all the negatives — as Moragas had noted (see Chapter 3) — relating to Aboriginal issues had been removed from the image of Aboriginal culture that was presented to the world. It has already been noted in Chapter 3 that any hope that the Games would advance reconciliation and help create a more tolerant and inclusive Australia was soon dashed after 2000. Kevin Dunn noted that there was even a small backlash in the tabloid press after the closing ceremony when the band 'Midnight Oil' appeared with the word 'sorry' on their shirts. Dunn noted that this action generated irate letters and hostile editorial comment in Sydney's tabloid newspaper, the *Daily Telegraph*.[14]

It would be easy to argue that there were few, if any, benefits to indigenous communities as a result of their Olympic involvement. However, some indigenous people believed that the Games led to small gains and even a measure of empowerment. Four Aboriginal Land Councils signed a treaty, the Talbagoorlie Treaty (Talbagoorlie being an Aboriginal name for Port Jackson), to cooperate on a tender for an Aboriginal Centre at Olympic Park. Jenny Munro, chairperson of the Metropolitan Land Council, believed that this cooperation between the Land Councils was one of the most promising developments in three decades and boded well for future cooperation.[15] An indigenous arts and culture pavilion, set up and managed by the land councils at Sydney Olympic Park, showcased 'Aboriginal culture and artworks' and provided information on Aboriginal history.[16] There were also benefits for indigenous artists who were involved in a successful indigenous arts festival in 1997 (see Chapter 3).

The symbolic capital generated by the Olympic Games for Aboriginal Australia should not be dismissed out of hand. The Olympic torch first arrived in Australia at Uluru, a sacred place for indigenous Australia, and was then handed to the traditional owners of the land as a mark of respect. This simple ceremony was a powerful statement of Aboriginal ownership of this important site. Seeing the faces of the traditional owners on television was probably a rare occasion for many urban non-indigenous Australians.

None of these things, of course, confronted the many problems that face the majority of indigenous Australians; nor did they advance the cause of reconciliation to any significant degree. It is extravagant to believe that an international sporting event could act as a change agent in any substantial way for such entrenched problems. It is naïve to expect that the cultural presentation in the opening ceremony, which had to be spectacular, entertaining and accessible to a diverse global audience, could also convey social and political messages which changed the way that people think.

In the lead-up to the Games there were local protests against two Olympic facilities, the Bondi Beach Volleyball Pavilion and the Ryde Leisure and Aquatic Centre. There was also some disquiet in the Auburn local government area, which was adversely affected by the creation of Sydney Olympic Park within the council's boundaries.

The Bondi Beach Volleyball Pavilion

Bondi Beach was chosen as the place of the Olympic beach volleyball competition ahead of other possible sites, such as Maroubra, because it appealed to the international beach volleyball federation, to international television interests, such as NBC, and to the SOCOG Sports Commission. Staging the event at Sydney's most famous beach — one that has national iconic status — would advance the television appeal of this sport as it competed for media attention with 27 other sports.

There was initially no sustained public opposition to the staging of beach volleyball on Bondi Beach, which is located within the boundaries of Waverley Council. After a series of community meetings, the council gave its in-principle support to the facility at a meeting of 2 August 1997.

Tacit support changed to public outcry once the scope and time frame of the development became known in November 1998. The proposed 10,000 seat temporary stadium covered approximately 20 per cent of the beach, occupying the central location in front of the Bondi Pavilion. It was also revealed that the Olympic beach volleyball site would incorporate 34 per cent of Bondi Park, as well as Bondi Pavilion, Bondi Surf Bathers' Life Saving Club and Bondi Beach Public School grounds. Rather than being a temporary inconvenience for a month or two, the stadium timetable (from erection to removal) stretched from May to October 2000.

A resident action group, Bondi Olympic Watch (BOW), which was formed after the November 1998 announcement, held numerous protest meetings, lobbied Waverley Council and gave vent to public anger against the beach volleyball stadium and related developments. BOW pointed out that residents would be denied access to a significant section of the beach and to Bondi Pavilion, which was used for cultural events, for an extended period. There were also concerns that the normal life of the suburb would be disrupted by some 30 proposed road closures and overcrowding, and that the development would cause environmental damage to the beach. Local residents were also appalled by a lack of adequate community consultation and by OCA's 'steamroller' tactics.[17]

Although Waverley Council was opposed to the construction of the beach volleyball stadium from November 1998, the mayor of Waverley, Councillor Peter Pearce, recognised that the council could not stop the development because the Minister for Urban Affairs and Planning had the power to override the council's consent powers, as the pavilion was an Olympic development. In order to secure some positive outcomes for the residents, the council continued to uphold its previous in-principle agreement.

The stance of the council, backed by the sustained campaign of the BOW, resulted in some minor modifications to the development. The height of the stadium was reduced by six metres. A controversial bridge from the stadium to the VIP stand was scrapped.[18]

Pearce secured some other positive outcomes for the residents of Bondi, the most significant being an OCA contribution to improvements in the Bondi Pavilion, which included the installation of a passenger lift with disabled access, the repainting of the exterior walls of the pavilion, the refurbishment of the toilets and showers and improvements to the reticulation of electric power and communication. Lenskyj claimed that such improvements were required for the Olympic event and therefore did not amount to concessions made to the Bondi community.[19] Whether or not this was the case, the additions to the Bondi Pavilion did improve the facility and benefit the community in the long term.

There were other concessions that were directly attributable to the sustained protests of the Bondi community. OCA gave a grant of $30,000 to several community service groups and agreed to reimburse the council the sum of $1,219,571 for revenue shortfalls and operating costs. This money had not been originally offered by OCA.[20]

Kristy Owen noted that the erection of the stadium produced a negative legacy in that 'the alienation of community land and resources' created a precedent that might recur in future large-scale temporary events. Fortunately, she added, section 17 of the Master Agreement provided for the 'reinstatement of community, cultural and occasional users of the Pavilion at the conclusion of the Olympic period'.[21]

It was ironic that while the Beach Volleyball Stadium was one of the most controversial Olympic venues before the Games, there was no manifestation of community dissent during and after the Games. This was because the opposition to the stadium had been defused by then. The fears of disruption and overcrowding at the time of the Games proved unfounded, as did any fears of traffic chaos more generally. In fact, the beach volleyball event proved one of the most successful and popular of all the Olympic sports. The stadium was dismantled in October 2000 and the beach was restored to its former status without any undue fuss.

The Ryde Aquatic Leisure Centre

The Ryde Aquatic Leisure Centre (RALC), the site of some preliminary water polo matches, was another controversial development opposed by many residents in Ryde and nearby suburbs. The centre was erected on the site of the Ryde Swimming Centre, a facility that included six pools on land designated as a public park. The Olympic development was attractive to the Ryde City Council (RCC) because the existing 32-year-old swimming centre was reported to suffer from 'structural and operational problems, including poor water circulation and filtration, rusting and corroding steel supporting structures, and concrete cancer'.[22] The council also stated that it was a 'once in the lifetime opportunity' to redevelop the facility with the benefit of Olympic funding and design 'at a minimum cost to the taxpayers'.[23] It also believed that the proposed multi-purpose facility better served the sport and leisure needs of ratepayers.

The new facility was built in two stages. The first included an Olympic pool, built to FINA specifications, as well as 'a wave pool, a small hydro-therapy pool, and an indoor multi-purpose sports hall'. OCA was responsible for the construction of this stage. The second stage involved 'a health and leisure complex, including another 25-metre indoor pool, four outdoor tennis courts, a child minding crèche, function rooms and a restaurant'.[24] The cost of the facility was $24.5 million, of which RCC paid around $16 million and OCA and SOCOG $8.465 million. Except during the Olympic period RALC was operated by a private company, David Lloyd Leisure Pty Ltd. RCC signed a 50-year contract with this firm which involved an initial premium of $3 million and an annual leasing fee of $175,000. The creation of the RALC involved the demolition of the municipal swimming centre, so for two years Ryde residents had no access to a local swimming pool.

A Ryde Pool Action Group (RPAG) was formed to protest against:

   i)   tokenistic community consultation and a lack of transparency
        in government decision-making;

   ii) the inappropriate use of Olympic planning mechanisms
        and legislation; and

   iii) the impact upon the ownership or control of community
        facilities and services.[25]

The RPAG, like the BOW, appeared relatively late in the Olympic timetable because OCA's approval of the development application for the RALC did not take place until 8 December 1998. Some residents took particular exception to the replacement of a facility on public land with one that was privately run. Mark Burnside, a Ryde resident, complained that 'it is the first step in the chronic, long-term alienation and commercialisation of public land that must be stopped immediately'.[26] There were fears that higher prices charged by a private company might exclude a proportion of the Ryde community. The president of RPAG complained that 'streamlined Olympic processes are being used to give a leg up to a private operator to establish a private members' club on community land'.[27] There was also concern about the gap of two years between the demolition of the old swimming centre and the creation of a leisure centre.

While there was some community disquiet about the new facility and the processes by which it was created, a majority the citizens of Ryde and nearby suburbs have ultimately voted with their feet to approve the new facility. Patronage figures for the past few years have demonstrated that the fears that the RALC would be a private club for the rich have proved groundless. By 2005 the annual number of patrons at RALC was double that attracted to the Ryde Swimming Centre is its last years of operation. There were 324,681 patrons in 1995–96 and 326,104 in 1996–97. By contrast, RALC attracted around 500,000 patrons in 2003–04 and 678,000 in 2004–05. Although the operating surplus for 2004–05 is not yet known, it will undoubtedly be larger than the reported figure of $200,000 for 2003–04.[28]

The Ryde Aquatic Leisure Centre provides a model of constructive negotiation between an Olympic authority and a local council. OCA contributed funding and design expertise to this Olympic facility, but the development accorded with the local council's desire to provide a more contemporary facility that could address the leisure and recreation needs of the community. Although some members of the community feared that this Olympic development would lead to the privatisation of public land and the exclusion of sections of the community, the public support for the facility fully endorsed the actions of the RCC. The Olympic Games have therefore left an enduring and worthwhile legacy to the citizens of Ryde and its neighbouring suburbs.

Prices, rents and the cost of living

Many people in Olympic cities fear that an Olympic Games will result in negative side effects, such as price rises, increased rents and a higher cost of living, which will persist afterwards. KPMG even predicted in 1993 that the Olympic Games could add to inflation in NSW, with 'the greatest price effect' occurring during the year of the Olympics, with 'potentially over one percentage point being added to the NSW inflation rate, and over half a per cent being added to the Australian inflation rate'.[29]

Preuss examined price-level changes in six Summer Olympic Games cities from 1972 to 1996 and concluded that in four of the six cities there was no Olympic price increase, any increase being comparable to non-Olympic cities in the same country. He noted that while the cost of living 'exploded' in Sydney during the Olympic year, it probably occurred for non-Olympic reasons because there were similar jumps in the other Australian capital cities. Sydney's cost of living prices, like those of other Australian capital cities returned to the pre-Games level in 2001 and 2002. Preuss concluded that the Sydney Games in particular, and Olympic Games in general, did not result in 'a lasting increase in the cost of living'.[30]

Lenskyj argued that the Olympic Games had a negative effect on

It was convenient to blame the Games for rising rents and homelessness. However, a surging property market was the primary cause.

the availability of housing for low-income earners, with spiralling housing costs leading to evictions and greater homelessness. She quoted extensively from the surveys conducted by the Tenants' Union, Rentwatchers and other groups who believed that there was a crisis in housing and homelessness in the years leading to the Olympic Games. She highlighted a pithy statement from Rentwatchers in 2000 — 'you can't share the spirit if you can't pay the rent' — making it a chapter title in her book on the Sydney Games. Lenskyj claimed that rent increases and housing prices were worst in the Olympic corridor, a 12 kilometre spine stretching from the city to Homebush Bay to Parramatta, close to the major Olympic sporting action. Sydney house prices, she noted, rose by 7 per cent above inflation in the Olympic corridor in 1998, compared to the usual 2 per cent. However, Sydney house prices rose well above the inflation rate across the board, in non-Olympic as well Olympic suburbs. While property prices were escalating from 1996 to 2000, the inflation rate was declining from 2.6 per cent in 1996 to less than 1 per cent in 1997 and 1998 — the five-year increase in inflation from 1996 to 2000 being only 7 per cent. The 7 per cent increase in prices in the Olympic corridor (compared to the usual 2 per cent) is not as startling as it appears.

A 2001 study by Jones Lang LaSalle for Macquarie Bank came to a different conclusion to Lenskyj. The report suggested that the Olympic

Games only had a minor impact on the rental market and concluded that Sydney, like Atlanta, 'experienced little or no Olympic related boost'.[31] The study found that prices in the Olympic corridor increased by less then 0.5 per cent above the city average for 1996 to 2000.[32] Macquarie Bank entitled a market research paper, published in August 2000 'Olympics, What Olympics?' Melbourne University researcher Dr Richard Reed came to a similar conclusion, arguing that Sydney's prices 'remained largely unaffected by the Olympics'. The Olympic Games had an 'irregular impact' on the Sydney residential property market because while there had been a 'slight increase' in the prices in suburbs near the Olympic village there was 'no flow-on effect to the outer suburbs'.[33]

Increased prices in the Sydney market occurred because the housing market was over-heated by factors other than the Olympic Games, and had surged by about 50 per cent from 1996 to 2000 compared to the national average of 39 per cent. This was part of the regular cycle of the Sydney property market — which usually lasts from seven to ten years — with years of real estate boom are followed by years of relative stagnation and some decline before the property market takes off again. The buoyant pre-Olympic Sydney housing market did not flatten out until 2004 and by 2005 there was a reported decline in the Sydney housing market of 7 per cent.[34]

Lenskyj admitted that there may have been other, non-Olympic, reasons — which were possibly more important — for the increasing problems of housing and homelessness in the five years before the Games. She argued that there was:

> ... indisputable evidence of a widespread social problem of housing and homelessness that increased in the years before the Olympics. Whether the Olympics constituted the major cause or one of the many causes, the onus was on all levels of government to address the obvious crisis in housing by protecting tenants' rights and preserving affordable accommodation.[35]

Local government

'The Olympic business, not the sport but the bidding and development process, is an example of economic globalisation' noted geographer

Kevin Dunn, so there is a question as to how well local authorities can 'guard against some of the more nefarious aspects of globalisation'.[36] Dunn added that place competition associated with this mega sporting event had resulted in four problematic outcomes: the subsidising of private sector interests at the cost of public concerns, the dilution of local planning powers, the limitation of public participation in the development process, and the homogenisation of community opinion.[37] The size and prestige of the Olympic event and its strict unforgiving deadlines can provide the excuse for fast tracking development proposals, streamlining decision-making and undercutting community consultation. Albany Consulting found that Olympics advisory and consulting boards were never involved 'at the crucial formulation phases'. Public and external advice was only sought at the 'therapy end' of developments, to assist with the 'big-sell'.[38] As with all developments in NSW that are defined as significant most of the Olympic projects were exempted from the requirements to produce an Environmental Impact Statement (EIS).

Mosman Council

Dunn noted in 1997 that 'local authorities', notably local councils, believed that they 'have been largely locked out of the [Olympic] decision-making process' and that any local government involvement has been tokenistic at best.[39] He added that even councils that include Olympic sites within their boundaries have received 'very little information on key issues like anticipated transport flows' to assist council in the formulation of transport plans. The mayor of Mosman complained on 21 January 1997 about 'the apparent lack of commitment to putting in place mechanisms for an effective ongoing flow of information between SOCOG and local government'.[40] The executive officer of the Inner Metropolitan Regional Organisation of Councils echoed this view, stating that local government officers were 'frustrated by the lack of detail that Olympic authorities were providing about developments' and 'refusals to supply documentary materials'.[41]

Because Mosman is a harbourside council area, with its foreshores providing excellent vantage points to watch the yachting at no cost, Mosman Council had been keen to develop an Olympic plan. It wanted to assess how best the community could minimise some negative impacts, such as damage to the environment and traffic congestion, and maximise some positive benefits, such as tourism promotion and the involvement of the Mosman community in the Olympic Games. To help develop this plan, Mosman Council invited the Centre for Olympic Studies at the University of New South Wales to organise an Olympic forum on 24 October 1997. The forum was addressed by Olympic experts in transport, marketing and the environment as well as some representatives from the Olympic and Paralympic organisations. At this forum Dunn urged the council to bargain hard with SOCOG to ensure that the staging of the Games might expand rather than reduce community participation in planning systems in Sydney, which, he said, are facing the 'entrepreneurialist pressure of economic globalisation'.[42] The council subsequently engaged transport Professor John Black to organise a team of students to conduct a transport survey during a test event.[43] Mosman Council thus attempted to circumvent the problem of inadequate Olympic information by creating its own alternative research base. The council's action represented a constructive response enabling it and its community to have greater ownership of the Olympic event.

Auburn Council — the home of the Olympics

Sydney Olympic Park is located within the boundaries of Auburn local government area, a place of 'socio-economic disadvantage, with relatively lower incomes, higher proportions of dwellings being rented and very high rates of unemployment' in comparison with the Sydney metropolitan average. According to the 1996 census approximately 48.2 per cent of the 51,000 residents were born in a 'non-English speaking' countries.[44]

There were some positive benefits for Auburn because of its location. In the lead-up to the Games there was some 'Olympic-related employment' generated by construction work, the provision of food and beverage services for the larger venues, and housekeeping services for the village. There was also a housing legacy in the creation of high-standard residential developments at the athletes' and media villages. Though the Olympic authorities claimed that Auburn benefited from improved sporting and recreational facilities on its doorstep, Auburn Council questioned whether many of its residents would use facilities largely designed for elite athletes.[45]

In fact the positive legacy claimed by the Olympic authorities was outweighed by negative economic and social legacies. Auburn Council

The housing at the former Olympic Village is well designed and surrounded by trees and open space.

The market place at Newington provides a focus for the residents of the village.

lost a significant amount of rate revenue — approximately $1 million per annum, representing 5 per cent of the council's budget — after the abattoirs were closed in the 1980s and the Homebush Bay site declared exempt from rates. The loss was made worse when 'a section of rateable industrial land was transferred to Strathfield LGA' in 1992. In return the State Sports Centre was included in the Auburn LGA, so that the entire Sydney Olympic Park was within one LGA.[46] While Auburn received compensation for 18 months' worth of rates, a financial assessment prepared for OCA estimated that Auburn Council would continue to suffer a revenue shortfall until 2007.[47] Auburn chose not to pass on this revenue shortfall to its ratepayers, believing that they could ill afford this extra 5 per cent increase. Council's diminished rate revenue led a reduction in the funding of community and youth services programs. It is ironic that the people of one of the most disadvantaged local government areas have had 'to subsidise the Olympics'.

Auburn Council, like Mosman, was shut out of Olympic decision-making and provided with inadequate information. Council's efforts to seek compensation from OCA and the NSW Government fell on deaf ears. Auburn Council followed the example of Mosman Council, engaging the UNSW Centre for Olympic Studies to coordinate an Olympic forum on 30 April 1999, but, as one of the speakers noted, many of the strategies suggested 'might all be a bit late for Auburn City Council' given the advanced state of the Olympic timetable.[48] The view was also expressed at the forum that the council had not pushed its case sufficiently with Olympic authorities.

The creation of a suburb of Newington, the former athletes' village, may have created potential social problems for the Auburn Council because it represented a 'high socio-economic enclave' in an otherwise depressed local government area. Auburn Council expressed concern in 1999 about the social problems that may result from the 'tremendous social disparity' within the LGA.

The new housing estate at Newington

After the Games, the former Olympic Village was transformed into the suburb of Newington. The new suburb consisted on medium density housing, 850 three- and four-bedroom architect designed houses and 350 two- to three-bedroom apartments on the 94 hectare site, many

This monument at the former Olympic Village lists the names of the Australian Olympic team, who stayed there.

with commanding views of the surrounding parkland. The Olympic Village had been planned on the principles of sustainable development and energy efficiency through solar design.[49]

James Bell, sales manager of Mirvac Projects Pty Ltd — the company that built the village — stated that there was some initial nervousness about selling the project 'off the plan' from 1998 (for occupation after the Games) because of the area's past history as the abattoir site and because it was surrounded by the Silverwater industrial site. Another challenge in the marketing of the village was that 'all the dwellings were initially completed to an Olympic mode floor plan' so that they had to be stripped back to their respective shells and converted to residential dwellings. However, there was a reasonable market take-up from 1998 with typical three bedroom houses selling from $350,000 to $390,000 and four bedroom houses from $450,000 to $490,000 off the plan. There was a progressive increase in prices in later years.[50]

The market for Newington properties peaked in the three years after the Games. Bell believed that this occurred because 'we promoted Newington as a new suburb and a great place to live' rather than as the former Olympic site. It is also the only infill site located in such a convenient location surrounded by parklands and sporting facilities. Mirvac countered an infrastructure weakness of this new suburb by including a shopping centre and a local school in the development. By 2005, 90 per cent of the properties had been sold.

Matt Hamilton of Newington Village Real Estate noted that Newington properties had appreciated significantly in value by 2005: with three bedroom houses selling for $550,000 to $590,000 and four bedroom houses for $670,000 to $770,000. Because of the desirability of Newington as a place to live, an additional 300 properties had been built since 2000 making a total of 1800 dwellings there. The low resale figure of around 70 properties per year provided further proof of the popularity of the suburb.[51]

Newington has proved a popular suburb for Chinese-, Indian- and Korean-Australians. The opportunity to purchase new property at a reasonable price has been appealing to such groups. The suburb is also regarded as 'very safe', which is another attractive feature.[52] Although Auburn Council may have had some qualms about the integration of the suburb of Newington into its local government area, it appears that many middle-income earners regard the 1800 dwellings of the former Olympic Village and its surrounds as a desirable area to live.

Newington and the former media village at Lidcombe have not suffered the fate of the 1956 Olympic Games village at Heidelberg, which by the 1990s was reported to be an unattractive slum.[53] Instead, many of the properties were sold at premium prices, returning the NSW Government a profit of $2.5 million by 2003.[54]

Olympic education

The Olympic Games produced education outcomes for primary and secondary students as well as tertiary institutions (which are covered in Chapter 5).

Olympic education was included in Sydney's bid for the 2000 Olympic Games with the NSW Department of Education proposing a range of strategies for schools. After the bid was won each school in NSW was invited to integrate Olympic education and programs in the curricula. It was later reported that 1578 schools and as many as 431,403 students participated in Olympic education programs.[55]

Helen Brownlee was one of the key players in the development of the department's Olympic education strategy. She was manager of the School Sport Unit, president of the NSW Olympic Council and an executive member of the AOC. The Olympic education programs that were implemented included Pierre de Coubertin Awards for secondary students. De Coubertin was chosen because he exemplified 'the qualities of initiative, teamwork, sportsmanship and fair play'.[56] Other programs included Olympic awareness weeks, Olympic guest speakers and the adoption of athletes. The purpose of Olympic education was to add to student understanding of the Olympic movement and its values, to increase student knowledge of the Olympic and Paralympic Games and to enhance student sports participation.

Brownlee believed that the Olympic education programs associated with the Sydney Olympic and Paralympic Games resulted in a positive legacy. An evaluation conducted after the Games confirmed this claim in that all programs were rated positively. Although most of the Olympic education activities ceased in 2000, some continued. Pierre de Coubertin Awards continue to be made to secondary students and this successful NSW program has now been adopted in some other Australian states. As a result, the awards and Olympic education continue to be featured on the website of the NSW School Sport Unit.[57]

Susan Crawford, SOCOG's manager of the Olympic 2000 National Education Program from 1997 to 2000, played a pivotal role in the design, management and delivery of an ambitious and innovative educational program for Australia's 10,500 school communities. She noted that the status of the program and the resources devoted to it 'reflected an understanding of the significance of Olympic Education in terms of the potential legacy to be gained from the promotion of Olympism, and particularly the Olympic Ideals, to a nation's youth'. The objective was to create an enduring legacy that would last well beyond 2000.

SOCOG, in conjunction with the University of Wollongong, produced a multimedia Olympic resource kit — Aspire: 2000 Olympic Games Resource for Australian Schools — which was one part of the National Education Program. Described as 'the world's first multimedia Olympic education resource' Aspire was distributed to 11,400 Australian schools so that it could be accessed by the country's 3.2 million schoolchildren.

Other initiatives included O-News, an Olympic student newspaper, a 'Kids' area within the SOCOG website, and various enhancement programs, involving art and language programs. There were also opportunities for schoolchildren to be involved in the Games with the 'Olympic Welcome Program' and 'Escort Runners' for the torch relay.

Although Crawford was keen to evaluate SOCOG's education program, there was no evaluation of *Aspire* or any other aspect of the education program, so its impacts are unknown. It is also unfortunate that Crawford's proposal that the Post-Games Report detail 'the historical development of the program with recommendations for future Organising Committees', was not implemented.[58]

There have been ongoing Olympic education programs at the Powerhouse Museum (see Chapter 2) and at Sydney Olympic Park. John Johnstone, Education Services Manager at the Park, noted that there was a growing demand for field excursions in environmental education, geography and art. He added that the number of students involved in excursion classes have increased from 12,173 in 2002–03, to 14,000 in 2003–04 and 18,000 in 2004–05. Three classrooms had been established at the Field Studies Centre at Bicentennial Park catering from kindergarten to year 12. Ninety thousand students have also been involved in tours and interactive programs. The excursions were conducted by a fully qualified staff of 15.[59]

Olympic consultation with communities

This chapter has highlighted many examples that suggest inadequate community consultation in regard to Olympic developments. It has already been noted in Chapter 8 that environmental groups gave SOCOG and OCA a poor rating on such criteria. While this situation may be a result of tight deadlines and the large scale of operations, which make it difficult to comply with the established consultation procedures, these may have been excuses to centralise and streamline decision-making. Dunn expressed a fear that 'Olympic preparations are setting new benchmarks for planning, but quite low ones, especially in terms of community and local government involvement in significant developments'.[60]

One solution to this negative outcome might be a greater community consultation in the pre-bid period. Canadian Olympic scholar Bruce Kidd contended more than a decade ago that there should be improved consultation processes because entire communities, and not just sports people, are affected by the Games. Kidd argued that the IOC should require each candidate city to conduct:

> ... a social impact assessment and a public consultation before submitting its bid. The obligations of the host city are growing with each Olympics, while the IOC is taking more and more of the revenues for its own purposes. Entire communities — not just sports people — are affected by hosting the Games, and the calculation of social costs and benefits is no easy matter. At the very least, the decision to bid should be made in the context of full public information and widespread consultation ... The IOC must ensure that a Games bid represents more than the elites.[61]

Community consultation has advanced further in Canada than in any other country. The organisers of the Toronto bid for the 1996 Olympic Games developed a pre-bid public consultation process. This resulted in a formal social contract which covered a variety of impacts, such as housing.[62] This idea was carried further at the time of the successful Vancouver/Whistler 2010 Olympic Games bid. An independent organisation, the Impact of the Olympics on Community Coalition (IOCC), was set up to ensure 'that environmental, social, transportation, housing, economic and civil rights issues associated are addressed from a community perspective'. The IOCC aimed to ensure that the Vancouver Organising Committee for the Olympic Games kept 'the promises made by the Vancouver 2010 Bid Corporation'. The IOCC, which will continue to operate until 2010,[63] aims to ensure that the 'Olympics are for all' so that the host community benefits as a whole. The case can thus be made not only for improved community consultation at the time of an Olympic bid but during the years between the winning of a bid to the staging of an Olympic Games.

Sydney had an official watchdog group, the Green Games Watch 2000, which performed a useful monitoring and reporting service (see Chapter 8) but its brief related only to the environment. The idea of an ongoing community coalition that looks at all aspects of Olympic preparations is appealing. It is also desirable that the staging of an Olympic Games should not result in a loss of social capital, as Dunn termed it, or a 'residue of public mistrust' in city's planning. Greater openness, transparency and accountability on the part of Olympic organisations will have the opposite effect.[64]

The host community — winners or losers?

Bob Stewart made an interesting comment in 2005 in reference to the potential community benefit from the 2006 Melbourne Commonwealth Games. He noted that while there is much rhetoric at the time of a bid and in the lead-up to a mega sporting festival about a 'net community benefit', there are few attempts to define such benefits and discuss how they will be realised. Rarely, if at all, do the organisers of major sporting festivals review the net community benefit after the event.

> When it comes to deciding if the Games will actually produce a net community benefit, nobody really knows. There is an enormous amount of hyperbole surrounding the potential economic and social impact, but there is also an equal concern about the cost explosion and loss of amenity during the Games. In the end it will come down to the highly subjective view of whether the Games provided value for money. This is something the Melbourne and Victorian community can answer only after the Games have ended and the legacy from the Games becomes clearer.[65]

So what was the 'net community benefit' from the Sydney 2000 Olympic Games?

The creation of a modern sports precinct at Sydney Olympic Park — the primary promise made to the community — was realised and, after some initial difficult years, achieved a measure of public acceptance (see Chapter 6). The successful staging of the Rugby World Cup in 2003 at the former Olympic Stadium played an important role in restoring the public's faith in the Park.

It is unlikely that the Sydney and NSW community were Olympic winners, as Preuss believed, because of any 'general upswing in economic activity', leading to a stronger city and stronger state economic environment, even though the Games were judged to be successful. The citizens of NSW did benefit from the Olympic-related building boom from 1993 to 2000, when the state's unemployment figures were lower than any other state. However, the NSW economy was fuelled much more by other factors, such as the property boom, which produced escalating revenue for the NSW Government resulting in a succession of surplus budgets. After the NSW property bubble burst at the end of 2003, the

NSW economy lagged behind most other states. It was reported in the *Sydney Morning Herald* of 12 August 2005 that the number of full-time jobs in NSW from December 2003 had increased by only 3.3 per cent compared with 15.6 per cent in Queensland, 14.9 per cent in Western Australia and 12.4 per cent in Tasmania.

So is the lagging economy of NSW in 2005 a long-term result of the state's substantial Olympic investment? Probably not. The Olympic Games has left the NSW Government with some small recurring debts but the Games continue to enhance the state's export industries. There are more significant reasons for the state's lacklustre economic performance. Access Economics reported in September 2005 'that the stagnation in housing prices is a key problem' and has 'flow-on impacts' that are being felt in the retail sector.[66] At best the Olympic Games was a mild stimulus to the economy before the Games (particularly in terms of jobs in the construction industry).

By contrast, the efforts to add to the symbolic significance of Sydney Olympic Park may be considered a positive outcome for the host community, in that it helps to cultivate the rich public memory of the Games. The relocation of the cauldron and the erection of Games Memories, a path that acknowledges the role of volunteers, underscore the public significance of this precinct and acknowledge the role of athletes and volunteers. The creation of a future museum to Sydney Olympic Park, which outlines both the history of this unique Park and the staging of the Games there, would further add to this memory. Another identifiable benefit was the enhanced sporting and recreational infrastructure of Sydney Olympic Park.

The Sydney 2000 Olympic Games were strongly supported by the host community, and the opposition to specific venues was limited to particular localities and occurred at a late stage in the Olympic timetable.

However, as is the case at most mega sporting events, there was no planning for, or even a statement of, any 'net community benefit' beforehand, nor was there any evaluation afterwards. Although Sydney's Olympic organisations benefited from strong community support for the Games, there were limits to their openness, transparency and accountability. Dunn cautioned that some of the actions taken in the name of the Olympic Games may diminish the public's faith in the planning process if the longer term.

Chapter 10

THE PARALYMPIC GAMES

The status of the Paralympic Games has been elevated dramatically in the past two decades. When the first Paralympic Games were held at Rome in 1960, and thereafter every four years, they were quite separate from the Olympic Games. The staging of the Paralympic Games as a twin festival occurred first at Seoul in 1988, though there had been some previous attempts to twin the two festivals. The plan of the Los Angeles Olympic Organising Committee to stage a Paralympic Games at Los Angeles in 1984, in conjunction with the Olympic Games, was abandoned at the last minute so the Paralympic Games were actually held at two separate locations, at Stoke Mandeville in England and New York in USA. From 1988, however, it has become customary to stage the Paralympic Games a short time after the Olympic Games, making use of the Olympic venues. The increasingly close relationship between the IOC and the International Paralympic Committee (IPC) since 2000, and formal agreements between the two bodies, have ensured that an aspiring Olympic city must also submit a bid for the Paralympic Games (see below). The Olympic and the Paralympic Games are now one festival, consisting of two parallel events.

There are only brief references to the Paralympic Games in most Olympic histories and dictionaries because the Paralympic Games have been treated, until recently, as less important and peripheral to the Olympic Games. However, two recent volumes, *Keys to Success,* published three years after the Barcelona Games, and *Staging the Olympics,* published one year before the Sydney Olympic Games, have included chapters on the Paralympic Games, indicating greater acceptance.[1] A few articles and chapters have also been written on topics such as the media, disability awareness, the Paralympic Village and the history of the Games.[2] The staging of the 1st Paralympic Congress in 1992, in conjunction with the Barcelona Paralympic Games, demonstrated an increasing interest in Paralympic research. However, there remains a dearth of scholarly writing on the Paralympic Games, in stark contrast to the significant growth in academic Olympic studies. There is no authoritative history of the

A panel of international Paralympic scholars met at the UNSW Centre for Olympic Studies on 14 October 2000. Some of the scholars included Otto Schantz, France (left and partly obscured); Simon Darcy, UTS and Ian Jobling, University of Queensland (at the end of the table); Norbert Müller, Germany and Richard Cashman, UNSW (centre right) (Simon Darcy).

Paralympic Games, even though this festival raises a host of new issues about the nature of sport, the relationship between these parallel sporting events as well as the issues of diability and discrimination in sport.

Nevertheless, there are an increasing number of popular books on the Paralympic Games, including a book on the Paralympics by former IPC President Robert Steadward and Cynthia Peterson. There is also a small but growing literature on Australian Paralympic athletes. Sandy Blythe, a member of the wheelchair basketball team, published his autobiography, *Blythe Spirit*, in 2000. Amputee track athlete, Neil Fuller, also published his autobiography, entitled *One Foot in the Door*. Greg Jones, the father and coach of wheelchair track athlete, Lachlan Jones, produced a book about their joint experiences, *Walk a Crooked Mile*, in the same year. Respected journalist Ian Heads, who has written extensively on Australian sport, joined forces with Louise Sauvage, Australia's most prominent Paralympian and the one who was chosen to light the cauldron in 2000, to document her life.[3]

Any book on the impacts of the Olympic Games should include a discussion of the Paralympic Games, since they have become an accepted part of the Olympic festival. While there is a reference to the Cultural Olympiad in the Olympic Games Global Impact Project (OGGI) list of social indicators, the Paralympic Games are not mentioned. Landry suggested that the Paralympic movement had 'raised public consciousness' with respect to 'the philosophical concept and meaning of *human* performance'.[4]

There are many questions that can be posed about the Sydney Paralympic Games. Why were they assessed as the best ever? By what criteria should their outcomes be assessed? To what extent did they set new benchmarks for the Paralympic Games? Why did the Sydney and Australian public support the Games so enthusiastically?

There are also a number of longer term questions that can be posed. Did the Sydney Paralympic Games advance the cause of the Paralympic Games and Paralympian athletes in general and Australian Paralympians in particular? Did the staging of the Paralympic Games improve disability awareness and the infrastructure for disabled people?

It is also worth reflecting on the value of including some Paralympic events in wheelchair track in the Olympic Games since the winners receive no official medal, nor are they counted in the unofficial medal tally. Does a handful of demonstration events enhance the Paralympic cause? Do such events progress Olympic and Paralympic cooperation? There are also the issues raised by Landry as to whether the Paralympic Games can extend the idea of Olympism and whether his notion of Paralympism is implicit in Olympism.

The emergence of the new field of disability studies as a critical scholarly discipline in the last decade provides a fresh set of questions and new theory with which to examine of the Paralympic Games. Gerard Goggin and Christopher Newell published a book on *Disability in Australia: Exposing a Social Apartheid* (2005). Earlier, Rosmarie Garland Thomson wrote a book on *Extraordinary Bodies: Figuring Physical Disability in American Culture and Literature* (1997). Garland explored how representation attached meaning to bodies. Helen Meekosha, in an article entitled 'Superchicks, Clones,

Cyborgs and Cripples: Cinema and Messages of Bodily Transformations' (1999) explored how 'Hollywood is continually pumping out movies saturated with images of disability'.[5] Schell and Duncan published an article on the coverage of the American network CBC of the Atlanta Paralympics in the same year. 'Media, disability and Olympism' was the subtitle of an article by Goggin and Newell on 'Crippling Paralympics?' in 2000. Others, such as Simon Darcy in a number of articles, have examined the relationship of the Sydney Paralympic Games to the disability community and disability infrastructure.

It will be the task of this chapter to assess the outcomes of the Sydney Paralympic Games in three major areas — sport, infrastructure and disability awareness — as discussed below. Another aim will be to review the success of the Paralympic Games in the longer term, to consider whether the Sydney 2000 Paralympic Games, like the Olympic Games, are still considered the benchmark Games five years down the track (see earlier chapters). There is also the question as to whether the success of the Sydney Paralympic Games flowed on to Athens and will benefit future Paralympic cities, or whether any success occurred because of the specific Sydney context, which was a one-off success.

Paralympic outcomes: issues and criteria

It is more difficult to assess the Paralympic Games than the Olympic Games because of their recent origins and changing character. Before Seoul in 1988, the Paralympic Games were mostly held in a different city and even a different country to the Olympic Games though they were held in the same year. Rome in 1960 and Tokyo in 1964 were two rare occasions before 1988 when the Paralympic Games were held in the same city as the Olympic Games.

There is also an absence of criteria to compare one Paralympic Games with another even since 1988. There have been significant changes since then in the organisation of the Paralympic Games. Spectators were admitted free at Seoul in 1988 and Barcelona in 1992, but were required to purchase tickets at Atlanta in 1996 and Sydney in 2000. While Atlanta sold mostly individual tickets, Sydney introduced a special day pass of $15, enabling spectators to attend multiple sports events. So any comparisons of spectator numbers and tickets sold need to take these changes into account. The relationship between the Olympic and Paralympic organising committees changed from Atlanta to Sydney and will change for future Games (see below).

The IPC has yet to introduce a system of transfer of knowledge similar to the Olympic Games Knowledge Services (see Chapter 5) so there is less transfer of knowledge from one Games city to the next. There is no sustained evaluation of the impacts of a Paralympic Games other than the production of a one volume post-Games report, much smaller than the three-volume Olympic Post Games report, the *Official Report of the XXVII Olympiad*; the report will become four volumes after the 2008 Beijing Olympic Games.

However, there are even more fundamental reasons why it is difficult to assess the outcomes of specific Paralympic Games. There remains an ongoing debate about the nature of the festival and its objectives. Firstly, the Paralympic twin status is both a strength and a weakness. The link with such a prestigious global festival enhances the Paralympic Games, but at the same time it suggests that the Paralympic Games may not have the capacity to organise its own separate festival. While cities compete aggressively for the right to host an Olympic Games, they inherit the Paralympic Games as an obligation. The second issue relates to the nature of the Paralympic Games as a sports spectacle. Robert Steadward was inclined to view the Paralympic Games as an occasion to display how sport catered for a variety of disabilities. 'A new marketing orientation' has emphasised 'global sporting spectacle rather than an event representing the diversity of disability sporting endeavour'.[6]

The 'hierarchy of acceptability' is another problem faced by Paralympic organisers in that some athlete categories featured more prominently than others because they are more easily understood by the non-disabled majority who watch Paralympic telecasts.[7] Lea Ann Schell and Margaret Carlisle Duncan noted that athletes with certain kind of disabilities are more likely to appear in telecasts, such as athletes 'whose disabilities made them less obviously different or were more correctable'.[8] Wheelchair athletes are one category of disability more easily comprehended because the athletes appear to operate under similar constraints, which is not actually the case as some athletes have more upper body mobility than others. Athletes from other categories — amputees, cerebral palsy, blind and partially blind and intellectually disabled — stretch the sports public's understanding of the nature of athletic performance.

Olympic sport too has its sporting hierarchies. The public understands and relates more to some sports than others. Gymnastics is immensely popular across the board whereas sports such as fencing, handball, and judo appeal to narrower and more specialised audiences. Some sports, such as beach volleyball, are easily followed on television whereas others, such as sailing, are not.

However, the biggest challenge facing the promoters of the Paralympic Games is the complex and even baffling classification system. Athletes from the six disability categories are further sub-divided into numerous levels defining degrees of impairment. Athletes competing in track are allocated one of the 22 levels, which are grouped in five categories (T indicates track).

T11–13	Visually impaired
T20	Intellectual disability
T31–8	Cerebral palsy
T41–6	Amputee and les autre (the others)
T51–4	Wheelchair track

Swimmers compete in one of 14 levels which are grouped in three categories (S indicates swimming):

S1–10	Athletes with physical impairment (S1 have the most severe and S10 the least severe impairment)
S11–13	Visual impairment (S11 have little or no vision, S13 have greater vision)
S14	Intellectual disability

Whereas there is only one men's and one women's 100-metre sprint on the Olympic track, there are many 100-metre sprints at the Paralympic Games, which creates public confusion about the value of each event.

It is also less difficult to assess Paralympic outcomes because there is less a clear sense of objectives beforehand, other than to stage a successful Games. Disability scholar Simon Darcy noted that SPOC lumped together a range of challenges it faced in staging the Games which included 'raising awareness of the Paralympics; augmenting funds; keeping the momentum going after the Olympic Games, and attracting spectators to the Paralympics'. He believed that 'a secondary consideration was that the Paralympics brought the host city's community of people with disabilities an opportunity for a lasting legacy of accessible infrastructure (venues, transport, accommodation), a raised level of disability awareness and an improved position in society'.[9]

These challenges relate to three very large areas. Paralympic officials and scholars agree that the primary objective is to stage a successful Paralympic Games. There is also agreement that a secondary and subsidiary aim is to use the Games to improve the city's sports infrastructure for athletes with disabilities and to improve the city's disability infrastructure in general — in transport, access to buildings and so forth. A third possible aim, which gains coverage in the media and which appeals to politicians and community leaders, is that the Games may enhance disability awareness in society and improve the lot of the disability community. This is an aspect of the Games that appeals greatly to disability scholars but less so to the organisers of Paralympic sport, who prefer to emphasise the sporting character of the Games.

Assessment of the Sydney Paralympic Games

At their conclusion, the Sydney 2000 Paralympic Games received rave reviews which were as effusive as those for the Olympic Games. Dr Robert Steadward, president of the IPC, repeated the Samaranch accolade of 'the best-ever' Games and informed the crowd at the closing ceremony that 'you have completed a perfect festival of sport and friendship'. Dr John Grant, president of SPOC, enthusiastically elaborated on this assessment in the *Sydney 2000 Paralympic Games Post Games Report*, published in 2001:

> The support for the Paralympic Games was outstanding. The 2000 Paralympic Games smashed all our predictions — the largest number of athletes and delegations ever to compete at a Paralympic Games, unprecedented media coverage and record

Although the budget for the opening ceremony of the Paralympic Games was much smaller the Olympic Games, it was a stylish and much watched event (Simon Darcy).

crowds and ticket sales. More than 1.16 million spectators turned out in force to witness this spectacular international event showcasing some of the finest sporting talent in the world.[10]

The media and politicians talked up the significance of the Paralympic Games as a change agent (see below).

Table 10.1 documents the records set by the Sydney Paralympic Games in terms of their size and public support. The opening and closing ceremonies played to packed houses in the Olympic stadium (which seated over 110,000) and secured a record television crowd for the Australian Broadcasting Commission. By contrast, 66,257 attended the opening ceremony of the Atlanta 1996 Paralympic Games — with Christopher Reeve being a star attraction — and 57,640 attended the closing ceremony. Although the Greeks supported the 2004 Paralympic Games and the stadium was relatively full for the opening, it was only about 80 per cent full for the closing ceremony. This may have been due to the fact that the event had been cancelled and then reinstated because of a tragic bus crash.

Table 10.1 Some quantitative comparisons between Paralympic Games staged between 1988 and 2004.

	Athletes	Number of nations	Number of sports	Tickets sold	Television rights fees	Accredited media
1988 Seoul	3053	62	17	nil		1672
1992 Barcelona	3020	82	15	nil		1499
1996 Atlanta	3310	103	17	388,373	$500,000	2088
2000 Sydney	3843	122	18	1,160,000	$4,200,000	2440
2004 Athens	3837	136	19	800,000		3000

Disability scholars, by contrast, have been critical of the status of the Paralympic Games as a parallel event to the Olympics. Goggin and Newell, in their article 'Crippling Paralympics?', published a month after the Sydney 2000 Paralympic Games, claimed that the relationship between the two festivals was unequal. They claimed that disability had been relegated to the margins of the Olympic event and that the 'Paralympics and disability were nearly completely invisible in the Opening Ceremony [of the Olympic Games] and the tumultuous final Sydney stages of the torch relay'.[11] Goggin and Newell added that at the time of the Paralympic Games, the mainstream media recycled stereotypes of disabled athletes which are linked with the oppression of people with a disability in society. They added that too often the mainstream media depicted Paralympic athletes as '"supercrips" in sexy chairs (that is exceptional people with disabilities surmounting the impossible), or people with acquired rather than developmental disability'. Reeve's presence at the Atlanta opening ceremony added unwittingly to the 'supercrip' stereotype.[12]

Reflecting on the Sydney Paralympic Games in 2005, Darcy

acknowledged that they were 'exceptional' and an undoubted success as a multi-sport event. He added that 'the experience was the first time that many people with disabilities could share a common experience whether as spectators, volunteers, employees or participants'. However, he reported that 'there was pessimism within the disability community about the lasting legacy of the Paralympics' and there was cynicism about 'the number of politicians willing to support the Paralympics but normally unwilling to discuss disability issues'.[13]

However, Greg Hartung, president of the Australian Paralympic Committee (APC), contested Darcy's view and took a more optimistic view about outcomes, because he regarded the Paralympic Games primarily as a sports event. Hartung pointed to an improved environment for Paralympic athletes after 2000. He noted that there was a post-Games dinner at Canberra that attracted 70 parliamentarians and added that there was continuing government and private funding for Paralympic sport beyond 2000 (see below). There was also a continuing acceptance of Paralympian athletes by the Australian sports community, with 54 athletes gaining part-time scholarships at the Australian Institute of Sport. Although the value of such scholarships was small, with each around $1000, they constituted recognition of the value of Paralympic sport. Hartung also noted that the Australian Paralympic team had become more cohesive. Before 1990, the Australian Paralympic team amounted to a collection of separate disability groups under one flag, whereas they now have become more of a team being organised according to sport.

Despite some differing opinions about these issues, certainly it is clear that the first challenge detailed above — staging a successful Games — was met.

Organising the Games

It was not difficult for the Sydney Paralympic Games to better the Atlanta Paralympic Games because the organisation of the previous Games had obvious deficiencies and had been flawed from the start. Australian Paralympian basketball captain, Donna Ritchie, described the initial shambles that occurred:

> We got off that plane in Atlanta, there were no decorations.
> We went to Centennial Park which I was looking so forward

> to seeing. It was rubble; they had knocked it down … Atlanta
> was not ready for the Paralympic Games; the village was not
> ready; the venues were not ready …[14]

The problem for Atlanta was that the Olympic and Paralympic organising committees were quite separate and there was no relationship between the two. This resulted in a number of serious problems in the transition from one festival to another.

The Sydney Games organisers learnt from the mistakes of the Atlanta Paralympic Games in the same way that Sydney's Olympic organisers were determined not to repeat the mistakes of the Atlanta Olympic Games. The most important result was that SOCOG and SPOC, from their inception, had a good working relationship. There was also close coordination with the other Games-related organisations, OCA and ORTA. These were key reasons for the operational success of the Paralympic Games, as Simon Darcy noted:

> This allowed [for Paralympic] accommodation, venue
> management, sports competition, volunteers, medical, security,
> arts festival and marketing to be delivered by SOCOG. Two
> other organisations [which played key roles in the delivery of
> the Olympic Games] were integral to the operational success of
> the Sydney 2000 [Paralympic] Games. ORTA was responsible
> for public transport arrangements and OCA was responsible
> for the design, planning, development and operation of
> venues. Generally, OCA processes delivered an accessible
> Games experience through the planning, design, development
> and operations of venue precinct. Importantly the planning
> processes were designed to incorporate people with disabilities
> and disability organisations through the establishment of the
> Olympic Access Advisory Committee. The Committee was
> an essential part of the access planning process established in
> conjunction with the OCA *Access Guidelines*.[15]

Such organisation produced two important outcomes. First of all, the Sydney model of close liaison and a constructive operating relationship between the two committees appealed to the IOC, which advanced this idea to propose one organising committee for both Games (see below).

Secondly, Sydney delivered positive outcomes both for transport and access to Paralympic venues. It was clear that this cooperation yielded positive outcomes.

Infrastructure

Simon Darcy and Jane Woodruff have documented in a number of articles that the planning processes, largely delivered by OCA, 'delivered an accessible Games experience through the planning, design, development and operations of the venue precincts'.[16] This occurred because people with disability and disability organisations were included in the planning process and played a role in the Olympic Access Advisory Committee and in devising of OCA's Access Guidelines. The planning processes were evaluated and refined after an extensive number of test events. Even during the Games, OCA responded promptly to complaints that were made through the Olympic and Paralympic Disability Advocacy Service (OPDAS).[17] Another reason why OCA dealt with disability issues with some sensitivity was that David Richmond, its director, and Jane Woodruff, manager of co-ordination, both had a deep understanding of such issues because of past disability-related positions with the NSW Government. Richmond had been a senior public servant in health and was the author of the 1983 Richmond Report, which outlined new policies for the delivery of mental health services.

ORTA, and existing transport organisations such as the State Transit Authority (STA), had also demonstrated an increased sensitivity to the needs of the disabled population in the lead-up to the Games. After a complaint made to Human Rights and Equal Opportunity Commission (HREOC) in 1995, the STA had increasingly purchased low-floor busses, which have easier disabled access. The railway station at Sydney Olympic Park has excellent disability access provisions.

Woodruff outlined what she regarded as the strengths of the infrastructure process. Firstly, many different stakeholders worked in partnership so that expertise and knowledge was shared. Secondly, the disabled users of the infrastructure were 'directly involved in the decision making' and provided advice. As a result, designers and project managers were educated 'through direct control with people with disabilities'.[18]

However, the improved access at Sydney Olympic Park was only so good as the city and suburban network which fed into it. Access to

Disability scholar Simon Darcy enters a low-floor bus at Sydney Olympic Park (Simon Darcy).

Sydney Olympic Park contrasted with what was available in the existing public transport system which disabled people had to use to reach the Park. One problem was that only 5 per cent of railway stations were 'Easy Access' stations in 2000. Another problem was that while the publicly run STA attempted to increase the number of low-floor buses, private bus operators were reluctant to follow suit.

Darcy has also pointed out that there was also a radical contrast between the attitude of OCA and SOCOG to disability issues. He contended that SOCOG was 'deliberately obstructive in their process for dealing with disability and access issues' leading to a 'marginalising of disability and access issues'. Darcy noted that a number of complaint cases were made against SOCOG, relating to ticketing, information and transport issues, under the *Disability Discrimination Act 1992*. The most celebrated complaint was made by blind man, Bruce Maguire, who was unable to access SOCOG's official website and the Games ticket book because they were not available in an alternative format — in Maguire's case in braille. Despite orders in favour of Maguire by HREOC and the Federal Court, SOCOG refused to comply and manipulated the legal system to avoid compliance until after the Games were over.[19] Darcy believed that this occurred because of the pressure of planning the Games, the organisational culture of SOCOG and its sunset clause, and a lack of internal disability and access expertise.

Despite this, the executive officer of the Disability Council of NSW believed that the Paralympic Games had speeded up improvements in access infrastructure. He stated that:

> It is my belief that Sydney in particular has benefited from the Olympics by way of infrastructure … The society may have got there eventually but it would be a long time before it happened without the Olympics.[20]

Darcy added there were several other positive transport outcomes for people with a disability. Professionals were involved in the planning of venues, common domains, transport and future large events had developed useful knowledge of what was involved in an 'inclusive planning process'. There was also the development of an 'on-line access resource for planning accessible environments and events'.[21]

Darcy has argued that changes in disability access at the time of the Games — as welcome as they were — were not primarily a result of the Games. They built on, and speeded up, the previous efforts to improve disability services and infrastructure. Disability groups used the Games to consult, lobby and advocate better access conditions.

Financial and athlete outcomes

Compared to Olympic Games budget of approximately $3.5 billion, the income and expenditure for the Paralympic Games was exceedingly modest — about 5 per cent of the Olympic budget (see Chapter 4) — demonstrating the lesser status of the twin event. Almost half the revenue of $186.8 million came from government grants, and SOCOG funding though ticket sales and entry fees contributed significantly. However, sponsorship, contributing only about a quarter of revenue from television rights, was a miniscule part of the funding. Table 10.2 provides a detailed look at the funding sources. Table 10.3 shows the expenditure. As can be seen, the principal items of expenditure were Games operations, technology, and revenue generation.

The Australian Paralympic team marched in similar colours and uniforms to the Australian Olympic team and were warmly applauded by the Australian public (Simon Darcy).

Table 10.2 Revenue streams (*PPGR*)

Category	Amount
Government grants	$72.2 million
Sponsorship	$45.9 million
Ticket sale/entry fees	$32 million
SOCOG funding	$17.9 million
TV rights	$4.1 million
Other categories	$14.7 million
TOTAL	$186.8 million

Table 10.3 Expenditure (*PPGR*)

Category	Amount
Games Operations	$30.2 million
Technology	$24.5 million
Revenue Generation	$23.5 million
Administration	$15.4 million
Paralympic Village	$14.8 million
Sport	$9.5 million
Other Categories	$37.7 million
TOTAL	$155.6 million

The Games produced a surplus of $31.2 million, though these figures do not include infrastructure costs, which were borne by OCA and effectively by the NSW Government.

It is astonishing to note that while the substantial costs of the Olympic Games were underwritten by the state government — so that the taxpayers would cover any shortfall — this was not the case with the Paralympic Games. If the Games had run at a deficit, the Paralympic directors would have been responsible for the debt.[22]

The Sydney Paralympic Games were also treated differently from the Olympic Games in that international Paralympic teams had to pay entry fees, amounting in total to about $8 million, which basically covered the costs of accommodation and meals in the village. By contrast, the fees for international athletes were waived for the Olympic Games as well as their travel costs to Australia. The federal government, however, was persuaded to pay the entry costs of $500,000 for the Australian Paralympic team after significant negative media coverage about the relative inequity in government funding for the Olympic and Paralympic athletes.[23] This situation had changed by the time of the Athens 2004 Paralympic Games when, for the first time, competing countries were not charged entry fees. This provided further evidence of the improving status of the Paralympic Games.

Hartung contended in October 2000 that $30 million was required over the next four years 'just to maintain standards' in Paralympic sport.[24] He noted in 2005 that the public and private sectors had more than met these targets and that after the 2004 Athens Paralympic Games the federal government had committed the sizeable sum of $22 million, which was an increase from $14.5 million, for the preparations for the Beijing Paralympic Games.[25] As a result, Australia will be able to field a strong Paralympic team in 2008.

Grants to the Australian Paralympic Committee, from the Australian Sports Commission more than doubled between 1996–97 and 2003–04, continuing to increase after the staging of the Sydney Paralympic Games.

Unlike the Olympians there was no war chest for Paralympian athletes for the next Paralympic Games. While the Australian Olympic team more than maintained the size of its team in comparison with other national teams at Athens in 2004, the Australian Paralympic team was reduced from 278 to 144. However, this reduction was not simply a cost-cutting exercise. With some of the leading Australian Paralympians retiring in 2000 and with the reduction of the team because of the scrapping of the intellectually disabled category — which produced about 20 per cent of the Australian medals in 2000 — the Australian Paralympic team entered a rebuilding phase after 2000.

Table 10.4 Paralympic grants received from the Australian Sports Commission (ASC *Annual Reports*)

Year	Grant
1996–97	$1,850,000
1997–98	$ 995,000
1998–99	$1,975,000
1999–00	$2,239,500
2000–01	$2,090,000
2001–02	$3,080,000
2002–03	$3,500,000
2003–04	$3,800,000

Nevertheless, Australia performed well at Athens, finishing second in the unofficial medal table in the number of medals won. Although Australia finished fifth in the gold medal tally, only one gold medal separated third and fourth and another gold medal separated fourth and fifth. The Australian success at Athens was even more surprising given that by 2004 there were an increasing number of countries investing significant amounts of money and technical expertise to gain Paralympic success including China, Great Britain and Canada. Table 10.5 compares the medal tally for the top ten nations over two Games.

Table 10.5 Top ten nations in the unofficial medal table at the Atlanta 1996 Paralympic Games and their performance in the 2000 and 2004 Paralympic Games.

(Note that the place on the ladder is determined by the number of gold medals and not the total of medals).

	1996 gold-silver-bronze (total) medals achieved place on ladder	2000 gold-silver-bronze (total) medals achieved place on ladder	2004 gold-silver-bronze (total) medals achieved place on ladder
USA	46-46-65 (157) 1st	36-39-34 (109) 5th	27-22-39 (88) 4th
Australia	43-37-27 (107) 2nd	63-39-47 (149) 1st	26-38-36 (100) 5th
Germany	40-58-51 (149) 3rd	15-42-38 (95) 10th	19-28-32 (79) 8th
Great Britain	39-42-41 (122) 4th	41-43-47 (131) 2nd	35-30-29 (94) 2nd
Spain	39-31-36 (106) 5th	39-30-38 (107) 3rd	20-27-24 (71) 7th
France	35-29-31 (95) 6th	30-28-28 (86) 7th	18-26-30 (74) 9th
Canada	24-21-24 (69) 7th	38-33-25 (96) 4th	28-19-25 (72) 3rd
Netherlands	17-11-17 (45) 8th	NA	5-11-12 (28) 27th
China	16-13-10 (39) 9th	34-22-16 (72) 6th	63-46-32 (141) 1st
Japan	14-10-12 (36) 10th	NA	17-15-20 (52) 10th

NA Not applicable as did not finish in the top 10.

Media coverage

While the international media paid a record figure for the media rights to cover the Sydney 2000 Olympic Games — the figure paid by NBC for instance jumped from $US456 million in 1996 to $US705 million in 2000 — the Paralympic Games struggled to achieve significant media interest and it appeared that SPOC faced the prospect of paying the media to televise the Games, which had occurred at Atlanta. Channel 7, which held the Australian rights to Olympic Games television coverage, only expressed lukewarm interest in broadcasting the Paralympic Games and in one proposal requested the Paralympics to underwrite them to the amount of $3 million in case there was a shortfall in advertising revenue.[26]

However, the final outcome was that, compared to previous Paralympic Games, where television coverage was minimal, there were significant advances in the national and international television and web coverage at Sydney Paralympic Games. Whereas the opening ceremony was broadcast live in only one country, Germany, in 1996, seven countries broadcast the entire ceremony in 2000. The amount for the Paralympic television rights secured at Atlanta of $500,000 jumped to $4.1 million at Sydney.

When Channel 7 declined to broadcast the Paralympic Games, the Australian Broadcasting Corporation (ABC), which had provided some Paralympic television coverage in 1992 and 1996, came to the rescue. In March 2000 the ABC announced that it would televise the opening and closing ceremonies with a daily segment of highlights of one hour at 5.30 pm which was repeated, with updates, for another hour from 11.30 pm. The Seven network agreed to broadcast a daily one-hour package of highlights on its pay television network, C7 — however less than 15 per cent of the population subscribed to C7.

The ABC was agreeably astonished — and presumably Channel 7 was surprised — by a record ABC audience for opening ceremony which exceeded all expectations. It was watched by 4.2 million Australians and it achieved a peak rating of 49.2 per cent in Sydney — an unprecedented audience for the ABC and its highest ever audience.[27] The public interest persisted throughout the Games with the daily highlights package achieving respectable ratings of over 10 (for the 5.30-6.30 pm slot) and over 5 for the later time, surprisingly, given that these were non-peak times. Such was the public interest that the initial time slot was increased by 30 minutes from the third day of the Games.[28]

The prospect of a good audience for the closing ceremony encouraged the ABC to give the Paralympics priority over the popular series *SeaChange* and *Second Sight*. Although the Sydney audience was about 60 per cent of the size of that for the opening ceremony, it was impressive nonetheless.

The daily program was anchored by a popular presenter, Karen Tighe, who as a member of APC had an empathy for Paralympic sport and was positive about its value. Although broadcasters struggled with limited information about a host of matters — athlete biographies, past performances, records and even the timing of events — Tighe attempted to educate the audience about the nature of Paralympic sport and its complex classification system.

An even more serious problem for Paralymic television was the small amount of live footage. While the Sydney Olympic Broadcasting Organisation produced hundreds of hours of footage and included multi-camera coverage of every event — providing a smorgasbord from which national broadcasters could freely pick and choose their preferred footage — the Paralympics had multi-camera coverage for only two sports, athletics and cycling, and for the finals of only three other sports, basketball, swimming and tennis. A dearth of live footage was one reason why the ABC decided initially to show only several hours of Paralympic television each day.[29] Global-All Media Sports, which sold and transmitted Paralympic coverage around the world, signed up 100 countries, so the international television coverage easily surpassed Barcelona in 1992 and Atlanta in 1996.

Although the Paralympic media coverage in 2000 was dramatically less than the blanket Olympic media broadcasting in Australia and internationally, it represented a great advance on the level of coverage at Atlanta. None of the major (commercial) North American broadcasters were prepared to cover the Paralympic Games, and Paralympic officials had no choice but to purchase four hours of CBS time to show the Games. However, they had little control over what was broadcast because they had no editorial rights. CBS determined what would be shown and chose the commentators.[30]

Webcasting was a significant innovation at the Sydney Paralympic

Common domains, such as this one, provided space for people to gather during both Games (Simon Darcy).

Games which appeared set to revolutionise their international media coverage. In 2000 the New York-based company WeMedia appeared to be the shining knight to help the Paralympics to benefit from new technology. WeMedia had begun as a glossy lifestyle magazine in 1997 featuring 'cross-disability issues' targeting the 54 million Americans with disabilities.

The company experienced such a rapid rise in sales that by June 2000 it launched WeMedia Sports. Rick Gentle, the former producer of three Olympic Games for CBS Sports, became its executive producer. In 2000 WeMedia was a significant presence at the Paralympic Games, with 300 staff occupying eight separate rooms in the press and broadcast centres. In addition to its webcasting WeMedia owned the television rights for the Paralympic Games, which were shown on Foxsportsnet and Pay TV.[31]

WeMedia provided 100 hours of live webcasts during the Sydney Paralympics — about 10 hours per day — that included 'live streaming video, real-time audio, and "extensive" coverage of the entire event'.[32] The coverage was provided by We Media Inc., a division of WeSports, an online sports network for people with disabilities. The webcasting proved immensely popular, with a creditable audience of 8000 for the opening ceremony and web traffic reported to be doubling every day.[33]

The IPC was in a unique position to profit from the latest technology because the Paralympics are exempt from the IOC ban on moving pictures (of the Games) on the web. The IOC, by contrast, is reluctant to make use of the internet because of the opposition of television interests, which provide massive funds for the staging of the Olympic Games.

The IPC signed a 'multi-million-dollar deal' with WeMedia before the end of the Games for worldwide television broadcast and internet webcast rights for the next six years, including the next three Paralympic Games.[34] Steadward stated that it would boost the 'profile, credibility and visibility' of the Paralympics.[35] It promised to be the biggest outcome of the Sydney Paralympic Games. Unfortunately WeMedia was a casualty to the dot.com crisis and collapsed in 2001.[36]

The public response to the Games

By any reckoning, the support of the Sydney Paralympic Games was impressive. The number of spectators exceeded Atlanta by approximately 300 per cent and were almost 50 per cent more than Athens. The ABC was agreeably surprised by the public interest in its broadcasts and increased its coverage during the Games (see above). At the end of the Games the Paralympians, like the Olympians, were accorded the honour of a tickertape parade and civic reception in Sydney, which was repeated in the other capital cities.

Public support in 2000 undoubtedly contributed to the exceptional performance of the Australian team, which headed the medal table with a final medal tally of 63 gold, 39 silver and 47 bronze, after it had finished second to the USA at Atlanta in 1996. One reason for the success of the Australian team was the integration of Paralympic athletes into the Australian sports system. Fifty-four athletes in the Australian Paralympic team were current or former scholarship holders at the Australian Institute of Sport enabling Paralympic athletes access to a professional sports system and infrastructure. This elite group of 54 secured 62 per cent of the gold medals and 56 per cent of the overall medals.[37]

Darcy identified some of the reasons why there was so much public support for the Games. The Paralympic Games followed a successful

Olympic Games 'with its party atmosphere' and its 'psychic benefits'. The second largest sporting festival ever staged in Australia occurred just weeks after the Olympics enabling Sydneysiders and Australians to once again soak up the atmosphere of Sydney Olympic Park. It was another occasion for Australians to indulge in their passion for sport.

Darcy believed that two groups of people, who had not supported the Olympic Games, joined the 'Paralympic party'. First of all, there were those who had left the city for the duration of the Olympic Games, fearing that those who remained in the city would suffer from overcrowding, increased costs and other inconveniences, though none of these actually occurred. Secondly, 'there were those who supported the Paralympics as it was not perceived as a corporatised event'.[38] It appeared to many that Paralympians more so than the Olympians were more in tune with the ideals of de Coubertin of the joy of sport and participation.

SPOC also cleverly targeted school children and seniors in its *Reaching the Community Program*. Approximately 360,000 of the 1,160,000 spectators — over 30 per cent — were part of school and other organised groups. Another successful innovation that boosted numbers was the $15 *Day Pass Ticket*, which enabled the holder to attend multiple events on one day at an affordable price. Given that many spectators were not familiar with most Paralympic sports, it represented a shrewd marketing exercise to provide the audience with a taste of a number of sports.

Improved disability awareness?

Writing at the end of the Games, Australian Paralympian swimmer and captain, Priya Cooper believed that 'the Paralympics have transformed Australia's perception of people with disabilities' and added that this was a legacy that 'must be nurtured'. She added that the Games also left 'an everlasting social legacy' for a 'generation of schoolchildren who witnessed first-hand the Games and athletes of all nations will grow up appreciating our sporting skills and be more accepting of all people with disabilities'.[39]

Journalist Adele Horin believed that the Paralympics had 'raised the nation's consciousness' and was a 'positive and possibly life-changing experience for many Australians'. Many myths about disabled athletes were shattered in the process:

> If you saw the wheelchair rugby and basketball teams at the
> Paralympics, you would know people with disabilities are
> not always polite. Some are downright nasty, and others can
> be tough, aggressive, single-minded and focused on winning
> — like any top athlete … Gorgeous, articulate and fiercely
> competitive athletes banished pity from our minds.[40]

The public also learned from the media discourse that Paralympians
did not want to be regarded as courageous or brave — or referred to
as 'bravehearts' as did Tim Fischer, mayor of the Paralympic Village.
Jim O'Brien, chief executive of the NSW Wheelchair Sports, stated that
continuing reference to 'overcoming adversity … irked athletes'. He
added those who were born with a birth disability know 'no other state'
and would 'never consider themselves brave'. Paralympians, O'Brien
argued, 'want recognition more so than sympathy'.[41] Such debate allowed
Paralympic voices to be heard in the media.

Horin added that the athletes on display were 'special' and mostly
'moderately disabled' — who represented the 'glamorous' and 'gorgeous'
face of disability. There was another 'unpretty world of disabilities':

> It is the world of profound intellectual and mental disability.
> And here, families are drowning for lack of help, support and
> options. Their lives are unglamorous to the extreme; there's no
> time for sport, the pressures are unrelenting. A gold medal day
> is when a youngster feeds himself.[42]

Horin implied that the applause for glamorous athletes did not translate into a
broader understanding of the needs of the disability community as a whole.

Darcy reported that there was some anecdotal evidence that there
was a changed attitude, at least in the short term, by schoolchildren
and adults including volunteers — who underwent disability awareness
training — to people with disabilities. He added that 'unfortunately no
research was conducted to test this hypothesis [of changed attitudes
towards disability] before, during or after the Paralympics'.[43]

There is also the problem that a positive feeling to the 'supercrip'
athlete may not translate to the disability community. Meekosha has
argued that a fascination with the technology of performance, such as
the use of protheses and racing wheelchairs, can be interpreted that it
is the technology rather than the athlete that is the 'performer'. She has

referred to this fascination with technology, which devalues athletic performance, as the 'Cyborgs' of disability.[44] (The cyborg concept of a man-machine mixture had long been popular in science fiction but achieved practical realisation in the twentieth century when new human-technology applications played an important role in advancing Paralympic sport). After the Paralympic Games there were stories about how school-aged children urged their parents to buy them a wheelchair, because they thought wheelchair basketball was a cool sport.

Stephanie Peatling, in an article published in the *Sydney Morning Herald* on 16 October 2000 under the title 'Hot seats', provided an example of this fascination with the technology employed in Paralympic sport — which was state-of-the-art and expensive. Competition wheelchairs were 'highly technical pieces of equipment' with price tags of up to $10,000. Wheel quality was critical to success; a number of European companies make carbon-fibre disc wheels, which cost $2000 to $3000 a pair. Each sport had developed appropriate technology. Tennis wheelchairs have one wheel at the front, another at the back and two at the side to allow greater mobility. Peatling added that 'teams will have technicians on standby to attend to repairs and two mobile maintenance units, with about 50 staff, at the athletes' village'. She thus equated Paralympic sport with the glamour of Formula 1 motor racing, perhaps detracting from individual athletic performance.

The 2004 Athens Paralympic Games

The staging of the 2004 Games was a test for the Paralympic movement because Paralympic sport is less developed in Greece than Australia, the United States and Spain, the hosts of the three previous Paralympic Games. Whereas the Australian Paralympic team finished second in 1996 and first in 2000 in the unofficial medal table, Greece had finished a lowly 46th in 1996 (with one gold, one silver and three bronze medals) and 32nd in 2000 (with four gold, four silver and three bronze medals). It was reported at the time of the Sydney Paralympic Games that negotiations over the Athens Paralympic Games had 'all but broken down' with the IPC issuing a threat that it would not hand over the flag at the closing ceremony because a host city contract had yet to be signed. Fortunately such a contract was signed in 2001 — just three years before the Games.[45] The equivalent contract in Sydney was in place five years before the Games.

The staging of the 2004 Paralympic Games provided a litmus test as to whether any of the advances achieved in 2000 carried on to the next Games. Despite the exclusion of athletes from one of the six categories of disability — the intellectually disabled (see below) — the figures listed in Table 10.1 (above) indicated that Athens bettered Sydney in terms of the number of media, countries represented and sports. Although the number of spectators at Athens were considerably less than Sydney, they were more than double the figure of Atlanta. This was an impressive result, given that the Greeks achieved a modest number of medals, finishing 34th with three gold, 13 silver and four bronze medals.

The post-Games 'scandal' involving intellectually disabled athletes

One reason for the greater number of athletes at the Sydney 2000 Paralympic Games was that there were more events in four sports for intellectually disabled athletes: 244 athletes from 29 countries participated in basketball, swimming, table tennis and track and field — approximately 6 per cent to the total. After this sixth disability category had been recognised by the IPC in 1992, when parallel competitions had been staged at Madrid at the time of Paralympic Games in Barcelona in 1992, a small program of four events for intellectually disabled athletes was introduced at the Atlanta Paralympic Games. The cause of the intellectually disabled was championed by the president of the IPC Dr Robert Steadward, who ensured that there would be greater representation of all disability categories, including this one.[46]

Athletes in this disability category earned a significant proportion of the 63 gold medals won by the Australian team and two of Australia's star performers, who gained wide media coverage, came from this category. Seventeen-year-old Siobhan Paton won six gold medals in her seven events in the S14 category in swimming. Paton broke 10 Paralympic and eight world records to achieve the best result of an Australian athlete at a Paralympic Games. Paton was the AIS Junior Athlete of the Year in 2000 and won the APC award for the Paralympian of the Year. Lisa Llorens was the other athlete from this category who gained three gold medals in track and field. Laurens, who fancied that she moved like a cheetah, was another personality who attracted media interest. The only other Australian Paralympian to gain three gold medals was Tim Sullivan, a sprinter in the T38 (cerebral palsy) category.

Less than a month after the completion of the Paralympic Games, Carlos Ribagorda revealed in the Spanish magazine, *Capital,* on 21 November 2000, that he and other members of Spain's gold-medal winning men's basketball team were not intellectually handicapped. After a Spanish Paralympic Committee enquiry found that 10 of the 12 members were not eligible to compete, the IPC launched an investigation which raised serious questions about the administration of the eligibility criteria by the governing body, the International Sports Federation for Persons with Intellectual Disability (INAS-FID). It found that only about one-third of the competitors' forms had been properly completed. To deal with this blatant cheating and slackness in enforcing proper eligibility rules, the IPC took the drastic step of excluding intellectually disabled athletes from future Paralympics.[47] It also suspended the governing body, INAS-FID.

Anne and Ian Jobling believe that this decision was both unfair and unjust. They quoted an editorial in the *Courier Mail* of 1 February 2001 that this was an 'ill considered decision' and 'because of the corrupt actions of a few an entire category of Paralympians have been eliminated'. They note that the sport of powerlifting was treated differently. While Atlanta had no positive doping tests and Barcelona had just three, 11 athletes were expelled from the Sydney Paralympics of whom 10 were powerlifters. While the ten powerlifters received harsh individual penalties of three to four years the sport continued on the program.[48]

The Joblings believe that discrimination against intellectually disabled athletes occurred because some in the Paralympian movement were already uncomfortable with their inclusion. David Naylor pointed out in Toronto's *Globe and Mail* of 1 February 2001 that 'whereas with physical disabilities you can quantify a disability, with intellectual disabilities you can't … ' Dr Michael Riding, who as Medical Officer of the IPC oversaw the operation of the Paralympic classification system, questioned whether it was possible to 'certify' intellectual disability and added that 'unless you have a certified disability you shouldn't go to the Paralympics'.[49] However, the 2001 scandal related not to the certification of intellectual disability but the administration of the eligibility criteria.

While the Australian team was cleared of any improprieties, a significant number of Australian Paralympic athletes suffered from this blanket ban. The international careers of Siobhan Paton and Lisa Laurens effectively ended because they were unable to participate in the most prestigious sporting festival, the Paralympic Games. Interviewed on the ABC on 30 January 2001 Paton pleaded 'I hope that they [the IPC] look into it more deeply and revise it quickly, hopefully, please … [because] swimming was my whole entire life … it's basically my career'.[50]

Closer ties between the IOC and the IPC

In the last decade the IOC and IPC have moved much closer to each other. During the closing ceremony of the 1st Paralympic Congress in 1992 IOC President Samaranch 'unequivocally expressed his encouragement and support to the Paralympic Movement'.[51] After the Sydney Olympic Games Samaranch accepted the invitation of the IPC to attend the Sydney Paralympic Games.

At the time of the Paralympic Games IOC President Samaranch and IPC President Steadward signed the Cooperative Agreement between the IOC and the IPC based on, as Steadward put it, the idea that the Olympic and Paralympic family 'share a common vision of elite sport' and 'believe in international solidarity'. The agreement proposed IPC representation in IOC Commissions such as Evaluation for the Olympic Games, Coordination for the Olympic Games, Culture and Olympic Education, Athletes, Women and Sport Working Group and Radio and Television. The agreement also included the principle that the IPC president be co-opted as a member of the IOC.

President Samaranch confirmed his commitment to the linking of twin festivals stating that:

> staging the Paralympic Games shortly after the Olympic Games
> at the same venue has proven to be a successful arrangement
> in the past, which should be maintained in the future. The
> IOC will support the Paralympic movement in various ways in
> the coming years, including financial assistance.[52]

A second agreement was signed between the IOC and IPC in June 2001 which created greater synergies between the two organisations. The second agreement proposed the important and radical step of having just one organising committee for both Games — although this will not come until effect until Beijing in 2008 and Vancouver in 2010. However, the organising committees of Salt Lake City (2002), Athens (2004) and Turin (2006) were sufficiently impressed with this idea and formed one rather than two organising committees.[53] Thus the close liaison between SOCOG and SPOC leading up to 2000 was taken a step further achieving a positive outcome for the organisation of future Paralympic Games.

An amendment to the 19 June 2001 agreement between the IOC and the IPC was signed on 25 August 2003 by new presidents of IOC and the IPC, Jacques Rogge and Phil Craven. The agreement transferred the broadcasting and marketing responsibilities for the 2008, 2010 and 2012 Paralympic Games to the organising committees and, in return, stipulated that the IPC would receive $US9 million from the IOC for the 2008 Games, $US14 million for the 2010 and 2012 Games. Craven stated that 'the amendment lays an excellent foundation for the IPC's quest to fully develop the Paralympic Movement'. Rogge stated that 'the IOC is happy to support the IPC for these forthcoming editions of the Paralympic Games and, in so doing, to strengthen its relations with the Paralympic Movement'.[54]

Conclusions

Do the Paralympic Games have the potential to extend Olympism, as Fernand Landry suggested? Given the increasingly close relationship between the twin festivals it is likely that the Paralympic Games will extend the notion of what constitutes performance and even what constitutes sport. The Paralympic Games raise new questions about the complexity of individual sport and the criteria by which it should be measured. The *Olympic Charter* advocates that all persons have the right to participate in sport and that non-discrimination should be a part of sports practice. The Paralympic Games extends such accessibility and furthers non-discrimination.

There are many interesting questions to pose about the parallel events. Where will agreements between the IOC and the IPC lead in the future? Will it result in an alternative and more inclusive scenario

— which has not found favour with the IOC or the IPC — in which Paralympic sport will be included in the Olympic program?

The Sydney Paralympic Games created new benchmarks for the Paralympic Games. There were significant advances over previous Paralympic Games in both the quantity and the quality of the Sydney Paralympic Games. The Paralympians gained greater public recognition and media coverage than ever before. The closer link between SOCOG and SPOC pointed the way to greater cooperation between the Olympic and Paralympic movements and led to a succession of agreements between the IOC and the IPC which shored up the future of the Paralympic Games. The gap has narrowed between the twin festivals since 2000. The entry fees of international teams were waived for the Athens Paralympic Games. Beijing will provide an additional bonus in 2008 in that the city will pay the airfares of all international Paralympic teams.[55]

The Spanish scandal in 2001 took some of the gloss off the Sydney Paralympic Games, reminding the public that the Olympic Games have no monopoly on cheating. The summary dismissal of one of the six disability categories after such a short test run suggest that there is still some uncertainty about the what the Paralympics should be: whether they should be a sports spectacular or a festival which features the widest range of disability categories. The collapse of WeMedia in 2001 also brought to an end a promising experiment in webcasting.

While the Paralympic Games (and the Olympic Games) can and did change the operation of sport, it is unrealistic to expect that sporting festivals to change broader social public attitudes and to improve the lot of the disabled community as a whole. However, there were some significant changes in disability and access provisions before the Games commenced.

With the closer relationship between the two festivals, there is a strong case for the OGGI project to add some Paralympic indicators. This will assist with the transfer of knowledge for Paralympic Games as well as the Olympic Games, and will enable the Paralympic Games to be better organised and to be run more professionally.

Chapter 11

A Continuing Legacy

It is usually assumed that a city's legacy is planned before an Olympic Games and is implemented afterwards on a one-off basis. *The Bitter-Sweet Awakening* has suggested a contrary view: that legacy is dynamic and evolving rather than fixed. The impacts of the Sydney 2000 Olympic Games continue to resonate in 2005 as further outcomes become apparent. Some of these impacts were planned, others were more indirect and yet others represent new post-Games developments. Because of this, this study is a provisional rather than a final report of Sydney's legacy as it stands after five years.

Another finding of this book is that the assessment of legacy varies over time and according to the location of the beholder. Although Australian views of the Games were partly negative in 2001, by the time of the 2003 Rugby World Cup and the 2004 Athens Olympic Games Australians had more positive perspectives on the Games . The international perspectives of the Games, by contrast, have always been positive in that the Sydney Olympic and Paralympic Games have been and continue to be regarded as benchmark Games. Australian Olympic expertise continues to be much valued by aspiring Olympic cities as well as others that hope to stage major sporting festivals, such as the Commonwealth and Asian Games and even some world cups. The Australian Olympic caravan — occupied by those experts who were prominent in many fields before 2000 and who now serve as Olympic advisers and consultants — continues to roll on and will certainly be prominent at least until 2012.

The Bitter-Sweet Awakening demonstrates that the post-Games period is as fertile a field for research as the pre-Games period or the Games themselves. While there is a massive amount of research undertaken before and during the Games, there has been a dearth of post-Games analysis. This is surprising and regrettable because many of the interesting issues that appear before the Games continue afterwards — such as environmental, sports or tourist impacts. Olympic research agendas have been skewed and many questions raised before the Games have been left unanswered. The research agenda has therefore been incomplete.

It is puzzling why there has been such limited Australian interest in Sydney's solid and even impressive legacy achievements,. Sydney's initial post-Games years were 'bitter-sweet' — like Barcelona's — and the awakening to the realities of the post-Games world has not been easy. Sydney Olympic Park struggled in the year or two after the Games, as Chapter 6 has documented. A key reason that Sydney's legacy has not been properly acknowledged is that the Australian media gravitates towards a negative stance in its Olympic coverage. This occurred both before and after the Games. Perhaps this is a continuing manifestation of a sense of cultural inferiority or even, a fear of achieving and acknowledging excellence. Perhaps media negativity results, as Milton Cockburn suggested, from an inability to comprehend the big Olympic picture.

Sandy Hollway voiced these concerns when he lamented that Australia's post-Games achievements have not been properly recognised and documented. By capturing many continuing post Games impacts this book has attempted to rectify this neglect. A study of Olympic impacts not only provides a well-rounded report of the city's Olympic investment but is also of value for the organisers of any future Australian mega sporting event and for aspiring Olympic cities. This study will also provide new material that will add to the findings of the OGGI program.

This book has posed a number of questions. Has Sydney been tarnished by the 'winner's curse', as Evan Osborne suggested? Has the value of the Games been overstated? What has been the worth of the Games to the government, business and the community?

This close look at the post-Games environment in all its facets suggests some answers. Undoubtedly the bid and the lead-up period produced much hyperbole and overblown rhetoric about how the Games would change the city and country, advancing tourism, increasing sporting participation, improving the environment, enhancing identity and so forth. Many of these claims have been overstated and are unobtainable as well. However, contrary to what many in the media have suggested, there have been considerable ongoing benefits for government, business and the community, although some groups have benefited more than others. While there have been some opportunities missed and some additional costs and even burdens, a long-range view of Sydney's legacy suggests that the positive impacts have outweighed negative ones. It has been fortuitous for Sydney that the 2008 Olympic Games will be staged in Beijing and the 2012 in London, thereby extending the potential legacy benefits for Sydney.

The analysis in this book also makes it is clear that there is a greater need to plan for the post-Games environment and to establish institutions to develop appropriate post-Games policies. The challenge for post-Games organisations is not simply to wind down the Olympic infrastructure and to avoid additional costs, but also to access new Olympic investment opportunities. The successful Sydney-Beijing Olympic Secretariat is an example of such a constructive investment role. SBOS had the expertise and flexibility to search out and respond to new Olympic opportunities, such as those which occurred after Beijing won its bid for the Olympic Games in July 2001.

I hope that this book will encourage historians of other Olympic cities to undertake similar legacy studies. There is much interesting research to be done on comparing legacy experiences from one city to another.

There is also an ongoing need to continue to monitor Sydney's post-Games environment, and to capture further impacts. In order to do this, I will provide material for an Olympic legacy site that will be posted on the Walla Walla Press website (www.wallawallapress.com). This site will update and monitor future Olympic impacts, provide bibliographical suggestions and notes on Olympic archives and collections, thereby encouraging future research on legacy.

NOTES

(For abbreviations see p. viii)

CHAPTER 1

1   Weirick, 'Urban Design', p. 70.
2   Hiller, 'Assessing the Impact of Mega-Events', pp. 47–9.
3   Roche, *Mega-events and Modernity,* back cover.
4   For a discussion of Olympic reductionism see Moragas and Kennett, 'Olympic Cities and Communication'.
5   Preuss, *Economics of Staging the Olympics,* p. 25.
6   Gratton, 'The Media', p. 122.
7   Rogge press conference, Athens, 29 Aug. 2004 (newsdesk@athens2004.com). Transcript supplied by Patricia Eckert, Olympic Museum, IOC.
8   Rogge press conference, 29 Aug. 2004.
9   *SMH,* 7–8 Aug. 2004.
10 Channel 7 commentary, 14 Aug. 2004.
11 Reid, 'Some Say Games were Fool's Gold for Greece', *Orange County Register,* 31 Aug. 2004.
12 Quoted in Miah, OSN News Review, 14 Oct. 2004.
13 Reid, 'Some Say Games were Fool's Gold for Greece'.
14 Quoted in Miah, OSN News Review, 28 Oct. 2004,
15 Reid, 'Some Say Games were Fool's Gold for Greece'.
16 Stewart, 'The "Pro" and "Con" Cases for the 2006 Commonwealth Games', pp. 25–6.
17 Sydney Olympic Games Review Committee, Report to the Premier, p. 3.
18 Roberts and McLeod, 'The Economics of a Hallmark Event', p. 242.
19 Roche, 'Mega-events and Micro-modernisation', p. 562, quoted in Hiller, 'Assessing the Impact', p. 48.
20 Moraras and Botella, *Keys to Success.*
21 Moragas, Kennett and Puig, *Legacy of the Olympic Games,* p. 494.
22 Hiller, 'Toward a Science of Olympic Outcomes', pp. 102, 106–07.
23 Cashman, 'What is "Olympic" Legacy?', p. 33.
24 Preuss, *Economics of Staging the Olympics,* p. xiv.
25 Dubi, Hug and van Griethuysen, 'Olympic Games Management', pp. 403–13; see also Technical Manual Template, Version 1.0, IOC Department, supplied courtesy of Nuria Puig, Centre for Olympic Studies, IOC.
26 Dubi, Hug and van Griethuysen, 'Olympic Games Management', p. 405.
27 Sydney Olympics 2000 Bid Ltd, *Sydney 2000,* vol. 3, p. 33.
28 Lenskyj, *The Best Olympics Ever?*
29 Gordon, *The Time of Our Lives,* p. 91.

30   *Atlanta Journal and Constitution*, 13 July 1997.
31   Cashman, *The Myth of the Lokamanya: Tilak and Mass Politics in Maharashtra*, Uni. of California Press, Berkeley, 1975, pp. 75–97.
32   Geertz, 'Deep Play', p. 43.
33   Handelman, *Models and Mirrors*, quoted in Roche, *Mega-events and Modernity*, p. 16.
34   Cockburn, 'Is There Life after the Olympics?', p. 1.

CHAPTER 2

1   Gordon, *Time of our Lives*, p. xiii.
2   Gordon, *Time of our Lives*, p. vii.
3   *SMH*, 9 Sept. 2000.
4   *Age*, 10 Jan. 2004.
5   Interview with Sandy Hollway, 4 Aug. 2005.
6   Toohey, 'The Sydney 2000 Olympic Games', p. 10.
7   Kidd, 'The Myth of the Ancient Games', pp. 71–83.
8   See for instance, John Nauright, 'Reclaiming Old and Forgotten Heroes: Nostalgia, Rugby and Identity in New Zealand', *Sporting Traditions*, vol. 10, no. 2, May 1994, pp. 131–9.
9   Cashman, 'Australia', Brian Stoddart and Keith A.P. Sandiford, *The Imperial Game*, Manchester Uni. Press, 1998, pp. 34–54.
10   There is a good collection of nostalgic cricket paintings of the 18th century in David Frith, *Pageant of Cricket*, Macmillan, Melbourne, 1987.
11   Gordon, *Australia and the Olympic Games*, p. 224.
12   *MCC News*, Mar. 1987, no. 75.
13   Olympic cauldron text, Nov. 1999 display, AGOSOM.
14   Moragas, Moreno and Kennett, 'The Legacy of Symbols'.
15   Moragas and Kennett, 'Olympic Cities and Communication'.
16   Quoted in the *Good Weekend, SMH*, Oct. 2000.
17   Australian Associated Press, 10 Oct. 2000.
18   *Mercury*, 20 Oct. 2000.
19   Moragas, Moreno and Kennett, 'The Legacy of Symbols', p. 286.
20   Moragas, Moreno and Kennett, 'The Legacy of Symbols', p. 287.
21   Toohey, 'The Sydney 2000 Olympic Games', p. 7.
22   *SMH*, 6 Sept. 2001.
23   *SMH*, 6 Sept. 2001.
24   *Sun-Herald*, 16 Sept. 2001; *Sunday Telegraph*, 16 Sept. 2001.
25   Communication from Harry Hiller, 17 June 2005.
26   *SMH*, 9 Sept. 2001.
27   Such as Hanna, *Reconciliation and Olympism*; Cashman, *Olympic Countdown*; Cashman and Hughes, *Auburn Council* and *Mosman Council*; Thompson, *Terrorism and the 2000 Olympics*.

28 Quoted in the *Good Weekend*, *SMH*, Oct. 2000.
29 *Age, 10 Jan. 2004*.
30 Lenskyj, *The Best Olympics Ever?*, p. 131.
31 Toohey, 'The Sydney 2000 Olympic Games', p. 10.
32 Toohey and Veal, 'The Legacy of the Sydney 2000 Olympic Games'.
33 *SMH*, 24 Oct. 2004.
34 The figures for the usage of the Centre website were supplied by Petri
    O. Calderon Larjanko, Web Support Officer, Faculty of Arts and Social
    Sciences, and were located at the following sites.
    http://www.arts.unsw.edu.au/sitestats/webtrends/2001/olympic/index.html.
    http://www.arts.unsw.edu.au/sitestats/webtrends/2002/olympic/0102_
    0802/index.html.

2001

Hits Entire Site (Successful)	271,299
International Visits	53.68%
Visits of Unknown Origin	29.52%
Visits from Australia	16.78%

2002

Hits Entire Site (Successful)	657,675
International Visits	39.47%
Visits of Unknown Origin	45.45%
Visits from Australia	15.07%

35 Interview Rick Matesic, 26 Jan. 2005; see also the Sydney Olympic
    Volunteers website.
36 *PGR* (vol. 1, p. 169) stated that there were 46,967 Olympic volunteers
    however, Lynch ('Volunteers 2000', p. 85) stated that there were 40,917
    accredited Olympic volunteers and 12, 635 accredited Paralympic
    volunteers (making a total of 53,552). However, some individuals may
    have been accredited for both Games.
37 Lynch, 'Volunteers 2000'.
38 Walker and Gleeson, *The Volunteers*, p. xiii.
39 Communication from Laurie Smith, 16 Dec. 2004.
40 Communication from Laurie Smith, 16 Dec. 2004.
41 Communication from Brendan Lynch, 13 Dec. 2004.
42 *SMH*, 22-23 Jan. 2005.
43 Communication from Kevin Fewster, 30 Sept. 2005; Sydney 2000 Games
    Collection website.
44 Communication from Charles Leski, 17 Oct. 2005. See also the website of
    Charles Leski Auctions (www.leski.com.au).
45 *Advertiser*, 25 Nov. 2003.
46 The RWC-induced visitor numbers by state total of 110,250 indicate that

a majority of the 64,296 individuals attended more than one state. (DSRD, 'Review of Business and Economic Benefits', p. 32).

47   DSRD, 'Review of Business and Economic Benefits', p. 93.
48   DSRD, 'Review of Business and Economic Benefits', p. 94
49   DSRD, 'Review of Business and Economic Benefits', p. 92.
50   DSRD, 'Review of Business and Economic Benefits', pp. 38, 39, 52.
51   *Advertiser*, 25 Nov. 2003.
52   DSRD, 'Review of Business and Economic Benefits', p. 71.
53   *SMH*, 26 July 2004.
54   Toohey, 'The Sydney 2000 Olympic Games', p. 10.
55   International Olympic security conference, ATHOC 2004, quoted in Kennelly, 'Business as Usual', p. 21.
56   Moragas, Moreno and Kennett, 'The Legacy of Symbols', p. 287.
57   *SMH*, 22, 23 Aug. 2005.
58   *Australian*, 22, 23 Aug. 2005; *SMH*, 22, 23 Aug. 2005.
59   Moragas, Moreno and Kennett, 'The Legacy of Symbols', p. 288.
60   Interview with Kevin Fewster, 12 Oct. 2005.

CHAPTER 3

1   Hiller, 'Mega-Events, Urban Boosterism and Global Strategies', p. 451.
2   *SMH*, 3 Nov. 2001.
3   MacAloon, 'Olympic Ceremonies', pp. 29–31.
4   Preuss, *The Economics of Staging the Olympics*, pp. 204–5.
5   Moragas, Moreno and Kennett, 'The Legacy of Symbols', p. 279.
6   Benedict *et al*, *The Anthopology of World Fairs*, pp. 6,7, 9 quoted in Roche, *Mega-Events and Modernity*, p. 16.
7   MacAloon, *Rite, Drama, Festival, Spectacle*, quoted in Roche, *Mega-Events and Modernity*, p. 165.
8   Roche, *Mega-Events and Modernity*, p. 166.
9   *SMH*, 25 Sept. 1993.
10   *SMH*, 25 Sept. 1993.
11   Booth and Tatz, 'Swimming with the Big Boys', p. 4.
12   Birch, *Master of Ceremonies*, p. 224.
13   Birch, *Master of Ceremonies*, pp. 221–4.
14   Hermann, 'Sale of the Millennium', pp. 173–82.
15   Birch, *Master of Ceremonies*, p. 224.
16   Malouf, 'Australia's British Inheritance', p. 28.
17   Davison, 'The Imaginary Grandstand', pp 13–14.
18   Smith, ABC *Sports Factor*.
19   Quoted in World Socialist website (www.wsws.org, 22 Sept. 2000).
20   *Australian*, 19 May 2001. Some other prominent persons were Dan Potra, Rhoda Roberts, Nigel Jamieson, Peter England, Dein Perry and Eamon D'Arcy.

21 ' Media Guide, Opening Ceremony', pp. 65–6.
22 'Media Guide, Opening Ceremony', pp. 69–70.
23 Bell, 'Innocence of the Olympic Pageant'; 'Media Guide, Opening Ceremony', p. 25.
24 *PGR,* vol. 2, p. 56.
25 Bell, 'Innocence of the Olympic Pageant'.
26 *PGR,* vol. 2, p. 57.
27 Bell, 'Innocence of the Olympic Pageant'.
28 Bell, 'Innocence of the Olympic Pageant'.
29 *SMH*, 31 Mar. 2001.
30 Bell, 'Innocence of the Olympic Pageant'.
31 Moragas and Kennett, 'Olympic Cities and Communication'.
32 ATC, 'Brand Australia', 10 July 2004.
33 Magdalinski, 'Cute, Loveable Characters', pp. 83, 85.
34 Magdalinski, 'Finding Fatso'.
35 Magdalinski, 'Cute, Loveable Characters', p. 87.
36 Hiller, 'The Urban Transformation of a Landmark Event', pp. 128–34.
37 Website of *Sports Illustrated* (www.sportsillustrated.cnn.com/olympics/newa/2001/10/01/montville_mascot/).
38 Magdalinski, 'Finding Fatso'.
39 Preuss, *The Economics of Staging the Olympics*, p. 48.
40 *SMH*, 3 Nov. 2000.
41 *SMH*, 2 Oct. 2000.
42 *Australian*, 16–17 Sept. 2000.
43 Hanna, *Reconciliation in Olympism*, p. 91.
44 Quoted in Bell, 'Innocence of the Olympic Pageant'.
45 Hermann, 'Sale of the Millennium', p. 178.
46 *Sunday Life*, 12 June 2005.
47 *SMH*, 31 Mar. 2001.
48 Moragas and Kennett, 'Olympic Cities and Communication'.
49 Good, 'The Cultural Olympiad', pp. 163–4.
50 Stretton, 'Culture in the Sydney 2000 Olympic Games', p. 210.
51 Stretton, 'Culture in the Sydney 2000 Olympic Games', p. 210.
52 *PGR*, vol. 2, p. 305.
53 Meekison, 'Whose Ceremony is it Anyway?', p. 194.
54 *PGR*, vol. 2, p. 303.
55 Good, 'The Cultural Olympiad', p. 166.
56 Good, 'The Cultural Olympiad', p. 167.
57 García, Urban Regeneration and Arts Programming', p. 108.
58 Good, 'The Cultural Olympiad', p. 164.
59 García, 'Enhancing Sport Marketing', pp. 203, 214–15.
60 García, 'Enhancing Sport Marketing', pp. 205, 216.

61 Cockburn, 'Is there Life after the Olympics?'.
62 Cockburn 'Is there Life after the Olympics?'.
63 Moragas and Botella, *Keys to Success*, p. 77.

CHAPTER 4

1 IOC, *Sydney 2000 Marketing Report*, front section.
2 Payne quoted in ATC, 'Olympic Games Tourism Strategy', p. 2.
3 Communication from Ray Spurr, 11 Aug. 2005.
4 Preuss, *The Economics of Staging the Olympics*, p. 61.
5 Chalip, 'Tourism and the Olympic Games', pp. 195, 200.
6 Communication from Ray Spurr, 11 Aug. 2005.
7 PWC Report, 'Business and Economic Benefits', p. 93.
8 Chalip, 'Tourism and the Olympic Games', p. 195; Sydney 2000 Games Information website.
9 Chalip, 'Tourism and the Olympic Games', p. 204.
10 Preuss, *The Economics of Staging the Olympics*, p. 194.
11 Searle, 'The Urban Legacy of the Sydney Olympic Games', p. 125.
12 Chalip, 'Tourism and the Olympic Games', p. 195.
13 PWC Report, 'Business and Economic Benefits', p. 2.
14 *PGR*, vol. 1, pp. 274–5.
15 OCA, *The Sydney 2000 Olympic and Paralympic Games*. According to this report SOCOG's revenue   was $2832.9 million and expenditure was $2424.6 million with legacy contributions assessed at $468.1 million.
16 OCA, *The Sydney Olympic and Paralympic Games*, p. 25; *PGR*, vol. 1, pp. 274–5.
17 OCA, *The Sydney Olympic and Paralympic Games*, p. 6.
18 OCA, *The Sydney Olympic and Paralympic Games*, p. 22.
19 Prime Minister and Cabinet website.
20 Shoebridge, 'After The Games: It Is Time For The Real Gold Rush', *Business Review Weekly*, 6 Oct, 2000, p.14.
21 OCA, *The Sydney Olympic and Paralympic Games*, Appendix 1.
22 PWC Report, 'Business and Economic Benefits', p. 8.
23 PWC Report, 'Business and Economic Benefits', p. 15.
24 Morse quoted on Tourism Australia website, 23 Feb. 2001.
25 Aust. Government, Dept of Industry, Tourism and Resources, 'Australia's Tourism Industry Fact Sheet', 8 Feb. 2005.
26 Spurr, 'Tourism', pp. 155-6.
27 Chalip, 'Tourism and the Olympic Games', pp. 196–7.
28 Duran, 'The Impact of the Olympic Games on Tourism', p. 3.
29 Duran, 'The Impact of the Olympic Games on Tourism'; see also Moragas, *Keys to Success*.
30 Spurr, 'Tourism', p. 154.

31   ATC, 'Olympic Games Tourism Strategy', p. 5, ATC website.
32   PWC Report, 'Business and Economic Benefits', p. 101.
33   *Olympic Impact*, no. 1, 1996.
34   Morse, quoted in ATC, 'Olympic Games Tourism Strategy'.
35   ATC, 'Olympic Games Tourism Strategy', p. 7.
36   PWC Report, 'Business and Economic Benefits', p. 55.
37   Preuss, *The Economics of Staging the Olympics*, p. 59; ABS, 1999, 2000.
38   Lisa Southgate, 'Hotels run bad last in Games', *Australian*, 11 May 2001.
39   *Atlanta Blues* (video).
40   Preuss, *The Economics of Staging the Olympics*, p. 63.
41   *Financial Review*, 11 Apr. 2001.
42   Quoted in Spurr, 'Tourism', pp. 148–9.
43   Preuss, *The Economics of Staging the Olympics*, p. 52.
44   Morse, quoted in ATC, 'Olympic Games Tourism Strategy'.
45   Tourism Forecasting Council, *The Economic Effect*.
46   Preuss, *The Economics of Staging the Olympics*, p. 59.
47   Spurr, 'Tourism', p. 153.
48   PWC Report, 'Business and Economic Benefits', p. 105.
49   *Northern Territory News*, 24 Jan. 2003.
50   ABC, 20 Nov. 2003.
51   ABC, 13 Apr. 2005.
52   ATC, 'Olympic Games Tourism Strategy', p. 24.
53   SCVB website.
54   Chalip, 'Tourism and the Olympic Games', p. 201.
55   Duran, 'The Impact of the Olympic Games on Tourism', pp. 9–10.
56   Chalip, 'Tourism and the Olympic Games', p. 201.
57   Information provided by researchers from SVCB.
58   *SMH*, 4–5 Oct. 2003.
59   Communication from Peter Hook, Accor, 11 Oct. 2005.
60   Jones Lang LaSalle, 'The Impact of the Olympic Games' (Jones Lang LaSalle website). p. 8.
61   PWC Report, 'Business and Economic Benefits', p. 14.

CHAPTER 5

1   Jones Lang LaSalle, 'The Impact of the Olympic Games' (Jones Lang LaSalle website), p. 4.
2   Preuss, *The Economics of Staging the Olympics*, pp. 65–7.
3   PWC Report, 'Business and Economic Benefits', Executive Summary.
4   OBR, Fact Sheet, 29 June 1999.
5   PWC, 'Business and Economic Benefits', pp. 44–5.
6   PWC, 'Business and Economic Benefits', p. 67.
7   PWC, 'Business and Economic Benefits', p. 4.

8   DSRD, 'Review of Business and Economic Benefits', p. 96.
9   DSRD, 'Review of Business and Economic Benefits', p. 96.
10   *Australian,* 21 July 2005.
11   *Hansard*, NSW Legislative Council, 11 Mar. 2004, pp. 7096–7 and 17 Mar. 2004, pp. 7363–4; Media release by Mark Vaile, Minister for Trade, 16 Apr. 2004.
12   Interview with Sandy Hollway, 4 Aug. 2005.
13   Media release, 16 Apr. 2004 (http://www.trademinister.gov.au/releases/2004/a05–04.html).
14   *SMH*, 24 Oct. 2004.
15   Austrade website.
16   *Hansard*, NSW Legislative Council, 11 Mar. 2004, pp. 7096–7 and 17 Mar. 2004, pp. 7363–4.
17   DSRD, 'Review of Business and Economic Benefits', p. 96.
18   Xinhua News Agency, 17 Feb. 2004.
19   Bloomfield, *Australia's Sporting Success*, p. 211.
20   Bloomfield, *Australia's Sporting Success*, p. 212.
21   Bloomfield, *Australia's Sporting Success*, p. 213.
22   *Australian*, 21 July 2005.
23   *SMH*, 31 Mar. 2005.
24   *SMH,* 28–29 May 2005.
25   ABC *Four Corners*, 'The Road to Wembley'.
26   *Australian*, 4 Apr. 2005.
27   *Australian,* 18 July 2005.
28   Cashman and Toohey, *Contribution of the Higher Education Sector*, p. 66.
29   Toohey and Halbwirth, 'The Sydney Organising Committee'.
30   Information provided by Craig McLatchey and Melissa Kimmerly, 26 May 2005.
31   Cashman and Toohey, *Contribution of the Higher Education Sector*, p. 71.
32   Cashman and Toohey, *Contribution of the Higher Education Sector*, pp. 4, 72.
33   Cashman and Toohey, *Contribution of the Higher Education Sector*, p. 69.
34   Cashman and Toohey, *Contribution of the Higher Education Sector*, pp. 58–61.
35   PGR, Games Workforce, p. 6.
36   Cashman and Toohey, *Contribution of the Higher Education Sector*, p. 45.
37   Cashman and Toohey, *Contribution of the Higher Education Sector*, pp. 67–7.
38   Interview, Peter Holden and Helen Kebby, 5 July 2005.
39   Cashman and Toohey, *Contribution of the Higher Education Sector*, pp. 55–7.
40   *PGR*, vol. 1, p. 368.

CHAPTER 6

1   Dunn and McGuirk, 'Hallmark Events', pp. 18–32; Winchester, Kong and Dunn, *Landscapes*, p. 134.

2   Gordon, *The Time of Our lives,* p. 85.
3   Dunn and McGuirk, 'Hallmark Events', pp. 18–32.
4   Moragas and Botella, *Keys to Success,* p. 45.
5   Moragas and Botella, *Keys to Success,* p. 46.
6   Searle, 'The Urban Legacy'.
7   Weirick, 'Urban Design', pp. 74–5.
8   Weirick, 'Urban Design', pp. 75–6.
9   *PGR,* vol. 1, p. 386.
10   Aquatic Centre, *Annual Report,* 2003–04; *Park News,* issue 2, Jan. 2004.
11   Toohey and Veal, *The Olympic Games,* p. 206.
12   *PGR,* vol. 1, p. 133.
13   *PGR,* vol. 1, p. 133.
14   Gordon, *Inside the Games,* p. 84.
15   Webb, *The Collaborative Games,* p. 165.
16   Toohey and Veal, *The Olympic Games,* p. 206.
17   Sydney Olympic Park website.
18   *SMH,* 9 Sept. 2001.
19   *SMH,* 11 Aug. 2001.
20   *SMH,* 11 Aug. 2001.
21   ABC *Four Corners,* 'The Road to Wembley'.
22   *Australian,* 8 Aug. 2001.
23   *Australian Financial Review,* 22 Aug. 2001.
24   *SMH,* 11 Jan. 2001.
25   Sydney Olympic Park website, 23 July 2003.
26   OCA, *Millennium Parklands: The Growing Legacy,* (video).
27   Weirick, 'A Non Event?', p. 82.
28   *SMH,* 16, 17 Mar. 2005.
29   *SMH,* 12 Apr. 2005.
30   *SMH,* 15 July 2005.
31   SOPA *Annual Report,* 2002–03, p. 8.
32   SOPA *Annual Report,* 2002–03, p. 16.
33   SOPA website.
34   *SMH,* 26 May 2004, 19-20 Feb. 2005.
35   Communication from David Humphries, manager, SuperDome. 17 Oct. 2005 and SOPA website.
36   *SMH,* 21 Aug. 2004.

CHAPTER 7

1   Cashman, *Sport in the National Imagination,* p. 173.
2   Bloomfield, *Australia's Sporting Success,* pp. 34–43.
3   Daly, *Quest for Excellence,* p. 17.
4   Vamplew, *Oxford Companion to Australian Sport,* p. 42.
5   Hogan and Norton, 'The "Price" of Olympic Gold', p. 203.

6   Hogan and Norton, 'The "Price" of Olympic Gold', p. 203.
7   Sydney Olympic Games Review Committee, Report to the Premier of New South Wales, p. 3.
8   OCA, *The Sydney Olympic and Paralympic Games*, p. 91.
9   Gordon, *The Time of our Lives*, pp. 57, 66.
10   Gordon, *The Time of our Lives*, p. 66.
11   Gordon, *The Time of our Lives*, p. 70.
12   Gordon, *The Time of our Lives*, p. 64.
13   Adjusted upward from $88.5 million in 2001 to $88.9 million in 2002.
14   Cashman and Hughes, 'Sydney 2000', pp. 216–25.
15   Bloomfield, *Australia's Sporting Success*, pp. 101–02.
16   Embrey, 'Sports for All?', p. 284.
17   Bloomfield, *Australia's Sporting Success*, p. 200.
18   Figures provided by Michael Salmon, Librarian, Amateur Athletic Foundation of Los Angeles.
19   OCA, *The Sydney Olympic and Paralympic Games*, p. 7.
20   *SMH*, 26 July 2003; *PGR*, vol. 1, p. 377; Information provided by Simonetta Lo po', Marketing Co-ordinator, Penrith Whitewater Stadium, 17 Sept. 2005.
21   *PGR*, vol. 2, p. 389.
22   *SMH*, 26 July 2004.
23   *PGR*, vol. 2, p. 388.
24   *SMH*, 26 July 2003.
25   *PGR*, vol. 1, p. 380.
26   *SMH*, 26 July 2004.
27   Frawley and Toohey, 'Shaping Sport Competition', p. 20.
28   Elphinston interview transcript.
29   Frawley and Toohey, 'Shaping Sport Competition', pp. 21–2.
30   Frawley and Toohey, 'Shaping Sport Competition', p. 23.
31   Elphinston interview transcript.
32   De Coubertin, quoted in Hai Ren, 'Olympic Games and Mass Sport Participation'.
33   Veal and Toohey, 'The Legacy of the Sydney 2000 Olympic Games'.
34   Ren, 'Olympic Games and Mass Sport Participation'; Cashman, 'The Relationship between Elite and Mass Sport', pp. 29–36.
35   Hoberman, 'Sportive Nationalism and Globalization', pp. 233–8.
36   NCCRS, *The Impact of the Olympics on Participation in Australia*; ASC, 'Impact of Hosting the Sydney 2000 Olympic and Paralympic Games'.
37   Coles, *Report of the Australian Sports Institute Study Group*, p. 14, quoted in Hogan and Norton, 'The "Price" of Olympic Gold', p. 212.
38   Bloomfield, *The Role, Scope and Direction of Recreation in Australia*.
39   NCCRS, *The Impact of the Olympics on Participation in Australia*.
40   Veal and Toohey, 'The Legacy of the Sydney 2000 Olympic Games'.
41   Hogan and Norton, 'The "Price" of Olympic Gold'.

42 Veal and Toohey, 'The Legacy of the Sydney 2000 Olympic Games'.

CHAPTER 8

1   Lenskyj, *Inside the Olympic Industry*, p. 155.
2   Preuss, *Economics of Staging the Olympics*, p. 81.
3   Quoted in Lenskyj, *Inside the Olympic Industry*, p. 165.
4   Quoted in Lenskyj, *Inside the Olympic Industry*, p. 165.
5   Prasad, 'How Green is Green Enough in 2000?', p. 6.
6   Greenpeace website.
7   Cashman and Hughes, *The Green Games*; Greenpeace website.
8   Cashman and Hughes, *The Green Games*, pp. 14–16.
9   Cashman and Hughes, *The Green Games*, p. 97.
10 Cashman and Hughes, *The Green Games*, p. 34.
11 Cashman and Hughes, *The Green Games*, pp. 96–109; Michael Knight, OCA media conference, 24 July 1997.
12 Cashman and Hughes, *The Green Games*, p. 97.
13 Cashman and Hughes, *The Green Games*, p. 107.
14 Cashman and Hughes, *The Green Games*, p. 97.
15 Cashman and Hughes, *The Green Games*, p. 99.
16 Prasad, 'How Green is Green Enough?'.
17 Reuters, 27 Oct. 1997.
18 Cashman and Hughes, *The Green Games*, p. 99.
19 SOCOC, *Our Environment* (video).
20 *PGR*, vol. 1, p. 353.
21 Prasad, 'How Green is Green Enough?'.
22 Prasad, 'Environment', p. 86.
23 Prasad, 'Environment', p. 86.
24 Greenpeace report, 15 Aug. 2000.
25 Cashman and Hughes, *The Green Games*, p. 15.
26 Reuters News, 29 Mar. 1999.
27 GGW 2000 archived website.
28 Michael Knight, OCA media conference, 24 July 1997.
29 Quadrant Research, 29 Feb. 2000, quoted in PWC Report, 'Business and Economic Benefits', p. 15.
30 Black, 'Transport', pp. 98–9.
31 Black, 'Transport', pp. 99–100; *PGR*, vol. 1, p. 158.
32 *Daily Telegraph*, 28 Nov. 1996.
33 Cashman and Hughes, *The Green Games*, p.15.
34 Green Games Watch 2000 archived website.
35 *Financial Times*, 29 May 1997.
36 Prasad, 'Environment', p. 91.
37 Green Games Watch 2000 archived website.
38 Earth Council Review, 1997, pp. 16–17.

39   GGW 2000 Newsletter 10, Spring 1999.
40   Cashman and Hughes, *The Green Games*, p. 108.
41   Lenskyj, *Inside the Olympic Industry*, p. 167.
42   Lenskyj, *Inside the Olympic Industry*, p. 162.
43   Lenskyj, *Inside the Olympic Industry*, p. 171.
44   Preuss, *Economics of Staging the Olympics*, p. 81.
45   Prasad, 'Environment', p. 92.
46   Prasad and Snow. 'The Shiny Side of Gold', p. 87; 'Examples of Successful Architectural Innovation of PV', 482.
47   ORTA, *Nothing Bigger than This*, p. 98.
48   *PGR*, vol. 1, p. 167; ORTA, *Nothing Bigger than This*, p. 91.
49   ORTA, *Nothing Bigger than This*, p. 104.
50   'Greenpeace Olympics Report card', 15 Aug. 2000.
51   'The Greenpeace Olympic Environmental Guidelines', Greenpeace website.
52   AAP, 25 Nov. 1999.
53   Formerly archived at http://www.deh,gov.au/events/greengames/whygreen.html, updated 20 June 2004.
54   BOCOG website.
55   'How Green are the Games?', Greenpeace website.
56   Weirick, 'Urban Design', p. 82.

CHAPTER 9
1   Hiller, 'Mega-Events, Urban Boosterism and Growth Strategies', p. 451.
2   Preuss, *Economics of Staging the Olympics*, pp. 22–3.
3   Lenskyj, *The Best Olympics Ever?*, p. 131.
4   Lenskyj, *The Best Olympics Ever?*, pp. 173–7.
5   Its website is archived at http://www.cat.org,au/pissoff/ at Pandora, Australia's Web Archive
6   Cashman, Richard, 'Impact of the Games on Olympic Host Cities'.
7   Communication from Bruce Kidd.
8   Lenskyj, *The Best Olympics Ever?*, p. 39.
9   *SMH*, 12, 13 Sept. 2000.
10   Lenskyj, *The Best Olympics Ever?*, p. 208.
11   Lenskyj, *The Best Olympics Ever?*, p. 41.
12   Shannon, 'The Friendly Games?', pp. 27, 33, 34.
13   Godwell, 'The Olympic Branding of Aborigines', p. 256.
14   Communication from Kevin Dunn', 20 Sept. 2005.
15   Munro, 'Treaty between the Sydney Land Councils', pp. 9–12.
16   Hunter, 'The Indigenous Expo at Homebush Bay', pp. 26–30.
17   Lenskyj, *The Best Olympics Ever?*, p. 189.
18   Owen, *The Local Impacts*, pp. 27–8.
19   Lenskyj, *The Best Olympics Ever?*, p. 196.

20 Owen, *The Local Impacts,* pp. 25–6.
21 Owen, *The Local Impacts,* p. 26.
22 Owen, *The Local Impacts,* pp. 20.
23 *SMH,* 21 May 1998.
24 Owen, *The Local Impacts,* pp. 20.
25 Owen, *The Local Impacts,* p. 21.
26 Lenskyj, *The Best Olympics Ever?*, p. 193.
27 Owen, *The Local Impacts,* p. 22.
28 Figures supplied by Ryde City Council courtesy of Paul Hartmann. RALC.
29 KPMG Peat Marwick, *Sydney Olympics 2000.*
30 Preuss, *Economics of Staging the Olympics*, pp. 259–61.
31 Jones Lang LaSalle, 'The Impact of the Olympic Games' (Jones Lang LaSalle website), p. 13.
32 Jones Lang LaSalle, 'The Impact of the Olympic Games' (Jones Lang LaSalle website), p. 13.
33 *UniNews*, vol. 13, no. 17, 20 Sept.–4 Oct. 2004.
34 *SMH,* 12 Aug. 2005.
35 Lenskyj, *The Best Olympics Ever?*, p. 106.
36 Dunn, 'The Olympics Locally', p. 20.
37 Dunn, 'The Olympics Locally', pp. 20, 23.
38 Albany Consulting quoted in Dunn, 'The Olympics Locally', p. 32.
39 Dunn, 'The Olympics Locally', pp.31-2.
40 Letter to SHOROC, 21 Jan. 1997, p. 2, quoted in Dunn, 'The Olympics Locally', p. 32.
41 Green Games Watch Newsletter, issue 6, 1997, p. 8, quoted in Dunn, 'The Olympics Locally', p. 32.
42 Dunn, 'The Olympics Locally', p. 33.
43 Black, *Coping with Olympic Traffic.*
44 Owen, *The Local Impacts,* pp. 28–9.
45 Owen, *The Local Impacts,* pp. 30–1.
46 Owen, *The Local Impacts,* pp. 30–1.
47 Communication from Kristy Owen, 5 Sept. 2005.
48 Dunn, 'Auburn under the Olympics', p. 32.
49 Mirvac, *Newington*, p. 31.
50 Communication from James Bell, 15 Sept. 2005.
51 Communication from Matt Hamilton, 14 Nov. 2005.
52 Communication from James Bell, 15 Sept. 2005.
53 Bagnall, 'Hell of a Village', *Bulletin*, 9 Nov. 1993.
54 *SMH,* 26 July 2004.
55 Brownlee, *Share the Spirit*, p. 153.
56 Brownlee, *Share the Spirit*, pp. 51–4; NSW Dept of Education and Training website.

57 Dunn, 'The Olympics Locally', pp. 31–3.
58 Crawford, 'The Sydney National Olympic Education Program'; Toohey, Crawford and Halbwirth, 'Sydney's Olympic Legacy and Educational Resources'; AOC, *The Olympic Education Kit*.
59 Communication from John Johnstone, 20 Oct. 2005.
60 Dunn, 'Auburn under the Olympics', p. 28.
61 Kidd, 'The Toronto Olympic Movement', p. 164.
62 Kidd, 'The Toronto Olympic Movement', pp. 154–67.
63 Website of the Impact of the Olympics on Community Coalition.
64 Dunn, 'Auburn under the Olympics', p. 26.
65 Stewart, 'The "Pro" and "Con" Cases', pp. 25–6.
66 *SMH*, 20 Sept. 2005.

CHAPTER 10

1   Landry, 'The Paralympic Games of Barcelona '92', pp. 124–38; Hughes, 'The Paralympics', pp. 170–80.
2   Goggin and Newell, 'Crippling Paralympics'; Darcy, 'A Games for Everyone?', 'Planning for Disability and Access at the Sydney 2000 Games', 'The Disability Legacy'; Sainsbury, 'The Athletes at the Paralympic Village'; Schell and Duncan, 'A Content Analysis'; Steadward, *History of the Paralympic Games.*
3   Louise Sauvage with Ian Heads, *Louise Sauvage: My Story*, HarperSports, Sydney, 2002; Steadward and Peterson, *Paralympics*; Neil Fuller, *One Foot in the Door*; Lachlan Jones, *Walk a Crooked Mile*, 2000; Sandy Blythe, *Blythe Spirit*, Pan Macmillan, Sydney 2000.
4   Landry, 'The Paralympic Games of Barcelona '92', p. 127.
5   Meekosha, 'Superchicks, Clones, Cyborgs and Cripples', p. 24.
6   Darcy, 'The Disability Legacy', p. 13.
7   Schell and Duncan, 'A Content Analysis', p. 46.
8   Schell and Duncan, 'A Content Analysis', p. 44.
9   Darcy, 'The Disability Legacy', p. 10.
10 PPGR, p. 2.
11 Goggin and Newell, 'Crippling Paralympics', p. 72.
12 Goggin and Newell, 'Crippling Paralympics', p. 79; Goggin and Newell, 'Fame and Disability'.
13 Darcy, 'The Disability Legacy', p. 13.
14 Cashman and Hughes, *Mosman Council*, p. 11.
15 Darcy, 'The Disability Legacy', p. 12.
16 Darcy, 'A Games for Everyone?', 'Planning for Disability and Access at the Sydney 2000 Games'; Woodruff, 'The Legacy of the Sydney 2000 Games'.
17 Woodruff, 'The Legacy of the Sydney 2000 Games'.
18 Darcy, 'The Disability Legacy', p. 13.
19 Darcy, 'The Disability Legacy', p. 13.

20 Darcy, 'The Disability Legacy', p. 15.
21 Darcy, 'The Disability Legacy', p. 15.
22 *SMH*, 18 Oct. 1999.
23 Information supplied by Greg Hartung.
24 *SMH*, 14 Oct. 2000.
25 *SMH*, 20 Oct. 2000.
26 *SMH*, 20 Oct. 2000.
27 Tremblay, 'The Media and the Paralympic Games'.
28 Tremblay, 'The Media and the Paralympic Games'.
29 *Australian*, 26 Oct, 2000..
30 Schell and Duncan, 'A Content Analysis', p. 30.
31 *SMH*, 23 Oct. 2000.
32 Goggin and Newell, 'Crippling Paralympics', p. 77..
33 *SMH*, 23 Oct. 2000.
34 *Paralympian*, no. 4, 2000, p. 3.
35 SMH, 23 Oct. 2000.
36 Tremblay, 'The Media and the Paralympic Games'.
37 ASC, *Annual Report,* 2000–01.
38 Darcy, 'The Disability Legacy', p. 11.
39 *SMH*, 1 Nov. 2000.
40 *SMH*, 4 Nov. 2000.
41 *SMH*, 18 Oct. 2000.
42 *SMH*, 4 Nov. 2000.
43 Darcy, 'The Disability Legacy', p. 14.
44 Meekosha, 'Superchicks, Clones, Cyborgs and Cripples', pp. 24–8.
45 *SMH*, 12 Oct. 2000.
46 Steadward and Peterson, *Paralympics.*
47 IPC, *Investigation Commission, Summary Report*, 2001.
48 Jobling and Jobling, 'Sydney 2000 for Athletes with Intellectial Disability'.
49 *Globe and Mail* (Toronto), 1 Feb. 2001, quoted in Jobling and Jobling, 'Sydney 2000 for Athletes with Intellectial Disability', p. 11.
50 ABC 7.30 Report, interview with Kerry O'Brien.
51 Landry, 'The Paralympic Games of Barcelona '92', p. 136.
52 *Paralympian*, no. 4, 2000, p. 3.
53 *Paralympian*, no. 3, 2003, p. 1.
54 *Paralympian*, no. 3, 2003, p. 1.
55 Information supplied by Greg Hartung.

BIBLIOGRAPHY

Adair, Daryl, Bruce Coe and Nick Guoth, *Beyond the Torch: Olympics and Australian Culture,* ASSH Studies, no. 17, Melbourne, 2005.

Andersen, Arthur with the Centre for Regional Economic Analysis, University of Tasmania, Economic Impact Study of the Sydney 2000 Olympic Games, 1999.

AOC, *The Olympic Education Kit*, Sydney, n.d.

ASC, *Annual Reports.*

Bale, John and Mette Krogh Christensen, eds, *Post-Olympism? Questioning Sport in the Twenty-first Century*, Berg, Oxford, 2004.

Benedict, B. *et al*, *The Anthopology of World Fairs*, Scolar Press, London, 1983.

Birch, Ric, *Master of Ceremonies: An Eventful Life*, Allen & Unwin, Sydney, 2002.

Black, John, *Coping with Olympic Traffic: Mosman Council Special Event Transport*, Centre for Olympic Studies UNSW, Sydney, 2000.

_____ 'Transport', Cashman and Hughes, ed., *Staging the Olympics*, pp. 93–105.

Bloomfield, John, *Australia's Sporting Success: The Inside Story*, UNSW Press, Sydney, 2004.

_____ *The Role, Scope and Direction of Recreation in Australia*, Dept. of Tourism and Recreation, Canberra, 1973.

Booth, Douglas and Colin Tatz, '"Swimming with the Big Boys" The Politics of Sydney's 2000 Olympic Bid', *Sporting Traditions*, vol. 11, no. 1, Nov. 1994, pp. 3–23.

Brownlee, Helen, *Share the Spirit: The Involvement of School Students in the 2000 Olympic and Paralympic Games*, Sydney, NSW DET, Sydney, 2002.

Cashman, Genevieve and Richard, *Red, Black and Gold: Sydney Aboriginal People and the Olympics*, UNSW Centre for Olympic Studies, monograph no. 2, Sydney, 2000.

Cashman, Richard, *Olympic Countdown: Diary of the Sydney Olympics*, Walla Walla Press, Sydney, 1999.

_____ *Sport in the National Imagination: Australian Sport in the Federation Decades*, Walla Walla Press, Sydney, 2002.

_____ 'The Impact of the Sydney 2000 Olympic Games on the Host Community: The Future of Sydney Olympic Park', Adair *et al*, *Beyond the Torch*, pp. 101–14.

_____ 'The Relationship between Elite and Mass Sport', *Journal of Asiana Sport for All*, vol. 6, no. 1, 2005, pp. 29–36.

_____ 'What is "Olympic" Legacy?', Moragas, Kennett and Puig, *The Legacy of the Olympic Games*, pp. 31-42.

Cashman, Richard and Anthony Hughes, eds, *Auburn Council Olympic Forum*, Centre for Olympic Studies UNSW, Sydney, 1999.

―――― *Mosman Council: Forum on the Impacts of the Olympics 24 October 1997*, Centre for Olympic Studies UNSW, Sydney, 1998.

―――― *Staging the Olympics: The Event and its Impact,* NSWUP, Sydney, 1999.

―――― 'Sydney 2000: Cargo Cult of Australian Sport', D. Rowe and G. Lawrence, eds, *Tourism, Sport, Leisure: Critical Perspectives,* Hodder, Sydney, 1998, pp. 216–25.

Cashman, Richard and Kristine Toohey, *The Contribution of the Higher Education Sector to the Sydney 2000 Olympic Games*, Centre for Olympic Studies UNSW, Sydney, 2002.

Cashman, Richard, Kristine Toohey, Simon Darcy, Caroline Symons, Bob Stewart, 'When the Carnival is Over: Evaluating the Outcomes of Mega Sporting Events in Australia', *Sporting Traditions*, vol. 21. no. 1, Nov. 2004, pp. 1–32.

Chalip, Laurence, 'Tourism and the Olympic Games', Moragas, Moreno and Kennett, *The Legacy of the Olympic Games*, pp.195–204.

Coles, A., *Report of the Australian Sports Institute Study Group,* Dept. of Tourism and Recreation, Canberra, 1975.

Crawford, Susan, 'The Sydney National Olympic Education Programme' 2000 (http://www.ioa.org.gr/books/reports/2001/R2001_498.pdf) pp. 498–505.

Daly, John, *Quest for Excellence: The Australian Institute of Sport in Canberra,* AGPS, Canberra, 1991.

Darcy, Simon, 'A Games for Everyone? Planning for Disability and Access at the Sydney 2000 Games', *Disability Studies Quarterly*, vol. 21, no. 3, 2001, pp. 70–84.

―――― 'The Disability Legacy' of the Sydney 2000 Paralympic Games', Cashman *et al*, 'When the Carnival is Over', pp. 10–16.

―――― 'The Politics of Disability and Access: The Sydney 2000 Games Experience', *Disability & Society*, vol. 18, no. 6, 2003, pp. 737–57.

Davison, Graeme, 'The Imaginary Grandstand', Bernard Whimpress, ed., *The Imaginary Grandstand: Identity and Narrative in Australian Sport*, ASSH, Adelaide, 2002, pp. 12–26.

―――― , 'Welcoming the World: The 1956 Olympic Games and the Representation of Melbourne', *Australian Historical Studies*, no. 109, Oct. 1997, pp. 64–76.

DSRD (with KPMG), 'Review of Business and Economic Benefits arising from Rugby World Cup' *2003*, 28 Feb. 2005.

Dubi, Christophe, Pierre-Alain Hug and Pascal van Griethuysen, 'Olympic Games Management', Moragas, Kennett and Puig, *Legacy of the Olympic Games*. pp. 403–13.

Dunn, Kevin, 'Auburn under the Olympics: Lessons from Globalisation', Cashman and Hughes, *Auburn Council Olympic Forum*, pp. 20–9.

_____ 'The Olympics Locally: Learning the Lessons from Economic Globalisation', Cashman and Hughes, *Mosman Council*, pp. 26–35.

Dunn, Kevin M. and Pauline M. McGuirk, 'Hallmark Events', Cashman and Hughes, *Staging the Olympics*, pp. 18–32.

Embrey, Lynn, 'Sport for All? The Politics of Funding, Nationalism and the Quest for Gold', Schaffer and Smith, eds, *The Olympics at the Millennium*, 272–86.

Frawley, Stephen and Kristine Toohey, 'Shaping Sport Competition: The SOCOG Sports Commission and the Planning and Delivery of Sport at the Sydney 2000 Olympic Games', Daryl Adair *et al*, *Beyond the Torch*, pp. 15–27.

García, Beatriz, 'Enhancing Sports Marketing through Cultural and Arts Programs: Lessons from the Sydney 2000 Olympic Arts Festivals', *Sport Management Review*, no. 4, 2001, pp. 193–219.

_____ 'Urban Regeneration, Arts Programming and Major Events', *International Journal of Cultural Policy*, vol. 10, no. 1, 2004, pp. 103–18.

Geertz, Clifford, 'Deep Play: Notes on the Balinese Cockfight', Geertz, *The Interpretation of Cultures*, Hutchison, London, 1975, pp. 412–53.

Godwell, Darren J., 'The Olympic Branding of Aborigines: The 2000 Olympic Games and Australia's Indigenous People', Schaffer and Smith, eds, *The Olympics at the Millennium*, pp. 243–57.

Goggin, Gerard and Christopher Newell, 'Crippling Paralympics? Media, Disability and Olympism', *Media International Australia*, no. 97, Nov. 2000, pp. 71–83.

_____ *Disability in Australia: Exposing a Social Apartheid*, NSWUP, Sydney, 2005.

_____ 'Fame and Disability: Christopher Reeve, Supercrips and Infamous Celebrity', *M/C Journal*, vol. 7, no. 5, 2004.

Good, Debra, 'The Cultural Olympiad', Cashman and Hughes, ed., *Staging the Olympics*, pp. 159–69.

Gordon, Harry, *Australia and the Olympic Games*, UQP, Brisbane, 1994.

_____ *The Time of Our Lives: Inside the Sydney Olympics*, UQP, Brisbane, 2003.

Gratton, Reg, 'The Media', Cashman and Hughes, *Staging the Olympics*, pp. 121–31.

Handelman, D., *Models and Mirrors: Towards and Anthropology of Public Events*, CUP, Cambridge, 2nd ed., 1998.

Hanna, Michelle, *Reconciliation in Olympism: Indigenous Culture in the Sydney Olympiad*, Walla Walla Press, Sydney, 1999.

Headon, David, '"Plastic Roos and Christine Anu" — Australia on Show in 2000', *Olympic Impact*, no. 1, 1996, pp. 1–2.

Hermann, Enno, 'Sale of the Millennium: The 2000 Olympics and Australia's Corporate Identity', *Media International Australia*, no. 94, 2000. pp. 173–83.

Hiller, Harry H., 'Assessing the Impact of Mega Events: A Linkage Model', *Current Issues in Tourism*, 1998, pp. 47–57.

_____ 'Mega-Events, Urban Boosterism and Growth Strategies: An Analysis of the Objectives and Legitimations of the Capetown 2004 Olympic Bid', *International Journal of Urban and Regional Research*, 2000, pp. 439–58.

_____ 'The Urban Transformation of a Landmark Event: The 1988 Calgary Winter Olympics', *Urban Affairs Quarterly*, vol. 26, no. 1, Sept. 1990, pp. 118–37.

_____ 'Toward a Science of Olympic Outcomes', Moragas Kennet and Puig, *Legacy of the Olympic Games*. pp. 102–9.

Hoberman, John, 'Sportive Nationalism and Globalization', John Bale and Mette Krogh Christensen, eds, *Post–Olympism? Questioning Sport in the Twenty-first Century*, Berg, Oxford, 2004, pp. 177–88.

Hogan, Kieran and Kevin Norton, 'The "Price" of Olympic Gold', *Journal of Science and Medicine in Sport*, vol. 3, no. 2, 2000, pp. 203–18.

Hughes, Anthony, 'The Paralympics', Cashman and Hughes, *Staging the Olympics*, pp. 170–80.

Hunter, Shane, 'The Indigenous Expo at Homebush Bay', Cashman, G. and R., *Red, Black and Gold*, pp. 25–9.

IOC, *Sydney 2000 Marketing Report*, Lausanne, 2001.

Jones Lang LaSalle, 'The Impact of the Olympic Games on Real Estate Markets', (http://www.joneslanglasalle.com/publications/global_insights_0106/).

Kidd, Bruce, 'The Myth of the Ancient Games', A. Tomlinson and G. Whannel, eds, *Five Ring Circus: Money, Power and Politics of the Olympic Games*, Pluto, London, 1984, pp. 71–83.

_____ 'The Toronto Olympic Movement: Towards a Social Contract for the Olympic Games', Robert Barney *et al*, eds, *Proceedings: First International Symposium for Olympic Research*, University of Western Ontario, Canada, 1992, pp. 67–77.

KPMG Peat Marwick (in association with the Centre for South Australian Olympic Studies), *Sydney Olympics 2000: Economic Impact Studies*, 1993.

Landry, F., 'The Paralympic Games of Barcelona '92', Moragas and Botella, *Keys to Success*, pp. 124–38

Lenskyj, Helen Jefferson, *Inside the Olympic Industry: Power, Politics and Activism*, State University of New York Press, Albany, 2000.

_____ *The Best Olympics Ever? Social Impacts of Sydney 2000*, State University of New York Press, Albany, 2002.

Lynch, Brendan, 'Volunteers 2000 — The Sydney Experience', Cashman and Toohey, *The Contribution of the Higher Education Sector*, pp. 84–96.

MacAloon, John, 'Olympic Ceremonies as a Setting for Intercultural Exchange', Miquel de Moragas *et al*, eds, *Olympic Ceremonies: Historical Continuity and Cultural Exchange*, pp. 29–43.

———— ed., *Rite, Drama, Festival, Spectacle*, The Institute of Human Issues, Philadelphia, 1984.

Magdalinski, Tara, '"Cute, Loveable Characters:" The Place and Significance of Mascots in the Olympic Movement', *Olympika*, vol. 13, 2004, pp. 75–92.

———— 'Finding Fatso Amongst the Ancient Rubble: A Story of One Wombat's Arse and its Historical Antecedents', conference paper, ASSH Melbourne, July 2005.

Malouf, David, 'Made in England: Australia's British Inheritance', *Quarterly Essay*, issue 12, 2003, pp. 2–66.

Media Guide, 'Opening Ceremony of the Games of the XXVII Olympiad in Sydney', 15 Sept. 2000, SOCOG.

Meekison, Lisa, 'Whose Ceremony is it Anyway? Indigenous and Olympic Interests in the Festival for the Dreaming', Schaffer and Smith, eds, *The Olympics at the Millennium* pp. 182–96.

Meekosha, Helen, 'Superchicks, Clones, Cyborgs and Cripples: Cinema and Messages of Bodily Transformations', *Social Alternatives*, vol. 18, no. 1, Jan. 1999, pp. 24–8.

Mirvac Lend Lease Development, *Newington: A New Suburb for a New Century*, Sydney, n.d.

Moragas, Miquel de and Miquel Botella, eds, *The Keys to Success: The Social, Sporting, Economic and Communications Impact of Barcelona '92*, Centre for Olympic Studies, Autonomous University of Barcelona, Barcelona, 1995.

Moragas, Miquel de, Ana Belen Moreno and Christopher Kennett, 'The Legacy of Symbols: Communication and the Olympic Games', Moragas, Kennett and Puig, *Legacy of the Olympic Games*. pp. 279–88.

Moragas, Miquel de, Christopher Kennett and Nuria Puig, eds, *The Legacy of the Olympic Games 1984–2000*, IOC, Lausanne, 2003.

Munro, Jenny, 'Treaty between the Sydney Land Councils', Cashman, G. and R., *Red, Black and Gold*, pp. 8–11.

Nadarajan, B., '2000 Sydney Paralympic Games: A Coming of Age', *Olympic Review*, 26, 36, pp. 5–8.

NCCRS, *The Impact of the Olympics on Participation in Australia: Trickle Down Effect, Discouragement Effect or No Effect?* ABS, Adelaide, 2001.

OCA, *The Sydney 2000 Olympic and Paralympic Games: A Report on the Financial Contribution by the New South Wales Government to the Sydney 2000 Games*, OCA, Sydney, 31 Mar. 2002.

Official Report of the XXVII Olympiad (Post-Games Report), 3 vols, Sydney, 2001.

Olympic Impact, journal of the UNSW Centre for Olympic Studies.

ORTA, *Nothing Bigger than This: Transport for the Sydney 2000 Olympic and*

Paralympic Games, ORTA, Sydney, 2001.

Owen, Kristy Ann, *The Local Impacts of the Sydney 2000 Olympic Games, Processes and Politics of Venue Preparation*, UNSW Centre for Olympic Studies, Sydney, 2001.

Park News, magazine of Sydney Olympic Park.

Prasad, Deo, 'Environment', Cashman and Hughes, ed., *Staging the Olympics*, pp. 83–92.

_____ 'How Green is Green Enough in 2000? Achieving and Assessing the Green Olympics', *Olympic Impact*, no. 1, 1996, pp. 6–7.

Prasad, Deo and Mark Snow, 'Examples of Successful Architectural Integration of PV: Australia', *Progress in Photovoltaics: Research and Applications*, John Wiley, 2004. pp. 477–83.

_____ 'The Shiny Side of Gold: Solar Power in Sydney 2000', *Renewable Energy World*, July- Aug. 2000, pp. 77–87.

Preuss, Holger, *The Economics of Staging the Olympics: A Comparison of the Games 1972–2008*, Edward Elgar, Cheltenham, 2004.

PricewaterhouseCoopers, 'Business and Economic Benefits of Sydney 2000: A Collation of Evidence', produced for DRSD, Sydney, 2002 (http://www.business.nsw.gov.au/facts.asp?cid=309).

Roberts, E.J., and P.B. McLeod, 'The Economics of a Hallmark Event', Geoffrey J. Syme *et al*, eds, *The Planning and Evaluation of Hallmark Events*, Avebury, 1989, pp. 242–9.

Roche, Maurice, 'Mega-events and Micro-modernisation: On the Sociology of New Urban Tourism', *British Journal of Sociology*, vol. 43, 1992, pp. 563–600.

_____ *Mega-events and Modernity: Olympics and Expos in the Growth of Global Culture*, Routledge, London, 2000.

Sainsbury, Tony, 'The Athletes at the Paralympic Village', Miquel de Moragas *et al*, *Olympic Villages: A Hundred Years of Urban Planning and Shared Experiences*, IOC, Lausanne, 1997, pp. 173–9.

Sauvage, Louise with Ian Heads, *Louise Sauvage: My Story*, HarperSports, Sydney, 2002.

Schaffer, Kay and Sidonie Smith, eds, *The Olympics at the Millennium: Power, Politics and the Games*, Rutgers University Press, Piscataway, 2000.

Schell Lea Ann 'Beez' and Margaret Carlisle Duncan, 'A Content Analysis of CBS's Coverage of the 1996 Paralympic Games', *Adapted Physical Activity Quarterly*, 1999, pp. 27–47.

Searle, Glen, 'The Urban Legacy of the Sydney Olympic Games', Moragas, Kennett and Puig, *The Legacy of the Olympic Games* , pp.118–26.

Shannon, Naomi, 'The Friendly Games? Politics, Protest and Aboriginal Rights at he XII Commonwealth Games, Brisbane, 1982', Ian Warren, ed., *Buoyant Nationalism: Australian Identity, Sport and the World Stage, 1982–1983*, ASSH Studies, no. 14, Melbourne, 2004, pp. 1–57.

Smith, Laurie, *Living is Giving: The Volunteer Experience,* Playright Publishing,

Sydney, 2001.

Spurr, Ray, 'Tourism', Cashman and Hughes, ed., *Staging the Olympics*, pp. 148–56.

Steadward, Robert D. and Cynthia J. Peterson, *Paralympics: Where the Heroes Come,* One Shot Holdings, Edmonton, 1997.

Stewart, Bob, 'The "Pro" and "Con" Cases for the 2006 Commonwealth Games', Cashman *et al,* 'When the Carnival is Over', pp. 21–6.

Stretton, Andrea, Stretton, 'Culture in the Sydney 2000 Olympic Games', Norbert Müller, ed., *Coubertin and Olympism; Questions for the Future*, Walla Walla Press, Sydney, 1998, pp. 207–11.

Sydney International Aquatic Centre, *Annual Reports.*

Sydney Olympic Games Review Committee, *Report to the Premier of New South Wales,* 1999.

Sydney Olympic Park Authority, *Annual Reports.*

_____ 'Arts and Cultural Strategy 2005 to 2015', Sydney, 2005.

Sydney Olympics 2000 Bid Limited, *Sydney 2000: Share the Spirit* [Sydney bid books], 3 vols. Sydney. 1991.

Sydney 2000 Paralympic Games Post-Games Report, 1 vol., Sydney, 2001.

Taylor, T., ed., *How You Play the Game: Sport and Human Rights*, University of Technology, Sydney, 1999.

The Paralympian, the official newsletter of the IPC.

Thompson, Alan, ed., *Terrorism and the 2000 Olympics,* ADFA, Canberra, 1996.

Toohey, K., and A.J. Veal, *The Olympic Games: A Social Science Perspective*, CABI Publishing, Wallingford, 2000.

Toohey, Kristine, Susan Craawford and Sue Halbwirth, 'Sydney's Olympic Legacy and Educational Resources,' *Orana,* Mar. 2000, pp. 14-20.

Toohey, Kristine, 'The Sydney 2000 Olympic Games', Cashman, 'When the Carnival is Over', pp. 3–10.

Tourism Forecasting Council, *The Olympic Effect: A Report on the Potential Tourism Impacts of the Sydney 2000 Games,* Commonwealth of Australia, Canberra. 1998.

Tourism New South Wales, Tourism Olympic Forum, Sydney, 2000.

Vamplew, Wray *et al, Oxford Companion to Australian Sport*, OUP, Melbourne, 1997.

Vollrath, Andrea, '"Eternity Games": Legacies and Collective Identity through Sports Events', Adair, *Beyond the Torch*, pp. 83–93.

Walker, Max and Gerry Gleeson, *The Volunteers*, Allen & Unwin, Sydney, 2001.

Webb, Tony, *The Collaborative Games: The Story Behind the Spectacle*, Pluto Press, Sydney, 2001.

Weirick, James, 'A Non Event? Sydney Olympics', *Architectural Australia*, vol.

85, no. 2, Mar./Apr., 1996, pp. 81–3..

_____ 'Urban Design', Cashman and Hughes, ed., *Staging the Olympics*, pp. 70–82.

Winchester, Hilary P.M., Lily Kong and Kevin Dunn, *Landscapes: Ways of Imagining the World*, Pearson Prentice Hall, Harlow, 2003.

UNPUBLISHED PAPERS:

ASC, 'Impact of Hosting the Sydney 2000 Olympic and Paralympic Games on Participating in Sport and Physical Activity in Australia', unpub. paper, Sport Development Unit, ASC, Canberra, 2001

ATC, 'Brand Australia', 10 July 2004.

_____'Olympic Games Tourism Strategy', summary, Feb. 2001.

Bell, Philip, 'The innocence of the Olympic Pageant, 2000: Australia as Fun and Funny', conference presentation, 2000.

Cashman, Richard, 'Impact of the Games on Olympic Host Cities' (http: www. blues.uab.es/olympic.studies/)

Cockburn, Milton, 'Is There Life after the Olympics?', typescript of an address to the Public Affairs Convention, Canberra, 23 Nov. 2000.

Duran, Pere, 'The Impact of the Olympic Games on Tourism: Barcelona, the Legacy of the Games', trans for the Centre for Olympic Studies, Barcelona, 2004.

Elphinston, Bob, transcript of an interview by Stephen Frawley.

Jobling, Anne and Ian, 'Sydney 2000 for Athletes with Intellectual Disability', paper prepared for the UNSW Centre for Olympic Studies', 2001.

Moragas, Miquel de, and Chris Kennett, 'Olympic Cities and communication'. Centre for Olympic Studies, Autonomous University of Barcelona.

Olympics Business Roundtable, Fact Sheet, 1999.

Ren, Hai, 'Olympic Games and Mass Sport Participation', conference paper, Beijing, May 2004.

Toohey, Kristine and Sue Halbwirth, 'The Sydney Organising Committee of the Olympic Games and Knowledge Management: Learning from the Experience', UTS and KnowledgeScape Pty Ltd.

Tremblay, Dominique, 'The Media and the Paralympic Games'.

Veal, A.J., and Kristine Toohey, 'The Legacy of the Sydney 2000 Olympic Games: Some Observations', Canberra Chapter of ASSH, Olympic Flame conference, Apr. 2004.

Woodruff, Jane, 'The Legacy of the Sydney 2000 Games for People with Diabilities', Sydney 2000 Games Forum, 6 Apr. 2001.

WEBSITES AND ELECTRONIC SOURCES:

Amateur Athletic Foundation of Los Angeles website (http://www.aafla.org). This website includes publications from the former UNSW Centre for Olympic Studies.

Austrade website (http://www.austrade.gov.au/).

ATC website (http://www.australia.com).

BOCOG website (http://en.beijing2008.com/)

Green Games Watch 2000 archived website (http://www.nccnsw.org.au/member/ggw/projects/FrequentlyAskedQuestions/faq2.html)

Greenpeace, archived Olympic site(www.greenpeace.org.au/archives/olympics/reports.html)

———— 'Greenpeace Olympics report card', 15 Aug. 2000 (http://www.greenpeace.org.au)

Impact of the Olympics on Community Coalition (http://www.olympicsforall.ca/).

Miah, Andy, OSN News Review, a quarterly digest of Olympic news (email@ANDYMIAH.NET)

NSW Dept. of Education and Training (http://www.sports.det.nsw.edu.au).

Pandora, Australia's Web Archive, National Library of Australia, has archived many Olympic sites (http://pandora.nla.gov.au).

Prime Minister and Cabinet website (http://www.pmc.gov.au)

Sydney Convention and Visitors Bureau website (http://www.scvb.com.au/).

Sydney Olympic Park website (http://www.sydneyolympicpark.nsw.gov.au).

Sydney Olympic Volunteers website (http://groups.msn.com/sydneyolympicvolunteers).

Sydney 2000 Games Collection (Powerhouse Museum) (http://www.powerhousemuseum.com/Sydney2000games/).

Sydney 2000 Games Information website, (http://www.gamesinfo.com.au).

Tourism Australia website (http:www.atc.net.au/).

VIDEOS

ABC *Four Corners*, (Ticky Fullerton, producer), 'The Road to Wembley', 5 Sept. 2005.

ABC *Atlanta Blues,* 1996, screened on 26 Feb. 1997.

ATC, *Australian Games,* 1997.

Beyond Products/ABC, *The Games*, 4 videos, 1999.

IOC/TWI and Channel 7, *The Dream,* 2 videos, 2000.

OCA, *Millennium Parklands: The Growing Legacy*, (video) OCA, Sydney, 1998.

SOCOG, *Our Environment — Our Olympic Legacy*, SOCOG, 1998.

THESES

Garcia, Beatriz, Towards Cultural Policy for Great Events', unpub. PhD, Autonomous University of Barcelona, 2002.

Haxton, Peter, "The Perceived Role of Community Involvement in the Mega-Event Hosting Process: A Case Study of the Atlanta 1996 and the Sydney 2000 Olympic Games, unpub. PhD, UTS, 2000.

Kennelly, Millicent, '"Busines as Usual:"How Elite Athletes Frame Terrorism Post 9/11', unpub. Bachelor of Arts, Sport and Exercise Management Hons thesis, UTS, 2005.

INDEX

OLYMPIC BOOKS PUBLISHED BY WALLA WALLA PRESS

Janet Cahill, *Running Towards Sydney 2000: The Olympic Flame & Torch*, 1999.

Richard Cashman, *Olympic Countdown, Diary of the Sydney Olympics*, 1999.

Stephanie Daniels and Anita Tedder, *'A Proper Spectacle': Women Olympians 1900–36*, 2000.

Michelle Hanna, *Reconciliation in Olympism: Indigenous Culture in the Sydney Olympiad*, 1999.

Manfred Messing and Norbert Müller, eds, *Focus on Olympism*, 2000.

Norbert Müller, ed., *Coubertin and Olympism: Questions for the Future*, 1998.

Dennis H. Phillips, *Australian Women at the Olympic Games*, 3rd ed., 2001.